Editorial

1	ERRORSMITH
15	JASSS
26	Track Down Fiction
34	JOHN MAUS
45	RENICK BELL
56	ANNA HOMLER
66	MMODEMM
74	OSSIA
85	GABBER ELEGANZA
97	We Are Time
98	ALESSANDRO CORTINI
110	COUNTRY MUSIC
122	Soundtexte
126	Substanzia Nigra
130	FURTHER REDUCTIONS
144	Basslines
148	PETER REHBERG
161	RUSSELL HASWELL
170	IPEK GORGUN & CERAMIC TL
172	ANGOISSE
174	CHRISTOPH FRINGELI, SIMON CRAB & NIGEL AYERS
188	JAY GLASS DUBS

D1688217

ERROR-SMITH

GETTING AROUND TO IT

Interview:
Marc & Guy Schwegler
Photography:
Lendita Kashtanjeva
Additional image:
James Hoff, "Left of Launch," 2017

The album *Superlative Fatigue*, released last year on PAN, gave the project Errorsmith the attention it deserves—and to many it felt like a long time coming. Behind the pseudonym is the Berliner Erik Wiegand, whose other projects, MMM and Smith N Hack, were celebrated by certain DJ circles for a handful of releases but were also mostly only known among a small community of dancefloor lovers. However, for almost two decades now, Wiegand has played a special role in the German capital's techno scene— a scene still often portrayed from the outside as one-dimensional. While he is, on the one hand, symptomatic of this Berlin scene and its development over the years (the great sense of freedom after the fall of the wall; first releases via the vinyl institution Hard Wax; work as a synthesizer developer for Native Instruments), on the other hand Errorsmith's techno is very much at odds with what is commonly considered "the Berlin sound." It's too overloaded, too close to expressive rave, too outward-looking, and above all too happy. On his older releases, there are only traces of harshness or aggression, and on his latest album there's none of either. Wiegand's music strikes a critical balance between emotional involvement and serious technical and musical know-how.

Marc and Guy Schwegler met Wiegand in a Kreuzberg café during *CTM* Festival after the latter had already played a set in December in the Lucerne Klub Kegelbahn. Lendita Kashtanjeva snapped photos of the likeable Berliner on both occasions.

Marc Schwegler: I found the title of your album *Superlative Fatigue* interesting in relation to the theme of *CTM* Festival, where you performed and for which we've come to Berlin. The theme "Turmoil" refers especially to current political, technological, and ecological upheavals and challenges. Your album title seems to refer to the exhaustion we're all experiencing more and more, especially in light of the turmoil of media hysteria that moves in ever-faster cycles and constantly strives for new historical and political superlatives.

One might speculate, then, about a conceptual superstructure... But I've read that you work on lists for your titles, fill them with terms and words you like, and then use them for tracks later. Is that right?

Erik Wiegand: I took that idea from Mark Fell. When we were looking for a title for our joint *Protogravity* EP on PAN in 2015, he said "I have a special list—I'll take a look." I found that to be a good course of action, especially because my working titles tend to be pretty hair-raising—things like "Wild Bass" or "Joker Pitcher"... And having to think of official titles under pressure is no fun at all. But if I have a list, I look through it and try to find something that fits. Mostly it's not descriptive—it's just a feeling. In the best case, the music and the title form a common image. In "I'm interesting, cheerful and sociable," I thought the title fits—the synth sound in the piece sounds a bit like a hysterical voice, and the title is a self-description on a personal ad—I thought that was great. I would never get the idea that I hear a piece and a title just emerges. The words have to come from a very different planet and then, in the best case, they connect. Sometimes it doesn't work so well, but the method has helped me a lot. For me it's also important that my pieces have titles. There are people who just call a track "A3" or something. That discloses nothing; it's too sober for me. If a piece has an interesting title, people are more likely to listen to it. For me, everything worked out so well with the title, and with the cover, too. I couldn't imagine a better cover.

MS The James Hoff cover came to you via Bill Kouligas of PAN?

EW Yes, exactly. Bill had tried a few things but wasn't really satisfied. The day before the delivery, when the pressing plant was already waiting, Bill said he still wanted to try something different. He asked me what I could imagine. I just said: "Yeah... it could be color gradients, a little crazy?" I don't know if he'd already thought of James before that. I mean, of course I can say whether I like something, but I'm not determined to have things one way, and I don't have super specific ideas. I think James spent the next few hours rendering things and offering some sketches. He finished the cover incredibly quickly. If you've been working on something for a long time and then suddenly tomorrow it all has to be done and there isn't even a real cover... Anyhow, it all came together in one fell swoop.

MS This album was a long process for you. Do you tend to have trouble finishing things?

EW I find it difficult to get things to the point where they not only have potential but can also be played in public. When I'm ready for that, it usually means I've been at work for a long time. It's not that I'm too picky about small details. I'm very good at creating potentials or opportunities with the instruments I develop. For example, I have an idea for a synthesizer, and I'd like to know how it could sound, and then I think I could use it to do this music or that music. But then it feels like too much work for me, and I move on to the next sketch. I may have gotten that from my father. He used to play in a band that did wedding music—covers of songs by the German country western band Truck Stop or by Frank Sinatra. The program was ok for his generation. But actually my father is an engineer—he only did music as a hobby. What I'm getting at is that my father was always working his studio and at the same time dreaming about recording and composing. But he didn't actually manage to do that because he spent all his time fiddling around with parts and tools. So somehow he didn't get around to it—and I have this problem too, partially. I always have to make a concerted effort. That's why it always takes forever. Sure, I'm not just doing this one thing—developing synthesizers is a part of my income as well. But I always dream of finishing my own music. It also takes a physical toll and I feel really stressed when I don't manage to do so. I get really embittered and lock myself in—I've kind of neglected my friends over the last few years.

MS I was wondering if maybe collaborations are a good way for you to get around to making music.

EW Yes, for sure. That's always been clear to me. My collaborations have also all taken a while, but they were always a bit faster and more enthusiastic. Making music has also always been an occasion to spend time with friends…

MS And there's also someone there to say, "Ok, it's time to finish this"—right?

EW Yeah—the mere fact that someone is sitting next to you leads you to make different decisions. You realize, "Ok, I can't change that one detail in Reaktor just because I think it might be helpful—we'll just take what's there." Things go more in the direction of how people normally work—how any other musician works. Which is good. Not everyone has to develop their own tools in order to do good things. I'm completely open when it comes to that. Everyone can use what they want, and there are great things that have been created with very little technical effort.

MS Would you say that all of the technical development work is a part of your musical practice?

EW It's definitely an exchange. Sometimes the beginning of the musical process is technical: I'll have an idea for a feature or a sketch of a synthesizer, a starting idea. And that gives me my first musical ideas. Things are then generated on their own. This helps. Each instrument gives you an easy way. Let's say you have a keyboard with chromatic keys—then it makes sense to play chromatic melodies. Pretty banal. Or if you have a guitar, of course it's easy to strum the chords. If you know how to shape this tool yourself, then you know, "Ok, I have this one feature now, so I could do this or that kind of music." This always has a musical impact, not only in terms of a beautiful sound, but also more concretely in terms of potential to use the whole thing musically. For me, that's a big part of my drive to hear something new. It gives me a real push. I think that's my strength. I also see Razor, which I not only built for myself, but also for others, as part of my musical work. I can't separate it. Similarly, painters might mix their own colors and then see how that color can give a painting a whole new character. It gives me more possibilities and influences my music a lot. Sometimes it's the other way around, too: I'll be having a problem with one piece; something is missing—it's good but not quite right. I don't just say, "Ok, I could just add that one element," but rather: "Ah, I could change the synthesizer so that I can—for example—simply pitch all the elements of that track at the same time." A pretty simple idea. And that's how it works in the other direction. From the technical I go to the musical, and from the musical I go back to the technical.

MS And what's it like for you now that other people are working with Razor? Are there things that you're still discovering? Things that you hear or things people tell you about? Things you wouldn't have anticipated?

EW No, not yet, unfortunately. I have to say that a lot of things end up being relatively conventional. Often I can't even distinguish that it's Razor being used—I thought it would be much easier to hear. But there are three or four features that aren't available elsewhere. I'd be able to recognize those right away.

Guy Schwegler: Bist du darüber etwas enttäuscht? Man könnte sich ja drüber freuen, dass niemand den Synthesizer nutzt wie du—aber gleichzeitig hat man sich ja vielleicht etwas mehr erhofft? EW: Ich bewerte das nicht so stark. Ich finde es nur schon toll, wenn mir Leute schreiben, wie viel Spass sie damit haben, dass es ihnen Inspiration gegeben hat, ganz egal was sie damit machen. Und klar: Ich finde es schon auch super, wenn ich die Features selbst noch mal neu präsentieren kann. Früher hatte ich eher noch das Gefühl, ich könne meine eigenen Sachen nicht weggeben und dass zu viel von meiner Musik drinsteckt. Ich habe auch immer stark getrennt zwischen dem, was ich für mich gebaut habe und meiner Arbeit für Native. Ich habe ja vor Razor auch schon zu anderen Produkten beigetragen. Bei Razor war die Konstellation allerdings anders: Während ich zuvor eher an kleineren Prozessen beteiligt war, die Teil eines grösseren Paketes waren, ist Razor ein prominenter Release—ein eigenes Produkt, das auch mit meinem Künstlernamen ausgezeichnet ist. Es war mir klar, dass die Leute es benutzen würden, inklusive sämtlicher Features. Und das ist auch gut so. Hier sind meine Ideen, macht was damit.

MS: Kannst du uns etwas über deine Philosophie in Bezug auf das Verfahren der additiven Synthese erzählen? Was ist für dich der springende Punkt dabei? EW: Additive Synthese gibt es schon länger. Da gab es in den 80er Jahren auch schon entsprechende Hardware. Additiv heisst einfach nur, dass man den Klang gestaltet, indem man Klangwellen zusammenfügt. Das müssen gar nicht unbedingt Sinuswellen sein. Es können auch andere Wellenformen sein. Von vielen möglichen Syntheseformen—und es ist überhaupt nicht so, dass sie verpönt gewesen wäre und ich das Ganze sozusagen rehabilitiert hätte. Es ist vor allem eine Frage der CPU, weil es eine der rechenintensivsten Syntheseformen ist—bei Razor sind es bis zu dreihundertzwanzig Sinuswellen, die den Sound gestalten. Für mich handelt es sich aber deswegen um eine interessante Art von Synthese, weil man als Kontrollfreak—der ich auf jeden Fall bin—bei sehr vielen Sinusoszillatoren die Amplitude und Frequenz, das Panning und die Phase—also in welchem Zeitabschnitt der Sinuswelle man startet, wenn man die Taste drückt—bestimmen kann. So erhält man beinahe auf einer atomaren Ebene ein Mitbestimmungsrecht. Als Gegenbeispiel: Bei einem subtraktiven Synthesizer arbeitet man mit Oszillatoren, die ein breites Spektrum haben, und dann filtert man davon weg. Deswegen eben subtraktiv. Da hantiert man mit bestimmten Filter-Steilheiten: Man filtert die Höhen weg, die Tiefen—es sind technische Gegebenheiten. Dabei ist es sehr selten, dass man einen Filter antrifft, der beliebige Parameter und Extreme zulassen würde, denn technisch ist das im Analogen so oder so nicht möglich. Bei Razor ist das kein Problem, denn der Filter nimmt kein Audio weg, sondern arbeitet einfach mit der Amplitude der Sinuswellen. Man kann sich völlig beliebige Filterkurven ausdenken. Das wäre die Kurzfassung.

MS: Wie stark beeinflussen deine eigenen musikalischen Vorlieben den Entwicklungsprozess eines Synthesizers bis zu dessen Markteinführung? EW: Es fliesst auf jeden Fall so etwas wie eine musikalische Präferenz mit rein. Rave-Signals mit Razor machen, ist beispielsweise relativ einfach. Ich wollte aber nicht einen Synthesizer für einen Musikstil machen. Ich habe Freude an unterschiedlicher Musik und wollte das Produkt daher auf keinen Fall zu sehr zuspitzen. Mit dem Promovideo zu Razor, das diesen Dubstep-Track beinhaltet, war ich ja eigentlich sehr happy, weil es jede Menge Features zeigt. Der Track stammt nicht von mir, jemand anders hat ihn an einem Abend produziert—das hat mich umgehauen! Mir ist ehrlich gesagt immer noch völlig schleierhaft, wie man das hinkriegt. Anyway: Aufgrund des Videos scheint die Idee aufgekommen zu sein, dass es sich bei Razor um einen neuen Dubstep-Synth handelt. Das fand ich etwas schade—war aber wohl vorherzusehen. Klar habe ich etwas eingebaut, damit das Ganze *wobbeln* kann—weil ich das auch interessant finde. Ich bekomme aber positive Feedbacks von Leuten aus völlig unterschiedlichen Richtungen. Zum Beispiel habe ich eine Anfrage von einem Psychedelic-Glitch-Hop-Produzenten für ein Feature bekommen und der meinte, Razor sei sehr angesagt in dieser Szene. Das geht dann vielleicht so in die Skrillex-Richtung? Keine Ahnung. Aber auch Freunde wie Mark Fell, die eher aus diesem experimentelleren oder minimalistischeren Umfeld kommen, konnten sich damit anfreunden.

MS: Hat es im Verlauf deiner Karriere nie den Punkt gegeben, wo du dich in Bezug auf die Musik anders orientieren wolltest? Also dich weg von der Klubmusik zu bewegen—in eher akademischere Gefilde, in die Klangkunst oder so? EW: Es gab schon auch Berührungen mit eher akademischer Musik. Ich habe an der TU Kommunikationswissenschaften studiert, wobei das an der TU ein wilder Mix aus Kybernetik, Programmieren, Phonetik und Tonstudio war—auch mit Ausflügen in die elektroakustische Musik. Da gab es also gewisse Überschneidungen. Einer ehemaligen Freundin von mir, die Künstlerin ist, habe ich teilweise auch bei Installationen mit Reaktor-Patches und so geholfen. In meinem Freundeskreis kommen auch viele aus der Szene. Ich finde das alles schon interessant, aber meine Leidenschaft ist ganz klar die tanzbare Musik. Wenn es nur tanzbare Musik gäbe, würde mir nichts grossartig fehlen. Es ist sehr selten, dass mir etwas gefällt, ohne dass es einen gewissen körperlichen Aspekt hätte. Ich brauche das. Man könnte ja sagen, dass es sich bei tanzbarer Musik nur um eine Art

Guy Schwegler: Has that been disappointing for you? I could imagine you might be happy that no one uses the synthesizer like you do—but at the same time maybe you hoped for more?
EW I don't really evaluate it that much. I just love it when people write to me saying how much fun they have with it or that it gave them inspiration—it doesn't really matter what they do with it. And sure, I also think it's great if I can present the features in a new way again in my own music. I used to feel that I couldn't give away my own things—that too much of my music was in them. I've always made a big separation between what I built for myself and my work for Native. I contributed to other products before Razor, too, but with Razor the constellation was different. Whereas before I was involved in smaller processes that were part of a larger package, Razor is a prominent release, a product of its own that's also labeled with my stage name. It was clear that people would use all of its different features. And that was a good thing—"Here are my ideas, do something with it."
MS Can you tell us something about your philosophy regarding the process of additive synthesis? What's the jumping-off point for you?
EW Additive synthesis has been around for a while. The associated hardware already existed in the 80s. Additive simply means that you design sound by mixing sound waves together. They don't necessarily have to be sine waves—they can also be other waveforms. It's one of many possible forms of synthesis, and it's not at all the case that it had been frowned upon and that I rehabilitated it, so to speak. It's mostly a question of CPU, because it's one of the most computationally intensive forms of synthesis—with Razor there are up to three hundred and twenty sine waves shaping the sound. For me, though, it's an interesting kind of synthesis because as a control freak—which I definitely am—you can determine the amplitude and frequency, the panning and the phasing—that is, the period in the sine wave when you start and press the key—of lots of different sine wave oscillators. So you have control on an almost atomic level. As a counter-example: in a subtractive synthesizer, you work with oscillators that have a broad spectrum, and then you filter away from it. That's why it's subtractive. You work with certain filter slopes—you filter out the highs and/or the lows. They're technical factors. As a result, it's very rare to encounter a filter that would allow arbitrary parameters and extremes, because it isn't technically possible in an analogue setup. With Razor, though, this isn't a problem because the filter doesn't take away audio—it simply works with the amplitude of the sine waves. You can create any kind of filter curve imaginable. That's the short version.
MS To what extent do your own musical preferences influence the development of a synthesizer, up to its launch into the market?
EW There's definitely something like musical preference that flows into the process. Making rave signals with Razor, for example, is relatively easy, but I didn't want to make a synthesizer for a specific music style. I enjoy lots of different types of music and didn't want to over-specialize the product. I was actually really happy with the promo video for Razor—the one featuring that dubstep track—because it shows a lot of features. The track isn't mine—someone else produced it in one evening, which blew me away! To be honest, I still have no idea how anyone does that. But anyway, the video seems to suggest that Razor is a new dubstep synth, though. I thought that was a pity, but it was to be expected. Of course I built something in that makes the whole thing "wobble," but partly because I think that's interesting. But I've gotten positive feedback from people who come from completely different styles. For example, I got a request from a psychedelic glitch-hop producer for a feature. They said Razor was very hip in that scene. Maybe that's something similar to Skrillex? No idea. But even friends like Mark Fell

Dienstleistung oder so handelt und sie ist ja gerade im akademischen Bereich auch immer noch etwas verpönt. Die ziehen da immer noch ihre Grenzen: tanzbar, nicht tanzbar. Das hat mich eigentlich immer gestört. Es ist immer reizend, wenn jemand im tanzbaren Bereich etwas ausprobiert und nicht nur nach Schema arbeitet. Im Klub brauche ich alles—es muss in die Lende gehen, darf mich intellektuell aber auch nicht beleidigen.

MS: Man hört deinen Sachen ja an, dass du dich auch in ganz bestimmten Mikro-Genres sehr gut auskennst. Hast du denn auch persönliche Berührungspunkte und Kontakte zu den entsprechenden Szenen? EW: Ich bin ja jetzt lange etwas untergetaucht—habe lange nichts veröffentlicht und hatte deswegen auch eher weniger Kontakte. Ich bin jetzt auch nicht wahnsinnig viel ausgegangen. Aber mit den Radiosendungen, die ich für Berlin Community Radio gemacht habe, war es mir immer ein Anliegen, die Playlisten zu veröffentlichen und die entsprechenden Leute zu taggen. Ich freue mich ja auch immer drüber, wenn das Leute mit meiner Musik machen. Als ich bei Facebook damit begann, die Listen zu veröffentlichen, meldeten sich dann tatsächlich auch Leute, die meinten: «Hey cool, dass du das gespielt hast.» Und es ergeben sich dadurch schon auch Kontakte, die dir Dinge weiterschicken. Aber es gibt keinen engen Austausch. Ich bin noch immer etwas schüchtern und weiss auch nicht, ob die meine Sachen wirklich kennen. Ich will den Leuten auch keine Zusammenarbeiten vorschlagen, wenn sie nicht explizit sagen, dass sie meine Musik auch wirklich mögen. Ich würde mir aber sehr wünschen, dass es mehr Verknüpfungen gäbe und ich Leute träfe, deren Musik ich mag.

GS: Wie wichtig ist dir das Auflegen? EW: Es ist schon wichtig, aber nicht überlebenswichtig. Für mich ist es oft ein Realitätscheck. Ich gehe ja davon aus, dass ich tanzbare Musik mache. Aber gerade wenn man seine Musik im Mix hört, dann kommt der Moment der Wahrheit [lacht]. Nicht nur im Klub—selbst wenn man das zuhause macht. Andere Produzenten, die ich mag, die konzentrieren sich auf das Produzieren und die benutzen beispielsweise Samples—entsprechend können sie sich darauf konzentrieren, dass alles sitzt, dass es gut klingt, dass der Beat stimmt. Die sind also elaboriert bei all den Sachen. Bei mir ist es aber so, dass die Beats oder die Sequenzen eher geringe Komplexität aufweisen, ich aber viel über klangliche Variationen oder so raushole. Ich bin manchmal total beeindruckt, wie geil Sachen von anderen Leuten klingen—wie laut etwas klingt ohne gleich tot zu sein. Wie geil Sequenzen sind, die ich selber nicht hinkriegen würde. Und dadurch, dass man seine Musik dann in so einem Kontext hört, kommen die eigenen Stärken und Schwächen klarer durch. Das ist ein Aspekt, der mich am DJing interessiert. Oft stört mich beim Ausgehen auch, dass doch vieles sehr eintönig ist, so insgesamt gesehen. Ich würde eigentlich gerne zeigen, wieviel interessante Musik es gibt und wie viel Sinn es macht, keine Grenzen zu ziehen—sondern dass es ein musikalisches Universum gibt, das sich als Ganzes präsentieren lässt. Und nicht, dass man als House-DJ den ganzen Abend nur 128 bpm spielt. Das macht mir keinen Spass—es bleibt zu viel auf der Strecke. Wenn ich manchmal auflege und etwas schneller werde, dann kommen teilweise Leute, die meinen: «Boah, ist das schnell.» Ey, das ist nicht schnell! Es gibt alles! Ich habe Spass daran, alles Mögliche zu spielen und so weit wie möglich zu gehen, Stücke aus verschiedenen Genres zu mischen und in unterschiedlichen Geschwindigkeiten aufzulegen. Bei jedem Tempo und in jedem Stil gibt es etwas Tolles.

who come from a more experimental or minimalist background were able to enjoy it.

MS Has there ever been a point in your career when you've wanted to approach music differently? I.e. to move away from club music and towards a more academic domain—towards sound art or something similar?

EW I've definitely had contact points with more academic music. I studied communication science at the Technische Universität Berlin. It was a wild mix of cybernetics, programming, phonetics, and studio recording, with forays into electro-acoustic music. So there was some overlap. I also helped a former friend of mine with her installations—she's an artist—using Reaktor patches and things. Many of my friends also come from that scene. I think it's all really interesting, but my passion is definitely dance music. If there was only danceable music in the world, I wouldn't really yearn for anything more. It's very rare that I like things that don't have a certain corporeal aspect. I need that. You could say that dance music is just a kind of service or something, and it's still a bit frowned upon in academia. They always draw the line: "Is it danceable or not?" And that always bothered me. It's lovely when someone tries out something new in the realm of dance music and doesn't just work according to a pre-established scheme. When it comes to the club, I always need everything at once—I have to feel it in my hip, but it also shouldn't insult me intellectually.

MS Your music makes it apparent how well-versed you are in certain micro-genres. Do you have personal contact to or relationships with any of those scenes?

EW I've been kind of off the grid for a while now—I hadn't published anything for a long time and therefore had fewer contacts. I haven't been going out a whole lot. But with the radio mixes I've done for Berlin Community Radio, I've always made a point to publish the playlists and tag the appropriate people. I'm always happy when people do the same with my music. When I started to publish the lists on Facebook, people actually wrote me and said, "Hey, cool that you played that." And then contact is established and those people send you more things. But there's no real close exchange—I'm still a bit shy and am not sure if people really know my stuff. I don't want to suggest working together with people unless they explicitly say that they really like my music. But I'd very much like to have more connections and to meet more people whose music I like.

GS How important is DJing to you?

EW It's important but not vital. It's rather a reality check for me. I always assume that I make danceable music, but the moment of truth is when you finally hear your music in the mix [laughs]. And not just in the club—also when you do it at home. Other producers I like focus on producing and they use samples, for example, so they can concentrate on having everything sit right and sound good, and on having the beat right. All of the aspects are pretty elaborate. With me it's the case that the beats or the sequences are less complex, but I get a lot out of sonic variations or things like that. Sometimes I'm really impressed by how amazing things by other people sound—how loud something can sound without also sounding dead, how awesome certain sequences are that I would never be able to do myself. And your own strengths and weaknesses come through more clearly when you listen to your music in that context. This is one aspect of DJing that interests me. When I go out, I'm often bothered by how monotonous and homogenous things sound. I'd really like to show people how much interesting music there is out there and how much sense it makes not to limit yourself—that there's a musical universe that can be presented as a whole. A house DJ shouldn't just play 128 bpm all night. I don't enjoy that—there's too much that falls by the wayside. Sometimes, when I DJ and speed things up a little, people come and say, "Whoa, that's really fast." Come on—that isn't fast! Not in the grand scheme of things! I enjoy playing a little of everything and going as far as I can to mix pieces from different genres and play at different speeds. There are great things in every tempo and in every style.

GS Do you feel like you're part of a certain Berlin scene?

EW I don't know… everyone has their own individual view of a city. If it's the city you live in, you have a slightly less uniform, higher-resolution image. I'm part of a Berlin scene that centers around Hard Wax. Without Hard Wax I would never have started publishing things. Fiedel [Michael Fiedler, Wiegand's collaborator in the projects MMM] was a customer there. Through them, he understood how to selfpublish things and then suggested we do that. That was an important turning point. I'm critical of the Berlin nightlife, but that's kind of a privileged whining. Of course there's a certain homogeneity I don't like, but there have always been alternatives, smaller initiatives. The homogenization of club music is also an international phenomenon—house and techno are dominant worldwide—so why should Berlin be so different?

GS What, then, is important to you for your own music, regardless of the context in which you're operating?

EW My music is mainly about expressing myself. I always need a kind of catalyst with which to come to my feelings—typical for a man, you might say bluntly. But music helps me, in any case—making music does, too. For me it really is about emotional expression.

GS A nice way to close!

GS: Fühlst du dich eigentlich als Teil einer gewissen Berliner Szene?
EW: Ach... Jeder hat seine eigene individuelle Sicht auf eine Stadt. Wenn man da lebt, hat man ein etwas weniger einheitliches und höher aufgelöstes Bild. Ich bin Teil einer Berliner Szene, die Hard Wax nahe steht. Ohne Hard Wax hätte ich nie angefangen, Sachen zu veröffentlichen. Fiedel [Michael Fiedler—Kollaborateur von Wiegand bei MMM, Anm. d. Red.] war da Kunde und hat mitgekriegt, wie man selber Sachen veröffentlichen kann und dann entsprechend den Anstoss gegeben, dass wir das machen. Das war eine wichtige Wegstellung. Ich bin zwar kritisch, was das Berliner Nachtleben angeht, aber das ist schon auch etwas Jammern auf hohem Niveau. Klar gibt es eine gewisse Homogenität, die ich nicht mag, aber es gab immer auch Alternativen, kleinere Initiativen. Die Homogenisierung der Klubmusik ist auch ein internationales Phänomen—House und Techno dominieren weltweit. Warum sollte Berlin also da komplett anders sein?

GS: Was ist dir denn persönlich wichtig für deine Musik, unabhängig von dem Kontext, in dem du dich bewegst?
EW: Bei meiner eigenen Musik geht es mir vor allem um einen Ausdruck von mir selber. Ich brauche immer eine Art Katalysator, um zu meinen Gefühlen zu kommen—typisch Mann, könnte man sagen, jetzt ganz platt ausgedrückt. Aber Musik hilft mir dabei auf jeden Fall—auch das Machen. Mir geht es schon um den emotionalen Ausdruck.

GS: Ein schönes Schlusswort!

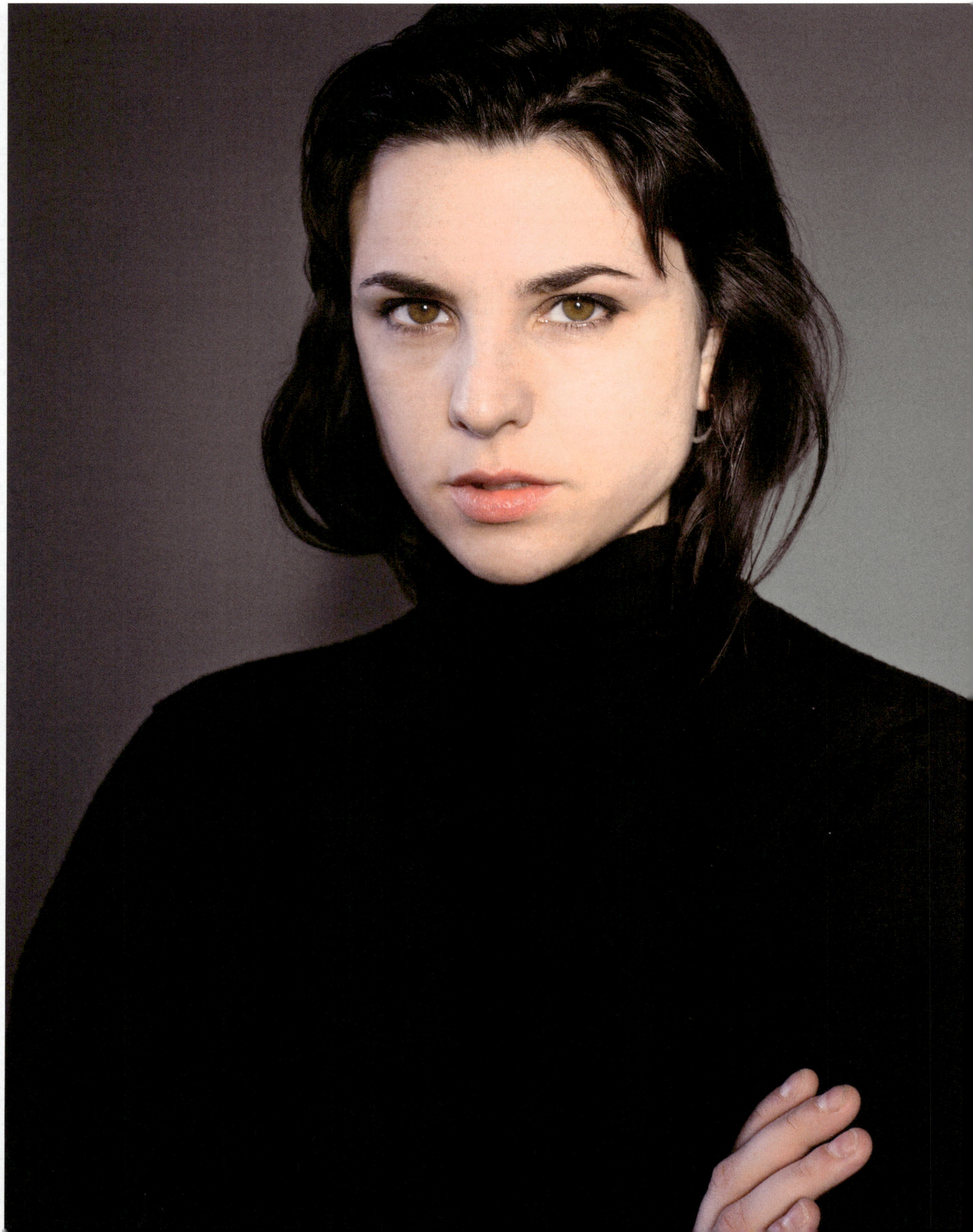

RADICAL PLACES
JASSS

Interview:
Samuel Savenberg,
Remo Bitzi
Photography:
Mai Nestor

"I guess the whole point behind playing records in this kind of situation is to remember what's the opposite of pretentious," writes Jasss about her contribution to the Ninja Tunes mix series, *Solid Steel*. The mix starts as anything but danceable, let alone catchy. A comment pops up at 1:12 minutes into the mix: "So do you first have to remind us of what pretentious is?" Social media is merciless. And yet Silvia Jimenez Alvarez, the woman behind Jasss, has hit the nail on the head with her proclamation. Curiosity coupled with a little bit of fuck-you attitude, and a huge love of music.

With her debut album *Weightless*, which appeared on the experimental label Ideal Recordings, Jasss navigates an impressive tightrope walk of childish curiosity and conceptual work; a difficult balancing act that has eluded many a producer. There is something very playful about the album, and various different sound recordings and samples are combined without overloading it. In this way, the album's title does it full justice.

Jasss was invited to DJ at Dampfzentrale in Bern at the end of 2017. Samuel Savenberg and Remo Bitzi met the musician beforehand for an interview.

«I guess the whole point behind playing records in this kind of situation is to remember what's the opposite of pretentious», schreibt Jasss begleitend zu ihrem Beitrag zur Ninja Tunes-Mixserie *Solid Steel*. Der Mix startet alles andere als tanzbar, geschweige denn eingängig. «So do you first have to remind us what is pretentious?», hallt es nach 1:12 Minuten Spielzeit in der Kommentarspalte zurück. Social Media ist eben gnadenlos. Und doch trifft Silvia Jiménez Alvarez, so der bürgerliche Name der Musikerin, mit ihrer Ansage den Nagel auf den Kopf. Neugier gekoppelt mit ein bisschen Fuck You-Attitüde und viel Liebe für die Musik.

Mit ihrem Debütalbum *Weightless*, das auf dem Experimental-Label Ideal Recordings erschienen ist, ist Jasss eine eindrückliche Gratwanderung aus kindlicher Neugierde und konzeptuellem Schaffen gelungen. Ein wichtiger Punkt, an dem schon der eine oder die andere Produzentin über Albumlänge gescheitert ist. Einerseits ist dem Album etwas sehr Verspieltes eigen, gleichwohl werden viele unterschiedliche Tonaufnahmen und Samples vereint, ohne dass das Ganze überladen wirkt. Im Gegenteil– der Titel wird dem Album durchaus gerecht.

Just zum Abschluss des Jahres 2017 wurde Jasss in die Berner Dampfzentrale zu einem Auftritt als DJ eingeladen. Samuel Savenberg und Remo Bitzi trafen die Musikerin davor zu einem Interview für zweikommasieben.

Remo Bitzi: Your influences were always highlighted in the reviews and festival announcements that I've read. I assume they probably popped up in one press release and then got copied all over… African dub or free-jazz—is it true?

Silvia Jiménez Alvarez: Yes of course those are influences, but so was almost everything else around. I remember at some point there was this one review… I mean a person that writes about music can write anything she or he wants, right? And if this person thinks, "I can totally hear the influence of this and that in the album," then that's probably true. But once a review gets published online and people start commenting and criticizing the critic, it gets complicated. "Yeah right, Africa. Jasss sounds very African." Well, I didn't say that. However, it's still true that I listened to a lot of that music because of my parents.

RB Could you please elaborate on how you grew up and the role of your parents and their taste in music?

SJA My parents are not artists or related to art at all. They are working class people, but well educated. I guess it was a way to escape from some things. They were still very young when they had me and it was a time in Spain with a lot of turmoil—a very politically-driven atmosphere. They had friends that were importing records—records that were not permitted in Spain. Same with books and art. My parents always lived in small towns and villages, so they had to search for these things. I think it was a way to not feel mediocre in a place where everything was indeed very mediocre and sad.

RB So, for that generation it wasn't a common thing to have access to these kind of records?

SJA No. Spain was closed. There were a lot of things that couldn't come in or out of the country.

RB So it was an extraordinary thing. Your friends at school didn't have access to the same music for example?

SJA I'd say that it wasn't until the last years of high school that I found other people with common interests. I'm not that old, but at the time and place where I grew up I didn't have access to much. I didn't run into electronic music until much later. You have to understand that I come from a village. And it's not like I grew up there and then moved to a big city. No. These villages are radical places.

RB Radical places—what do you mean by that?

SJA The people in the village would often reason with "it's always been like this." In the place that I grew up the macho attitude was so clear that it was already a parody. I didn't take it seriously as a kid, because for me it was a parody. There was no way you could believe what they were saying.

Samuel Savenberg: Would you say that you already had a different approach to music when growing up?

SJA Absolutely

SS And did you realize that as a kid?

SJA I did realize that I was attracted to different things than the others. Also the others weren't really communicative. And I always struggled a bit to find my place. I never got bullied or such but I didn't find a connection. I was able to function, I had my friends, but I guess a lot of people feel this way. At least a lot of people I've encountered much later know that feeling of alienation. Probably even some of those that I wasn't able to communicate with did. But for sure the music their parents were listening to and the way they were educated was really different.

RB Do you sometimes go back there to visit?

SJA Yes, I do. I will be back there in two days actually. And I think it's beautiful. There is a lot to learn from these situations. For example, we live in a time where everyone is super self-entitled to talk about and to criticize whereas in small places there is a lot of dogma and a lot of creepy stuff. But obviously this is not just black and white. So I ask myself, can I learn something from the social dynamics there? Sure I can.

Remo Bitzi: Mir ist aufgefallen, dass in Rezensionen wie auch Festival-Programmtexten etc. deine musikalischen Einflüsse viel Platz einnehmen. Ich gehe davon aus, dass das von einem Pressetext übernommen worden ist; etwas, das ja nicht neu ist, mir aber dennoch auffiel. Afrikanische Dub-Musik, Free-Jazz—was hat es damit auf sich?

Silvia Jiménez Alvarez: Meinetwegen darf ein Journalist schreiben, was er will. Wenn meine Musik bei jemandem Bilder oder Geschichten hervorrufen, dann ist das schön. Umso mehr, wenn ich das auch nachvollziehen kann. Gerade bei Sachen, die online publiziert werden, gibt es aber noch einen weitere Ebene: die der Kommentare. Diese ist in meinen Augen eher komplizierter. Es ist die Reaktion auf die Reaktion auf meine Kunst. Und das kann auch mühsam sein. «Ja klar, afrikanische Musik. Jasss wirkt ja so afrikanisch!», heisst es etwa. Dabei habe ich selbst das gar nicht behauptet. Um die Frage nach den Einflüssen zu beantworten: Das ist tatsächlich Musik, die ich viel gehört habe und somit hat sie auch mein Schaffen beeinflusst. Aber das gilt doch für alles, was einen umgibt. Ich bin mit vielerlei Musik aufgewachsen. Das habe ich meinen Eltern zu verdanken.

RB: Kannst du das ausführen?
SJA: Meine Eltern sind weder Musiker noch Künstler oder sonst irgendwie in eine entsprechende Szene involviert. Sie sind Teil der Arbeiterklasse, aber sie sind sehr interessiert und gebildet. Das ist heute aus mitteleuropäischer Sicht vielleicht gar nicht so einfach zu verstehen, aber ich denke, für sie war Musik eine Form von Eskapismus. Meine Eltern waren noch jung, als sie eine Familie gründeten. Sie selbst sind unter dem Franco-Faschismus aufgewachsen. Unruhen und Tumulte waren damals Teil des spanischen Alltags. Entsprechend war die Stimmung sehr politisch, was sich vermutlich auch im Konsum entsprechender Kunst, Musik und Literatur bei meinen Eltern manifestierte. Spanien war in vielerlei Hinsicht ein abgeschottetes Land. Meine Eltern hatten Freunde, die verbotene Schallplatten in das Land importierten. Das alles passierte nicht in grossen Städten, sondern wir reden hier von Dörfern und ländlichen Regionen. Ich glaube, all das war dem Versuch geschuldet, sich nicht durchschnittlich oder mittelmässig zu fühlen. Denn unter Franco war alles irgendwie normal und durchschnittlich. Aber auch traurig.

RB: Verstehe ich das richtig: Es entsprach nicht der Norm, sich für diese Art von Musik zu interessieren oder überhaupt Zugriff dazu zu haben?
SJA: Spanien war abgeschottet. Vieles fand weder ins Land rein noch aus dem Land raus.

RB: Wie war das denn für dich als Kind? War dir bewusst, dass du mit «anderen» Dingen oder Ansichten gross geworden bist als etwa deine Mitschülerinnen? **SJA:** Es hat lange gedauert, bis ich Mitmenschen fand, deren Interessen sich mit meinen deckten. Das war gegen Ende meiner Zeit am Gymnasium. Es ist ja noch gar nicht so lange her und ich will hier nicht alt klingen, aber da, wo ich herkomme, gab es für mich keine Möglichkeiten, auf Gleichgesinnte zu stossen. Ihr müsst verstehen: Ich bin in einem kleinen Dorf aufgewachsen. Und es ist nicht so, dass ich da aufgewachsen und danach sofort in eine grosse Stadt gezogen wäre, kaum war ich volljährig. Nein. Das hat mich schon geprägt. Ich denke, Dörfer sind Orte voller Radikalität.

RB: Orte voller Radikalität, wie meinst du das? **SJA:** Die Leute in diesen Dörfern argumentieren oft mit: «…weil es schon immer so war.» Da, wo ich aufgewachsen bin, war diese Macho-Attitüde sehr verbreitet. Aber sie war so überspitzt—für mich hat das beinahe wie eine Parodie gewirkt. Ich konnte dies bereits als Kind nicht ernst nehmen. Alles war auf die Spitze getrieben, man konnte es nicht für voll nehmen.

Samuel Savenberg: Würdest du sagen, dass du einen anderen Zugang zu Musik hattest als Kind? SJA: Klar, absolut.

SS: Und hast du das damals bereits so wahrgenommen? SJA: Ich habe mich für andere Dinge interessiert, und es fiel mir nicht so leicht, meinen Platz zu finden. Nicht, dass ich gemobbt oder ausgestossen worden wäre, aber es gab halt wenig verbindende Elemente mit anderen. So zumindest empfand ich es. Vielleicht ist das aber auch ein ganz normales Gefühl, wenn man erwachsen wird. Dieses Gefühl von Distanz und Fremdheit, das ist ja nicht der Kaste der intellektuellen Kulturinteressierten vorbehalten. Aber klar, es gab unübersehbare Unterschiede: Welche Musik zuhause gehört wurde oder über welche Themen am Familientisch gesprochen wurde.

RB: Fährst du noch oft in das Dorf zurück, in welchem du aufgewachsen bist? SJA: Ich fliege übermorgen zurück. Und ich freue mich. Wir leben ja gerade in einer Zeit, in der man gerne aus der Distanz beobachtet und kritisiert. In solchen Dörfern funktioniert das aber nicht. Da gibt es noch ganz andere Denkmuster. Trotzdem lässt sich nicht alles in Gut und Böse einordnen. Und ich frage mich: Kann ich etwas von den sozialen Dynamiken von da lernen? Klar kann ich das.

SS: Ich finde deine Beobachtung interessant. Es geht ja auch darum, dass man sich zunehmend in einer Blase wiederfindet, in der Ideale und Umgangsformen vorherrschen, die fernab der Realität sind. Und das kann als von oben herab wirken. SJA: Spricht man mit gewissen Leuten, die man oft in grösseren Städten antrifft, bekommt man oft den Eindruck, dass sie etwas sagen wollen im Stile von: «Wir haben die perfekte Welt und wir werden dich lehren, wie du richtig zu leben hast.» Man kann all seinen Freunden erzählen, wie man zu leben habe oder was Offenheit bedeute, aber Pepe aus meinem Dorf, den wird man nicht einfach so überzeugen können. Pepe sieht die Welt anders; und daran wird sich so schnell nichts ändern.

SS: Weiss Pepe denn, was du so machst? SJA: «Sie reist viel wegen ihrer Musik.» Das würde man wahrscheinlich in meinem Dorf zu hören bekommen. Ein wirkliches Interesse an meinem Schaffen gibt es kaum, denke ich.

SS: Du bist erst spät auf elektronische Musik gestossen. Du warst also nie ein Klub-Kid oder so? SJA: Ich mag den Klub als Ort. Aber würde mich nicht als Klub-Kid bezeichnen. Wenn ich einen Klub besuche, fühle ich mich wie ein Stalker.

SS: Welcher Aspekt am Klub interessiert dich? SJA: Für mich besitzt der Klub etwas Utopisches und Verträumtes. Es gibt das grosse Soundsystem. Wer auch immer Musik abspielt, ist im Besitz von viel Macht. Er entscheidet über Auswahl und Lautstärke. Das finde ich grossartig. Ich denke dabei daran, wie meine Freunde und ich früher abends zusammen in der Küche sassen und einander Musik vorspielten. Das war vor der Zeit von YouTube, entsprechend leidenschaftlich wurde gekämpft und diskutiert, um dann diejenige Glückliche zu sein, die ihre Musik den anderen abspielen konnte und somit die Macht hatte. Im Klub gibt es keine Diskussion darüber. Als DJ ist man verantwortlich und wenn es den anderen nicht passt, haben sie Pech gehabt. Sie können meinetwegen sogar reden, die Musik ist so wieso laut genug. Es gibt so viel tolle Musik und die Möglichkeit, diese in hoher Lautstärke anderen zu zeigen, ist grossartig. Musik zu entdecken, gibt mir schon einen Adrenalinschub, sie dann noch auf einem guten Soundsystem abspielen zu können umso mehr.

SS I think that is an interesting point. Because nowadays one can witness so many discussions where it seems everyone is trying to stand above everyone else…

SJA Yes, when speaking to some people—and this often happens in bigger cities—you get the impression that they want to say is: "We have the perfect world and we are going to teach you how to do it." You might go and tell your friends how to behave and to be open minded, but you are not going to tell Pepe from my village. No, Pepe's view of the world is a bit different and will probably stay that way.

SS Is Pepe aware of what you are doing now?

SJA Yes, he'd probably say: "She's traveling a lot because of her music." They are not really interested in what I'm doing.

SS Would you call yourself a club kid?

SJA I like the club, but I wouldn't call myself a club kid, no. I'd say I'm rather a little bit of a stalker when it comes to clubs.

SS Where did that fascination came from?

SJA The club has something utopic and dreamy… I mean it's the big soundsystem, the power to decide what is played and how loud. That for me is amazing, because if I hung out with my friends—and this was before YouTube was there—we would all go to war with each other when it came to who was in charge of what to play. Imagine that you don't have to fight with anyone because you have your slot and it's much louder. And everybody pays attention and everybody shuts the fuck up. Or doesn't shut up, which I wouldn't care about because it's loud enough. There's so much amazing music and it's so thrilling to play it out loud. It's really exciting for me to discover music. I guess it really gives me some kind of rush.

RB Because people are listening, or in general?

SJA Both. It really means something to me. It's not just the fun of it. I find it very touching for some reason. Of course not all situations are the same—when you play the closing slot at 10am then it's different, but there were certain gigs, moments where I listened to a bunch of stuff that I had been searching for and then was playing in a set and I'm just like, "wow." This thrill is the same as when I was a kid. It's so giving.

SS Is this also a reason why you DJ instead of playing live?

SJA I do play live. But I don't play live in a club context. I mean, it's difficult to say because I only have done it three times and these three times were perfect situations.

SS I guess the people coming to your concerts have different kinds of expectations depending on which record(s) they know.

SJA I mean, it's always the same process, right? First they hear the Mannequin EPs and so that is what they think I do; then they put on the album released on Ideal and they are confused; finally they go and see the live shows and are like: "Oh, she's doing something different than before…"

SS Do you like to play with these expectations?

SJA Yes, I love it. It's not that I really play with it, rather I get bored very easily and I don't think I should sacrifice the fact that I get really hungry to experience something new and that I get really excited. So I don't think I should sacrifice this so as not to let people down because they're expecting some specific sound or something. Because I could mix it all, you know… That's the good part of not having such a big fanbase: You can do whatever you want.

SS As an electronic musician people get to know you because of your productions. But then again, when they book you they expect you to DJ, which is probably something different. I guess this is confusing to the audience.

SJA I think the best thing is to just not give a damn. Because people have their own criteria and they will always have it. I think that's alright! I think it's fantastic when someone thinks that my music is shit. But I think it's my duty to not give a shit about that. I should not care; although, I have to pay the rent and get something to eat. But that's where the gold is at: When you don't give a shit, when you're a child. To be able to

RB: Weil da Leute zuhören oder grundsätzlich? SJA: Sowohl als auch. Musik bedeutet mir sehr viel. Und sie zu spielen auch. Das ist mehr als einfach nur Spass für mich. Es berührt mich! Klar gibt es unterschiedliche Situationen—morgens um 10 Uhr das Closing zu spielen, hat nicht denselben Reiz. Aber es kommt schon vor, dass ich in einem Set zum ersten Mal eine Neuentdeckung spiele und in der Situation richtig weggeblasen werde. Eben, das löst einen Schub aus.

SS: Diese Leidenschaft könnte gut als Begründung dienen, dass du als DJ und nicht als Livemusikerin unterwegs bist. SJA: Ich spiele auch live. Ob ich auflege oder live spiele, hängt vom Anlass ab. Für Live-Sets mag ich den Klub-Kontext nicht so sehr. Wenn ich aber ein Konzert im Rahmen eines Festivals spielen kann, dann mache ich das gerne. Bis anhin habe ich erst dreimal live gespielt, wobei alle drei Male unter perfekten Umständen stattfanden.

SS: Die Leute haben wahrscheinlich ziemlich unterschiedliche Vorstellungen davon, wie deine Live-Konzerte werden—je nach dem was sie von dir kennen. SJA: Es ist immer dasselbe, nicht wahr? Die Leute haben die EPs auf Mannequin gehört und haben ein entsprechendes Bild von mir. Kurz darauf erscheint die LP auf Ideal; etwas, das für leichte Verwirrung sorgt. Und dann besuchen sie ein Konzert von mir und es ist nochmal etwas ganz Anderes…

SS: Das stört dich aber nicht, oder? Also spielst du gerne mit der Erwartungshaltung des Publikums? SJA: Klar, ich liebe es. Ich würde es nicht als Spiel bezeichnen; mir wird einfach schnell langweilig. Und ich denke nicht, dass ich meine Lust, Neues auszuprobieren, den Erwartungen anderer unterordnen sollte, nur um auf Nummer sicher zu gehen. Letztlich habe ich aber das Glück, keine allzu grosse Fangemeinde zu haben, was eben auch mehr Freiheit bedeutet.

SS: Erwartungshaltungen in der elektronischen Musik sind ja ohnehin spannend. Man erlangt mit den eigenen Produktionen einen Bekanntheitsgrad, wird anhand dieser gebucht, und spielt dann meistens als DJ. Und obschon das Standard ist, sorgt das doch immer wieder für Verwirrung. SJA: Das Wichtigste bei alledem ist, sich nicht drum zu kümmern. Menschen haben ohnehin ihre eigenen Kriterien—und das völlig zurecht. Ist es nicht fantastisch, wenn jemand mein Schaffen richtig scheisse findet? Hauptsache es gibt eine Reaktion. Wie die ausfällt, sollte sich aber nicht auf meine Arbeit auswirken. Klar, am Ende des Tages muss die Miete bezahlt werden und Essen auf dem Tisch stehen. Trotzdem sollte man sein Ding durchziehen. Wie ein Kind… Ja, ich glaube, wie ein Kind voller Sturheit und Freude.

RB: Kannst du erläutern, was genau du damit meinst? SJA: Mit dem Alter wird man zynischer. Man beginnt, gewisse Sachen anders zu handhaben. Das sind Strategien, die durchaus Sinn machen, aber umso schwieriger wird es, diese zu dekonstruieren oder sich überhaupt vorzustellen, dass es für alles mehrere Möglichkeiten gibt. Es wird überhaupt schwieriger, seine Kreativität und Fantasie zu benutzen. Dies auf das Musikmachen zu übertragen, heisst: Man hat etwas aufgenommen, hat einen Loop daraus gemacht und dann hört man nicht auf, sich den anzuhören, voller Begeisterung darüber, wie er klingt. Dieses kindliche Gefühl, das ist wunderbar.

RB: Hast du das noch oft beim Produzieren? SJA: Ich habe in letzter Zeit wenig produziert, da ich viel unterwegs war. Es hat aber auch mit der Art und Weise zu tun, wie ich aufnehme. Wenn ich Musik mache, dann ist das eine bewusste Entscheidung. Da ist immer eine Stimmung, die ich festhalten möchte, ich gehe nicht einfach ins Studio und nehme ein paar Geräusche auf. Ich brauche schon ein Konzept.

RB: Wie gehst du bezüglich Sampling vor? Es scheint so viele verschiedene Soundquellen zu geben. Zum Beispiel die Stimme beim Track «Mother». SJA: Das ist meine eigene Stimme–also Sampling im weiteren Sinne. Aber was meint ihr genau?

SS: Ist es nicht eine grosse Herausforderung, mit so unterschiedlichem Material zu arbeiten? Gerade wenn du sagst, dass du mit sehr konkreten Ideen an die Sache herangehst. SJA: Ja, aber das kommt später. Ich brauche keine Melodie oder so, um zu beginnen. Ich brauche eine Stimmung. Alles andere ergibt sich in der Folge. Natürlich ist das zeitintensiv, aber das wurde noch nie zu einem Problem für mich. Ich weiss ja nicht, wie andere Leute produzieren, aber für mich ist das eine ziemlich emotionale Angelegenheit. Und ich glaube, das hört man der Musik an. Sie besitzt immer auch eine kitschige Komponente. Am Anfang bin ich damit jeweils noch vorsichtig, bevor ich dann zu mir sage: «Bring in the cheese». Mit dem Sampling ist es wie mit allen Elementen, die Teil der Musik werden. Zuerst gibt es eine Stimmung, die ein Profil, eine Textur erhalten muss. Ich habe neulich einen Song für eine Compilation gemacht. Das Stück basiert auf einer einfachen, süssen Synth-Melodie und wird durch einige Field Recordings ergänzt. Es handelt sich um Aufnahmen, die ich in der Nähe eines Swimmingpools gemacht habe. Der Track war fertig und ich legte ihn eine Weile zur Seite. Nach längerer Zeit hörte ich ihn mir wieder an und seit diesem Moment–ich kann mir nicht erklären, warum dem so ist–habe ich ein ganz konkretes Bild in meinem Kopf, wenn ich das Stück höre: Das Bild von meinem Vater in seiner Kindheit. Das ist sehr seltsam und steht eigentlich im Widerspruch zu dem, was ich anfangs gesagt habe. Weil offensichtlich dachte ich nicht an meinen Vater, als ich das Stück machte.

RB: Im Vergleich zu deinen früheren Veröffentlichungen ist dein Album ziemlich anders. Das waren dann also auch ganz andere Stimmungen? SJA: Nun, ich bin eine sehr launische Person. [Lacht] Ich arbeite bereits an und mit meinen nächsten Stimmungen. Aber dieses Mal wird es wohl ein wenig länger dauern.

SS: Würdest du dir wünschen, dass die Menschen beim Hören deiner Musik vom Entstehungsprozess und den Stimmungen wissen? SJA: Oh, auf keinen Fall, nein! Manchmal lese ich Kritiken und da werden regelrechte Geschichten erzählt, oder auch erfunden. «...es fühlt sich an, als ob man durch die Wüste fährt...» Aber da wird durch gar keine Wüste gefahren! [Lacht] Aus dem Grund möchte ich nicht, dass die Hörerinnen im Vorfeld bereits zu viel Hintergrundinformationen haben. Dadurch sagt man den Leuten unter Umständen nämlich, was sie zu fühlen haben. Aber wisst ihr, wozu ich gerne fähig wäre? Ich würde gerne meine Musik mit den Ohren Fremder hören können. Meine Musik mit neutralen Ohren hören zu können, wäre grossartig. Würde ich es mögen? Was würde ich anders machen?

RB: Lass uns zum Schluss über das Auflegen sprechen. Mir ist beim Anhören deiner Mixe aufgefallen, wie eklektisch diese ausfallen. Es gibt viele Variationen in Tempo und Stil. Das hat mich beeindruckt und ich wollte fragen, wie du das gerade auch in einem vollen Klub hinbekommst? SJA: Ich glaube, dass man das Klub-Publikum manchmal unterschätzt. Ich habe neulich in einem Kunstmuseum im Baskenland gespielt. Ich wurde gebucht und mir wurde gesagt, ich solle keine Tanzmusik spielen. Das habe ich auch gemacht und die Leute haben trotzdem richtig gefeiert und

think like a child. It's what you lose when you grow up.

RB Could you describe that a little more precisely? What part of being a child do you mean?

SJA The way I feel is that as you grow up, you get more cynical. You start creating roads and paths to follow. "This car goes this way, that car goes that way." It's very difficult to deconstruct that and imagine how you used to build these roads and how these roads are flexible. That's what we all try to come back to. For example when you make a sound that fascinates you or you come up with a loop and you say to yourself "Wow, this is the shit!" That's the feeling. It's beautiful.

RB Do you still have that when you work on music?

SJA I haven't had it in a while because I haven't had the time to work on new music. I was traveling a lot. It's also because of the way I record. I have to be in a working mood. Not just "okay, I'm gonna record some sounds." It's not conceptual but just like searching for a melody or so.

RB What about the samples that you use—there's a lot of sources, right? For example there is this one track, "Mother"...

SJA Oh, well that's actually a recording of me singing.

SS However, there's a lot of different sources—is it a challenge to make music with so much material?

SJA Yeah but that comes later. I don't need a melody, I need a mood to get started. The moment that I get into this mood, everything else comes together. Of course it still needs time, but I haven't had problems with this. I don't know how other people produce but for me it's a really emotional thing. And then this resonates in the music—it's almost a bit cheesy, which I try to hide. But then after a while I say to myself: "Ok, bring on the cheese!" [Laughs] As for the sampling, it's like with everything else. First there's the mood, then it needs a texture. There is this one track I made for a compilation. It's based on a really sweet and naive melody that I played on a synthesizer and it also has this sound of water. I recorded some people at a swimming pool. So I finished this track and was really happy with it. I didn't listen to it for about two months... But then, I listened to it again and ever since I can only think of my father when he was a kid. It's really strange. Because this hadn't been my intention back when I recorded the track. So it's somehow the other way around this time—the mood came after.

RB Compared to your earlier works your album is quite different. I guess you must have some pretty different moods?

SJA I am a very moody person. [Laughs] So yes, I am already working on my next mood but it's gonna take a little longer I guess.

SS Do you sometimes wish that people would know about your moods and how directly they affect your music?

SJA Oh, no, please not! Sometimes you read those long reviews that try to include a story that's just not there: "And then you're driving through the desert..." Let me tell you, you're totally not driving through the desert. But that's amazing. And therefore I don't want people to know the backstories because that would be a little bit like telling people what to feel. There is one thing though, that I would love to be able to do and that is to hear what I do without being me. To be able to judge myself with clean ears. Would I put that music out?

RB Let's come to an end with some DJ talk. I noticed in your mixes that there is quite a variation with tempi and styles. I'm pretty impressed by this and was wondering how you manage to do so in front of a club audience?

SJA Audiences are totally underestimated, it's crazy. For example I did this show in the Basque country in a contemporary art museum where I was booked to do a set that was not dance music. I got the best feedback that I ever had after playing. The other day I also played some heavy bass music during the Mannequin labelnight at Berghain's Säule. The Mannequin audience is normally not into that kind of stuff—in theory! However, you should have seen the people! Bodies are into rhythm, not into genres.

wir hatten eine tolle Zeit. Bei der letzten Mannequin-Labelnight in der Säule des Berghain habe ich fast nur Bassmusik gespielt. Man würde wahrscheinlich nicht davon ausgehen, dass das zusammenpasst–Bassmusik im Rahmen einer Mannequin-Labelnacht. Aber die Leute fanden es super. Körper mögen Rhythmus mehr als Genres.

MY T-SHIRT IN THE FIELD

Column:
Anna Froelicher

In the third iteration of her column, Anna Froelicher reconsiders her favorite t-shirt, which is soft and lies light on the skin; which comes from far away—from a bamboo-lined postcard shop on a faraway island, perhaps—; which is really just junk–should it be thrown away or kept?–; whose patterns imitate fantastical, imagined sounds; and which makes her look like an ethnomusicologist. After some circling, a text evolved that tells of field recordings, ghosts, and the longing for geographical authenticity in music consumption.

I throw on my big, short-sleeved T-shirt even when it's gray outside and even when the summer is long over. I sit down at a four-legged table or lie down on the carpet. The garment's rayon-viscose blend adjoins the wool under my feet. I undo the small button at the neck for free, relaxed breathing.

I want to deliver an invocation. Therefore, everything needs to be in place. At regular intervals, one of my previously-compiled playlist turns the 10 square meters of my room into a billowing rectangle, the fluffy ground of which acts as a sail and guides me through the air on a decelerated 70bpm. We're on the third track. I mumble his name—"Baozoo Khen"—to myself quietly and enjoy the long, imaginary "O" of a language I don't know. "Baozoo Khen" is on the album *Voices* by Laurent Jeanneau aka Kink Gong, which appeared two years ago on the label Discrepant. For the album, as the title suggests, the French sound artist worked primarily with human voices, all of which he recorded himself. The result is a mixture of original recordings with the "field," processed sounds, and computer-based sounds subsequently added in the studio. "Baozoo Khen" is one of those tracks for which the label "otherworldly beauty" provides a fitting, if old-fashioned or pre-postmodern, description. It almost doesn't matter whether the unfamiliar harmonies and nasal voices remain faithful to the traditional music cultures of their geographical origins (Jeanneau spent a long time in China, Vietnam, and Laos gathering recordings for *Voices*) or whether their non-halftone-based intensity is "only" a fantasy of Jeanneau's studio work, i.e. the product of software. Which would be nicer, anyway?

My t-shirt and I stand back up and walk a couple of steps. I pull out a book from a makeshift wall shelf. I open the first page and find a photo taken in 1916 in Washington D.C. and published by the Harris & Ewing Studio the same year. Against the backdrop of a canvas, a man with leather shoes and feather jewelry sits very upright in a wooden chair. He faces a metallic horn. The horn belongs to a phonograph, which is installed more provisionally than permanently on top of a wooden box. Behind the box sits a woman with her body directed towards the camera. She's wearing a white (although black-and-white photography isn't very precise in depicting color gradation) button-down blouse that blossoms into a bow at the neck. Her feet are likewise in leather shoes. The woman's gaze is directed downward to her hand, which seems to be doing something on the phonograph. The common title of this iconic image is *Frances Densmore* [editor's note: influential American ethnomusicologist] *using wax cylinder phonograph to record Mountain Chief, a Blackfoot Indian*.[1] However, as the American Folklife Center—an institution for ethnographic and historical music documentation in the U.S.—later noted, the description in the image title was incorrect. The photo actually depicted a *playback horn on the cylinder recorder*, which means that Densmore hadn't been recording the Mountain Chief—rather, they'd been listening to something together (and as a next step, the Mountain Chief would translate it for Densmore in a sign language).[2]

I close the heavy book with a loud *ptac* and return to my starting position on the now swirling and uneven floor. Track #4 of the playlist washes over me in waves, encouraging me to consider the big picture: an advancing industrial past, history as a mill? It's "Plucked From The Ground Towards The Sun" by Huerco S. (from *Colonial Patterns*, Software Records, 2013). From the thick of this molasses, I close my eyes and review the photo in my mind's eye, soaking it up as if it were water, letting it freeze and evaporate. I assemble the condensed drops together again in their funny, fisheye state, like pieces of a puzzle. The three protagonists in the photo—two humans and a phonograph, all in a familiar but outdated studio aesthetic–are ghosts of the past. All three are actually long dead, yet we feel we know them. As ghosts, they carry two faces—one that's ghoulish and haunting, and one that's conciliatory and wise. Track #5—"Lake," from Elysia Crampton's first EP under that name (Boomkat Editions, 2015)—communes with these ghosts and transports them to the shores of a mossy, swampy America.

Without the magic of the revised caption, the relationship constellation of the photo reminds me of a discussion at the festival *Digging in the Global South* in Cologne last year.[3] In a panel, the co-founder of SWP Records (he shall remain unnamed) presented the work of their small Belgian label, which has set itself the task of conserving traditional and minority music from the African continent via field recordings and releasing it on vinyl. As with other labels of this kind, the imagined audience is a small group of 'connoisseurs' living in the home countries of former colonial powers, all of whom can afford a leather wingback chair and adequate playback equipment: "We want you to enjoy a great sound, seated in your favorite chair opposite your hi-fi...".[4] The fact that the record covers prominently note the names of the relatively well-off field researchers from the global north and that the musicians on the recordings are credited merely via titles like *Malawi Grooves, Zambia Roadside*, and *Forgotten Guitars from Mozambique* suggests that the spirits of the colonial past continue to haunt us, and that the figures of history repeat themselves, if in slightly revised ways. The mostly very 'purely' staged releases stem from a gesture towards the undiscovered, towards things lost in oblivion (and therefore somehow especially authentic). The label owner's panel presentation sounds like an adventure report in which white rescue fantasies paint a picture of Africa flooded with Western culture ("McDonald's" is cited). The practice of field recording in a global context reveals itself here still, or once again, as a blind spot in a discourse about the power relations of documentation. And at the same time, the panel discussion still contains the same ambivalence shown in the picture in the book on my lap. SWP Records, as Frances Densmore did, have the means, the interest, and the desire to conserve lost or dying music, and thus to make it accessible to those interested or to (the idea of) those affected by the aforementioned loss—that's great, though, isn't it? And if my ears, miles away from the sources, are blessed with the opportunity to hear sounds I'd never deemed possible, that's really nice, though, isn't it?

Peder Mammerfelt's "Circumcision Dance" from the album *The Swedish Congo Records* (Archives Intérieurs, 2015), which snuck into my playlist as track #6, took field recordings as its basis but didn't work with them as actual material. For the project, the Swedish musician and label operator reinterpreted six 1950-released 78rpm recordings entitled *The Belgian Congo Records*. In "Circumcision Dance," the song's structure was decoupled from its original sound and spitted out in the form of zeros and ones. In this case, it wasn't a historical music recording from the so-called Belgian Congo of the 1930s that found its way into the coils of my speakers, but rather its synthetic, abstracted clone. Have the ghosts of the future crept into the past with the intention of liberating the analogue orchestras from their ethnified authenticity? If so, then at what price? Is the emancipated listener herself enough?

As I contemplate these questions I start to sweat a bit, and the fabric under my armpits sticks to my skin. The next track has rescued the abrupt close of track #6 with a smooth transition, and is bringing my flying carpet to a tranquil hovering position a few centimeters above the floor. The title of track #7 is "Mix 2 (Toulouse Low Trax Mix)." The performers are Ogoya Nengo and The Dodo Women's Group and the album is *On Mande Versions* (although in this case iTunes' conceptions of authorship have been pushed to their limits). On the track, which was released in 2017, vocals by the Kenyan singer Ogoya Nengo are electronically orchestrated, pitched, and fragmented by the much younger Toulouse Low Trax[5], a musician from the scene around Salon des Amateurs. "Mix 2" is mostly laid-back and not particularly exciting, but the lyrics, which contain the English phrases "Where is you?" and "Where I see you?" capture my interest in their fine aberration from the grammatical norm. Are they funny? And when I found the track on the WWW, did I click on it because the sound of the name Ogoya Nengo promised unknown excitement? Kind of like the O of the playlist's track #3 had?

I relax my shoulders and shake my head. A strand of hair falls in front of my face and I notice that it's gray–already? It feels as though someone has added a long silence to the end of "Mix 2," causing a big break before the next track, although this isn't really the case. The silence suddenly sounds metallic. A small burst of air passes through the fabric on my skin and makes the delicate membranes on my ear vibrate–membranes I never knew I had. I look down at myself, and my t-shirt has grown larger. It reaches down to my ankles. On my back, it has grown a long, wrinkled tail that connects seamlessly with the carpet. I turn my head to the mirror on the wall to the right of me and watch as my body slowly dissolves like warm wax. Although it all seems strange, I feel cozy and warm. This feeling is encouraged by the thought of Frances Densmore, the Mountain Chief, and the phonograph, which plays something for them and for itself, something these three very different characters can hear together, something I might even hear in my room on my laptop. What are you listening to, Mrs. Densmore? And you, Mr. Mountain Chief? And you, phonograph? And why do you all seem so alive?

---

1   http://www.loc.gov/pictures/item/2004667752/ (downloaded 11.02.18)
2   https://www.washingtonpost.com/national/health-science/smithsonian-archives-preserve-lost-and-dying-languages/2014/01/17/2a2c8218-74a1-11e3-8b3f-b166-6705ca3b_story.html (downloaded 11.01.18)
3   The festival was mainly dedicated to electronic music from Africa and the African Diaspora. Via various formats (lectures, concerts, panels, and club nights), on the one hand it offered a nuanced perspective on contemporary musical output, and on the other hand a (self-)critical reflection upon the role of Western agency in the interplay between positive othering, cultural appropriation, and hybridization.
4   http://www.swp-records.com/about (downloaded 11.02.18)
5   See also the interview with Toulouse Low Trax in zweikommasieben #15.

kotä

www.kotaerecords.com
www.kotaerecords.com
www.kotaerecords.com

gleb glonti   silk saw   elektroschit   ::vtol::
vlad dobrovolski   brinstaar   wolffflow   solo operator

Im dritten Teil ihrer Kolumne geht Anna Froelicher ein paar Schritte von ihrem Lieblings-T-Shirt aus, das leicht auf der Haut liegt; von weit her kommt, vielleicht und geht aus einem bambusbestückten Postkartenladen einer fernen Insel; das Trödel ist–kann das weg oder wird das noch gebraucht?; das durch seine Musterung Klänge imitiert, von denen sich nur phantasieren lässt; in dem sie wie eine Musikethnologin aussieht. Nachdem sie einmal im Kreis gegangen war, entstand ein Text über Field Recordings, Geister und den Wunsch nach geografischer Authentizität im Musikkonsum.

Ich werfe mir mein grosses, kurzärmeliges T-Shirt über, auch wenn es draussen grau ist und der Sommer lange vorbei. Ich setze mich auf dem Teppichboden gemütlich. Das Rayon-Viskose-Gemisch des Kleidungsstückes grenzt an ein Wollstoff unter meinen Füssen. Ich öffne den kleinen Knopf in der Nähe des Halses für ein ruhiges, freies Atmen.

Ich habe eine Anrufung vor. Hierfür muss alles seinen Platz haben. Eine zuvor zusammengestellte Playlist verwandelt die zehn Quadratmeter meines Zimmers regelmässig in ein waberndes Rechteck, auf dessen flauschigem Grund ich mit entschleunigten 70 bpm auf die Lüfte segle. Wir sind beim dritten Track, ich murmle seinen Namen einmal leise vor mich hin–«Baozoo Khen»–und geniesse das langgezogene, imaginierte O einer Sprache, die ich nicht kenne. «Baozoo Khen» befindet sich auf dem Album *Voices* von Laurent Jeanneau aka Kink Gong, das vor zwei Jahren auf dem Discrepant Label erschienen ist. Für *Voices* hat der französische Klangkünstler Jeanneau, wie der Titel schon sagt, vor allem mit ihm aufgezeichneten, menschlichen Stimmen gearbeitet. Entstanden ist eine Mixtur aus Originalaufnahmen des «Feldes», bearbeiteten Klängen und nachträglich hinzugefügten computerbasierten Sounds im Studio. «Baozoo Khen» ist einer dieser Tracks, bei dem das Etikett ausserweltlicher Schönheit wohl eine angemessene, wenn auch altmodisch vor-postmoderne Beschreibung zu liefern scheint. Fast könnte es unklar bleiben, ob die ungewohnten Harmonien und nasalen Stimmen ein Zeugnis über die traditionelle Musikkultur ihrer Herkunft ablegen (Jeanneau war für *Voices* lange in China, Vietnam und Laos unterwegs) oder ob ihre nicht halbtonbasierte Intensität doch nur eine Phantasie Jeanneaus Studioarbeit ist–das Produkt einer Software? Was wäre schöner?

Mit meinem T-Shirt stehe ich wieder auf und gehe ein paar Schritte. Aus einem behelfsmässig zusammengestellten Wandregal ziehe ich ein Buch hervor. Ich öffne die erste Seite und finde ein Foto, 1916 in Washington D.C. aufgenommen und im selben Jahr von Harris & Ewing Studio publiziert. Vor dem Hintergrund einer Leinwand zeigt es einen Mann mit Lederschuhen und Federschmuck, sehr aufrecht auf einem Holzstuhl sitzend. Sein Gesicht ist einem metallenen Trichter zugewandt. Der Trichter gehört zu einem Phonographen, der wohl mehr provisorisch als dauerhaft auf einer Holzkiste installiert wurde. Hinter der Kiste sitzt eine Frau, mit ihrem Oberkörper zu mir gerichtet. Sie trägt eine weisse (wobei sich die Farbigkeit in der Schwarz-Weiss-Fotografie nicht so genau bestimmen lässt) Knopfbluse, einen Halsende im Unterricht einer Fliege mündet. Ihre Füsse stecken ebenfalls in Lederschuhen. Der Blick der Frau ist nach unten auf ihre Hand gerichtet, die etwas von Phonographen zu richten scheint. Der geläufige Titel dieses ikonisch gewordenen Bildes ist: *Frances Densmore [einflussreiche US-amerikanische Musikethnologin, Anm. d. Verf.] using wax cylinder phonograph to record Mountain Chief, a Blackfoot Indian.* Wie das American Folklife Center–die US-amerikanische Institution für ethnographische und historische Musikdokumentation–jedoch später festzustellen konnte, war die Beschreibung der Bildhandlung nicht korrekt. Eigentlich würde die Momentaufnahme ein *...playback horn on the cylinder recorder...* zeigen, was bedeutete, dass Densmore den Mountain Chief in diesem Moment nicht aufnahm, sondern sie gemeinsam etwas anhörten (das Mountain Chief in einem weiteren Schritt für Densmore in Zeichensprache übersetzte).²

Ich schliesse das schwere Buch mit einem geräuschvollen *ptac* und lasse mich auf dem wabrig und uneben gewordenen Fussboden zu meiner Anfangsposition zurücktreiben. Track Nr. 4 der Playlist schwappt in Wellen an mir rüber und animiert dazu, sich auf das Wesentliche zu konzentrieren: fortschreitende, industrielle Vergangenheit, die Geschichte als Mühle? «Plucked From the Ground, Towards the Sun» von Hueco S. (von *Colonial Patterns*, Software Records, 2013). Inmitten dieser Melasse schliesse ich die Augen und lasse das Foto Revue passieren, sauge es auf als wäre es Wasser, lasse es gefrieren, verdampfen und puzzle die kondensierten Tropfen in ihrer komischen Fischaugen-Optik nochmal zusammen. Die drei Protagonist_innen auf dem Foto–zwei Menschen und ein Phonograph in einer vertrauten, aber aus der Mode gekommenen Studioästhetik–sind Geister der Vergangenheit. Eigentlich sind alle drei längst tot und doch glauben wir, sie zu kennen. Als Geister tragen sie zwei Gesichter, ein gruseliges und heimsuchendes und ein vermittelndes und weises. Track Nr. 5–*Lake* von Elysia Cramptons erster EP unter diesem Namen (Boomkat Editions, 2015) verbindet sich mit diesen Geistern und versetzt sie an das Ufer eines moosig-sumpfigen Amerikas.

Ohne die Magie der revidierten Bildunterschrift erinnert mich die Beziehungskonstellation des Fotos an eine Diskussion am *Digging in the Global South*-Festival in Köln letztes Jahr.³ Ein hier nicht namentlich zu nennender Mitbegründer von SWP Records stellte in einem Panel die Arbeit ihres kleinen, belgischen Labels vor, das sich zur Aufgabe gemacht hat, traditionelle und minoritäre Musik vom afrikanischen Kontinenten in Field Recordings zu konservieren und auf Vinyl zu veröffentlichen. Ähnlich zu anderen Labels dieser Art ist das imaginierte Publikum eine in den Heimatländern der ehemaligen Kolonialmächte angesiedelte Minderheit von «Kennern», die sich einen angemessenen Abspielanlage leisten können: «We want you to enjoy a great sound, seated in your favourite chair opposite your hi-fi...» Dass die Plattencover prominent die Namen der vergleichsweise finanzpotenten Aufzeichnerin aus dem globalen Norden platzieren, die Musiker der Feldaufnahmen jedoch oft unter vielversprechenden Titeln wie: *Malawi Grooves, Zambia Roadside* oder *Forgotten Guitars from Mozambique* subsummiert werden, lässt vermuten, dass die Geister der kolonialen Vergangenheit weiter spuken und sich die Figuren der Geschichte, wenn auch irgendwie verdreht, wiederholen. Die meist sehr pur inszenierten Veröffentlichungen leben von einer Geste des Unentdeckten, in Vergessenheit Geratenen (aber deswegen besonders Authentischen). Der Beitrag des Panels hört sich an wie ein Abenteuerbericht, mit einem weissen Rettungsphantasien ein von westlicher Kultur («McDonald's») überflutetes Afrika-Bild zeichnen. Die Praxis des Field Recordings im globalen Kontext offenbart sich hier–immer noch oder immer wieder–als blinder Fleck eines Diskurses um die Machtverhältnisse der Dokumentarischen. Und gleichzeitig steckt in der Diskussion des Panels dieselbe Ambivalenz, die auch das Bild in meinem Schoss zeigt: SWP Records oder auch Frances Densmore haben die Mittel, das Interesse sowie den Drang, verloren geglaubte oder aussterbende Musik zu konservieren und so Interessierten oder vom Verlust direkt Betroffenen (zumindest als Idee) zugänglich zu machen–ist doch toll? Und wenn dann noch meine meilenweit entfernten Ohren die Gelegenheit erhalten, nicht für möglich gehaltene Klänge zu hören–ist doch schön?

In Peder Mammerfelts «Circumcision Dance» vom Album *The Swedish Congo Records* (Archives Intérieurs, 2015), der sich als Track Nr. 6 in meine Playlist eingeschlichen hat, wurde auf der Basis von Field Recordings gearbeitet, die jedoch nicht als tatsächliches Material im Album vorkommen. Der schwedische Musiker und Labelbetreiber Mammerfelt interpretierte für sein Projekt sechs 1950 veröffentlichte 78 rpm Platten mit dem Titel *The Belgian Congo Records*. «Circumcision Dance» wurde die Struktur von ihrem Sound entkoppelt und in Form von 0 und 1 wieder ausgespuckt. Kein Sample historischer Musikaufnahmen aus dem sogenannten Belgisch-Kongo der dreissiger Jahre sollte in die Windungen meiner Lautsprecher finden, sondern nur ein synthetischer, abstrahierter Klon. Haben sich hier die Geister der Zukunft in die Vergangenheit eingeschlichen, mit dem Versuch, die analogen Klangkörper von ihrer ethnisierten Authentizität zu befreien? Aber zu welchem Preis: ist die emanzipierte Hörerin selbst genug?

Während ich über diese Fragen nachdenke, beginne ich leicht zu schwitzen und der Stoff unter meinen Achseln bleibt an der Haut kleben. Der nächste Track hat sich reibungslos an das abrupte Ende von Track Nr. 6 angereiht und bringt meinen fliegenden Teppich einige Zentimeter über dem Boden schwebend zum Ruhen. Der Titel von Track Nr. 7 lautet «Mix 2 (Toulouse Low Trax Mix)», die Interpretin heisst Ogoya Nengo and The Dodo Women's Group und das Album *On Mande Versions* (wobei iTunes hier offenbar an die Grenzen des eigenen Autorschafts-Konzepts kommt). Der Track, 2017 veröffentlicht, basiert auf Vocals der kenyanischen Sängerin Ogoya Nengo, dem aus dem Salon des Amateurs Umfeld stammenden jüngeren Toulouse Low Trax⁵ elektronisch instrumentiert, gepitcht und fragmentiert werden. «Mix 2» ist vor allem entspannt und nicht besonders aufregend, aber die Lyrics, zum Ende ich abwechslungsweise die englischen Worte «Where is you?» und «Where I see you?» verstehe, ziehen in ihrer feinen grammatikalischen Abwandlung mein Interesse auf sich. Ist das lustig? Und habe ich den Track im WWW angeklickt, weil der Klang des Namens Ogoya Nengo Spannendes zu versprechen hat? Fast so wie das O von Track Nr. 3 der Playlist?

Ich lockere meine Schultern und schüttle meinen Kopf. Dabei fällt mir eine Haarsträhne ins Gesicht. Ich bemerke, dass sie grau ist–so schnell? Obwohl es nicht so ist, fühlt es sich an, als hätte jemand etwas vorspielt, was diese drei doch so unterschiedlichen Gestalten gemeinsam hören können, ja, was sogar ich in meinem Zimmer an meinem Laptop noch hören könnte, unterstützt mein wohliges Gefühl. Was hören Sie, Mrs. Densmore? Und Sie, Mr. Mountain Chief? Und Sie, Phonograph? Und warum sind sie so lebendig?

---

1   http://www.loc.gov/pictures/item/
    2004667752/ (heruntergeladen am 11.02.18)
2   https://www.washingtonpost.com/
    national/health-science/smithsonian-
    archives-preserve-lost-and-dying-
    languages/2014/01/17/2a2e3218-74a1-11e3-
    8b3f-b166-6705ca3b_story.html
    (heruntergeladen am 11.01.18)
3   Das Festival war vornehmlich elektronischer Musik aus Afrika und der afrikanischen Diaspora gewidmet und bot in verschiedenen Formaten (Vorträge, Konzerte, Panels und Club-Nächte) einerseits ein differenziertes Bild des aktuellen musikalischen Schaffens, und gleichzeitig eine (selbst-)kritische Reflexion westlicher Zugriffe im Spannungsfeld zwischen positivem Othering, kultureller Aneignung und Hybridisierung.
4   http://www.swp-records.com/about
    (heruntergeladen am 11.02.18)
5   Siehe auch das Interview mit Toulouse Low Trax in zweikommasieben #15.

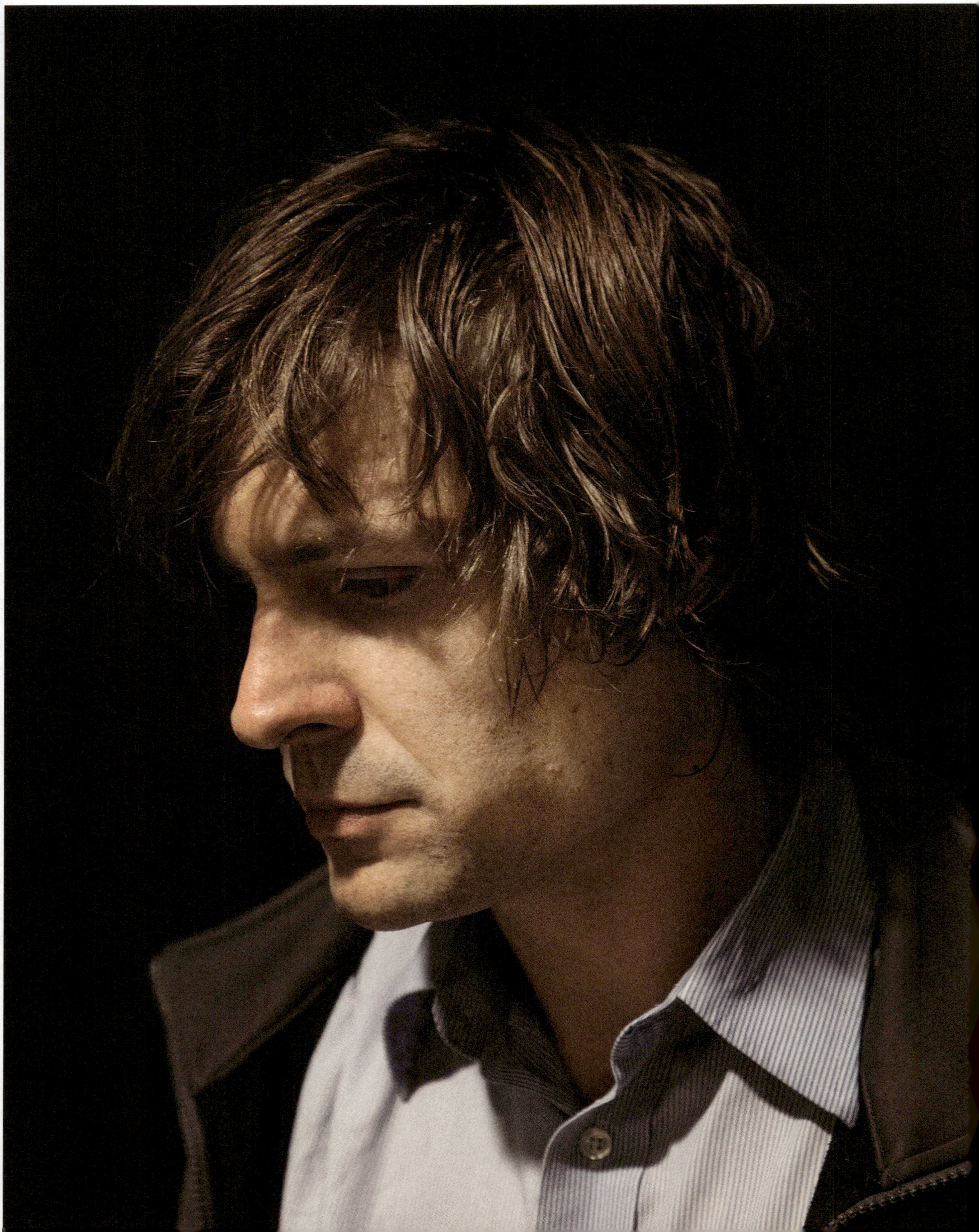

ON THE EDGE OF FOREVER
JOHN MAUS

Interview:
Helena Julian
Photography:
Kyle Tryhorn

In 2011, John Maus' *We Must Become the Pitiless Censors of Ourselves* instantly became a critical success, recognised for merging the parameters and paradoxes of pop and punk music with its enrapturing synth arrangements, haunting reduced lyrics and intellectual eclecticism. The album sent him on a world tour, though he was only to retreat from the music industry shortly after. Maus' live performances are iconic, emerging on stage with an almost exorcistic rituality, embodying both palpable anxiety and vulnerability, expelling fragments of lyrics as a way of reaching out into the void. Other than Maus' ferocious cries into the microphone there is no contact with the audience, neither hellos nor goodbyes, and yet audience members become increasingly mystified by his enigmatic performance, often flocking to join him on stage for an ecstatic, collective howling of the sparse lyrics.

Maus has spent the last six years revelling in a wealth of influences that seem external to the music industry, gradually gathering momentum, until finally emerging again, now with his newest album *Screen Memories* (2017). The following interview was conducted after a concert at the *Le Guess Who?* festival in Utrecht in November 2017, about two months into Maus' tour accompanying the album's release. The performance was again a true raptured exertion, with Maus exhausting his voice and body with an enthralling urgency, repeatedly spreading both arms and tilting his head upwards as a call for mercy from a bottomless vortex. Shortly after the show giving this interview, Maus was seemingly not out of breath at all, only his sweat drenched shirt and hair suggesting the rhapsodic concert had actually taken place.

Helena Julian: You've returned after six long years since your previous album release, *We Must Become the Pitiless Censors of Ourselves*. What have the past six years looked like for you?

John Maus: I keep saying that the previous years have gone by in what felt like two milliseconds. It feels like time is somehow accelerating, quickening. I spent roughly two years finishing my PhD dissertation in political science. At the time I also delved more into a feeling of responsibility that comes with the fact that my work had a bit of visibility. I became increasingly interested in the media, the technology, and the instruments in a way that I had never before. I built synthesizers from the circuit boards up. The last two years were spent composing and investigating different techniques and trying to find stuff to listen to. I guess a lot of that stuff will also be in the boxset the label is putting together (John Maus – *John Maus*, Ribbon Music, 2018). But all this time together felt like merely a week, I swear. There's some days that I woke up out of a fever dream thinking that I'm almost dead or have less than five minutes, or that nobody would be interested anymore and that I would have nobody to share the work with. It all moves too fast. Therefore, I was surprised that there was still any interest left after six years.

HJ: In these rapid years, what kind of work were you keeping close and listening to?

JM: When I was working on my dissertation it was mainly just the basic repository stuff that I like a lot but that you can't really take a lot from. When thinking of the post-war pop music idiom, you're not going to borrow anything from Mahler in a pop song, but when I started working on music I started investigating stuff that I could borrow. It's a process of looking under rocks. I listened to some of the library records of the *KPM 1000 Series*. For some reason I also got on a strange path to some of the music of the Chinese cultural revolution that lends itself to this idiom. They don't have the chromaticism that Western repertoire has, so the way they harmonize is very specific. As a way of finding inspiration I tried some things that were in keeping with this suspicion I had that one should have a relation to the technology that is involved in music-making. That one should be in complete command of the vanguard of that technology and in keeping with that, I wrote some programs with computational math software. I spent a lot of hours listening to these parameters that I had put in place, finally realizing that all I was hearing were precisely those rules that I had set up. I think I only went so far as to scratch the surface; it didn't go to shows as much as I thought it would. I listened to Ariel Pink's new record a lot, too—I'm always keeping tabs and sharing stuff with my little circle of friends that I started out with.

HJ: With your previous records in mind, I sense there is a different thematic impulse activating the new album. But I'm hesitant to define this motive. If anything, I would say it resonates like a "Songs of Experience" to your "Songs of Innocence."

JM: It's one of the things that I have been a bit morose about. I feel that in the first records, especially in the second one *(Love is Real, 2007)*, there was a sense of an assent; there was a flight, an audacity, a sort of affirmative conviction that is definitely lacking in this new record. The new work is much heavier and I've wondered if this is because of the little isolated place I wrote it from, being left to my own devices. Referring to the title of the new album, *Screen Memories*, I also feel I should recognize that everything became mediated through the news feeds and the screens around me. I can't shake the suspicion that there is this experience as opposed to an innocence or an optimism that perhaps recent global developments could have gone another way, while the actual news events of the past year have completely disregarded that option. I also realized while looking at the top 40s or the wider field of underground independent music: a lot of the tricks I had up my sleeve that set me apart in 2007

eine Rockshow. Genesis, Alan Vega—diese Leute. Das ist die Sprache, in der ich mich bewege und man kann dann diskutieren, inwiefern sich das mit Performancekunst kreuzt.

HJ: Ich mag, dass es da immer noch eine Ambiguität gibt in Bezug darauf, was ein Live-Konzert und was Performancekunst ist. Wenn ich über deine Show nachdenke, dann würde ich sagen, dass da weder ein reines Rock-Konzert noch Performancekunst präsentiert wird. Es handelt sich wohl eher um eine übergreifende Form, bei der die Aktion je nach Kontext und Ort anders gelesen werden kann. JM: Tatsächlich habe ich teilweise befürchtet, dass es einige Leute gibt, die an dem, was ich vorher gemacht habe, interessiert waren und die diesen Einbezug der Band wohl als Sellout wahrnehmen. Das, das die Sache so mehrdeutig macht, sogar radikal mehrdeutig, das es befragt, das ist die gleiche Logik, die auch hinter dem Album steht: Der Versuch, einer Sprache und ihren Parametern so strikt wie möglich zu folgen. Das ist, wie ich glaube, die Art und Weise wie man die Ambiguität und die Grenzen eines Werks untersuchen kann. Ich wünschte, ich hätte eine neue Maxime zu bieten. Ich fühle mich, als würde ich immer noch meinen Annahmen hinter *We Must Become the Pitiless Cencors of Ourselves* folgen. Mit dieser Platte sind diese Annahmen nun bestätigt worden. Die radikalsten Dinge scheinen immer aus einer gewissen Treue zu Konventionen zu entstehen; dann, wenn man einem Idiom bis zur Grenze seiner Belastbarkeit folgt. Je weiter man die Hülle dehnt, desto grösser werden die politischen Effekte. Es ist wie Beethoven im Unterschied zu Wagner. Während Wagner meinte, er wolle tun, wie es ihm beliebe und seine eigenen Harmonien kreierte, versuchte Beethoven, das perfekte Ding für die Wiener Kavaliere hinzubekommen und trieb diese Entwicklung bis in den Wahnsinn weiter. Oder auch jemand wie William Turner, der in seiner Sturm und Drang Periode ein Idiom immer weiter entwickelt, bis daraus beinahe schon Expressionismus wird—im 18. Jahrhundert! Es gibt jede Menge Beispiele, wie man einer Sache bis zum Zusammenbruch folgen kann; während man die Melodie der Sache selbst zu spielen beginnt.

HJ: Ich verstehe, dass der Einbezug der Band es ermöglicht, die Lesart der Form an sich zu befragen. Nachdem du mit der Platte nun tourst—was könnte eine andere mögliche Antwort auf diese Einbindung einer Live-Band sein? JM: Theoretisch wäre es möglich, das eine Antwort im Versuch bestünde, die Spannung dieser Form erneut fühlbar zu machen. Mit der Band wäre es toll, wenn man die Physik der Sache wieder mobilisieren könnte. Du hättest also nicht länger nur diesen hysterischen Körper auf der Bühne, hingerissen zur nackten Singularität, sondern darum herum würde sich eine physikalische Materialität winden, die nur mit Leib und Seele spielende Instrumentalisten erzeugen können. Aus dieser Überlegung heraus fasziniert mich der Gedanke, dass die gesamte Popmusik nach dem zweiten Weltkrieg nichts anderes ist als «Missbrauch von Heeresgerät». Eine Art Beschleunigung; Chiffriergeräte, Vocoder, Mischpulte, Tape, Raketen, Artillerie, Zerstörung. Und dann hast du all diese Teenager die dieses Zeug «missbrauchen»—diese Idee gefällt mir.

HJ: Was bedeutet es für dich, sich wieder einem Publikum auszusetzen nach sechs Jahren Pause? JM: Es ist etwas expliziter geworden, gerade im Zusammenhang mit dem, worüber wir gesprochen haben—die Schwere des neuen Albums im Gegensatz zur Unschuld der früheren Werke. Wie die Zeit zu rasen scheint und wie technokratische Ideologie um sich greift bis zur endgültigen Unversöhnlichkeit mit allem... Die

are just part of contemporary vernacular now. So if I wanted to keep pushing the post-war pop music idiom, it left me with fewer cards to play.

HJ The album also seems to be coming to terms precisely with this mediation.

JM Indeed. Much more than before, I felt that the medial dimension of music is to be mobilized, making the media a part of the expression. I can't repeat enough that I think that it is exactly the media that sets popular music in the last fifty years apart from all the earlier situations. It's interesting to remind ourselves that when people first heard a voice come out of a box they were horrified. The ghost leaving the machine, the object starting to talk; naked materiality itself beginning to talk for the first time.

HJ Thinking of pushing the idiom through mediation, the series of live shows will be performed with a live band. This differs immensely from the way you previously performed—solo, aided by recordings you sang along to, across, distorting, amplifying, emphasizing fragments as you moved through the song. What does the inclusion of a live band signify?

JM I didn't write the record with a live band in mind at all—it was the furthest thing from my mind. The band is a way of being able to comment on different modes of listening. A live situation calls for certain energy requirements. I feel the pulse should be faster. The details of the record are more complicated than anything than I had done before so it would probably take about seven performers on stage to literally play everything that is happening on the record. The inclusion of a band stems from a desire to share music, to bring the music to different places, to engage with a live situation.
In a less self-interested sense, I feel like part of a live situation that is all too often neglected is precisely the sonic dimension. A live performance brings you closer to being able to mobilise a physical dimension of sound that doesn't happen with a karaoke box. Aesthetically it settles any sort of confusion about what's taking place, whether it's a punk rock concert, a musical event, or some sort of performance-art work. I'm not operating in the performance art idiom; it's a rock-music show. It's Genesis and Alan Vega and all these kinds of folks. That's the idiom I'm in and I guess we could discuss to what extent that crosses with performance art.

HJ I appreciate that there is still some sort of ambiguity about what a live concert or performative work can be. Thinking about the show, what is presented isn't specifically a rock concert or a performative work. It's much more an accumulation of form in which the action is read by the specific context of where and how it is presented.

JM Indeed, part of me was worried that there would be a fraction of people interested in what I have previously done who would perceive the inclusion of a band as some sort of sellout move. The thing that made it ambiguous, even radically ambiguous, a sort of interrogation, was the same sort of logic behind the record; a way of trying to follow the idiom and its parameters as strictly as possible. That is the way I feel one is best able to interrogate the ambiguity and the limits of a work. I wish I had a new maxim to offer because I feel I'm still building on where my suspicions during *We Must Become the Pitiless Censors of Ourselves* tended to go. With this record, those suspicions seem confirmed. The most radical things almost always seem to come out of fidelity to convention, following the idiom to its breaking points. The further the envelope is pushed, the greater the political effects will be. It's like Beethoven as opposed to Wagner. Wagner stating I'm just going to do whatever and create my own harmonies while Beethoven tried to make the most perfect Viennese gallant thing, exploring this development into insanity. Or maybe even someone like William Turner who in his Sturm und Drang period just starts pushing the idiom further and further so that it becomes almost close to expressionism, already in the

Auseinandersetzung mit dem Publikum ist bewusst exorzistischer geworden, zumindest für mich ist es eine Art Exorzismus. Viel mehr als noch 2012, viel dringlicher. Der erste Track auf dem Album, «The Combine», ist sehr Johannes-der-Täufer-mässig, Heuschrecken und Honig, das Königreich ist nah... Es gefällt mir eigentlich nicht, dass diese Art von Assoziationen schon aufgerufen worden sind—dieses evangelische Ding—, aber es ist nun halt mal eine Lesart, die es gibt. Wenn ich jetzt in die Gesichter der Leute im Publikum schaue, angeleuchtet von den Handys, auf die sie schauen, dann erinnert mich das an die Art und Weise, wie die Scholastik das Böse als «ungeschaffenes Licht» zur Ontologie gemacht hat. Natürlich schauen sie alle aber nicht auf ihren Bildschirm sondern auf den Text, das Bild vor allem. Ach, diese ganze Silicon Valley Ideologie... Technologie an und für sich ist wohl zwischen oder jenseits von Gut und Böse, aber es ist die Ideologie, die sie rahmt—vor allem diese gnostisch-technokratische Achtsamkeit; Einheit und Fortschritt, wie sie alle von Intelligenz und Evolution schwärmen... Die Tastsache, dass dies mehr und mehr die gängige Ideologie zu sein scheint, hat in mir eine mir wichtige Unversöhnlichkeit genährt.

HJ: Wenn ich an die Lyrics auf dem neuen Album denke, dann scheinen die eine gewisse erkennbare Unmittelbarkeit zu haben. Gehe ich etwa die Lyrics zu «The Combine» im Kopf durch, da scheinen nicht mehr als zwei sich wiederholende Zeilen zu sein: «I see the combine coming, It's gonna dust us all to nothing». Kannst du Dir vorstellen, dass die Lyrics also wie Mantras funktionieren? JM: Ich würde in Bezug auf Lyrics generell eigentlich darauf wetten, dass sie das Schlimmste sind, was der Musik je passiert ist. Die Existenz von Versen als Synonym für Musik im Ganzen im populären Bewusstsein—das ist der Musik an sich ja eigentlich völlig fremd. Die Worte, die bleiben, sind eher nur reine Idiome. Es gibt so viele Beispiele, wie Sprache auch zu einem phonetischen Angriff auf Bedeutung werden kann; Sprache ist nun mal auch in einer bestimmten akustischen Materialität begründet. Also versuche ich, die Lyrics bis zum Maximum zu pushen. Bei manchen Texten auf dem neuen Album dachte ich, dass sie schon beinahe zu platt geworden sind—«Standing on the edge of forever, your pets are gonna die»... Da muss es irgendeine unbewusste Verbindung zu den Entwicklungen in der Politik gegeben haben, als ich das schrieb—die Wahlen in den USA waren ja kurz vorher. Auf eine Art hoffte ich, dass sie in einer Beziehung zu dem stünden, wie ich mich mit der Welt verbunden sah, während ich schrieb... Und ich dachte mir, das Apokalyptische könnte Anklang finden. Und dann sind da die Lyrics in «Bombs Away» am Ende des Albums, die wohl die philosophischsten Verse auf dem Album sind. Sie sprechen direkt darüber, was es heisst, zu mobilisieren. Und das ist weit entfernt von dieser linearen Zeit der Technokraten, bei denen sich vorwärts bewegen immer Fortschritt heisst, als ob Mobilisierung sich immer der Perfektion annähern würde... Aber obgleich ich versuche, diese Konzepte und Idiome zurückzuweisen, amüsiert es mich doch, wenn ich Kritiken lese, wo es nur heisst, ach, dieser 80er Jahre Retro Typ ist zurück in der Stadt mit seinem Hypnagogic-Pop-Retro-Synth-Coldwave Synthesizer Album, mit Songs über Landmaschinen... Ich sage dir, von jetzt an werde ich einfach nur noch sagen: «Alles chillig, ich bin chillig...»

HJ: Und chillig zu sein, das ist immer das Wahre... JM: (lacht) Ja, niemand will eine eiternde Wunde, die auf der Bühne rumschreit oder ein blendendes Licht. Die wollen alle nur, dass alles chillig bleibt, Ninja Turtle T-Shirts tragen und drauf spucken...

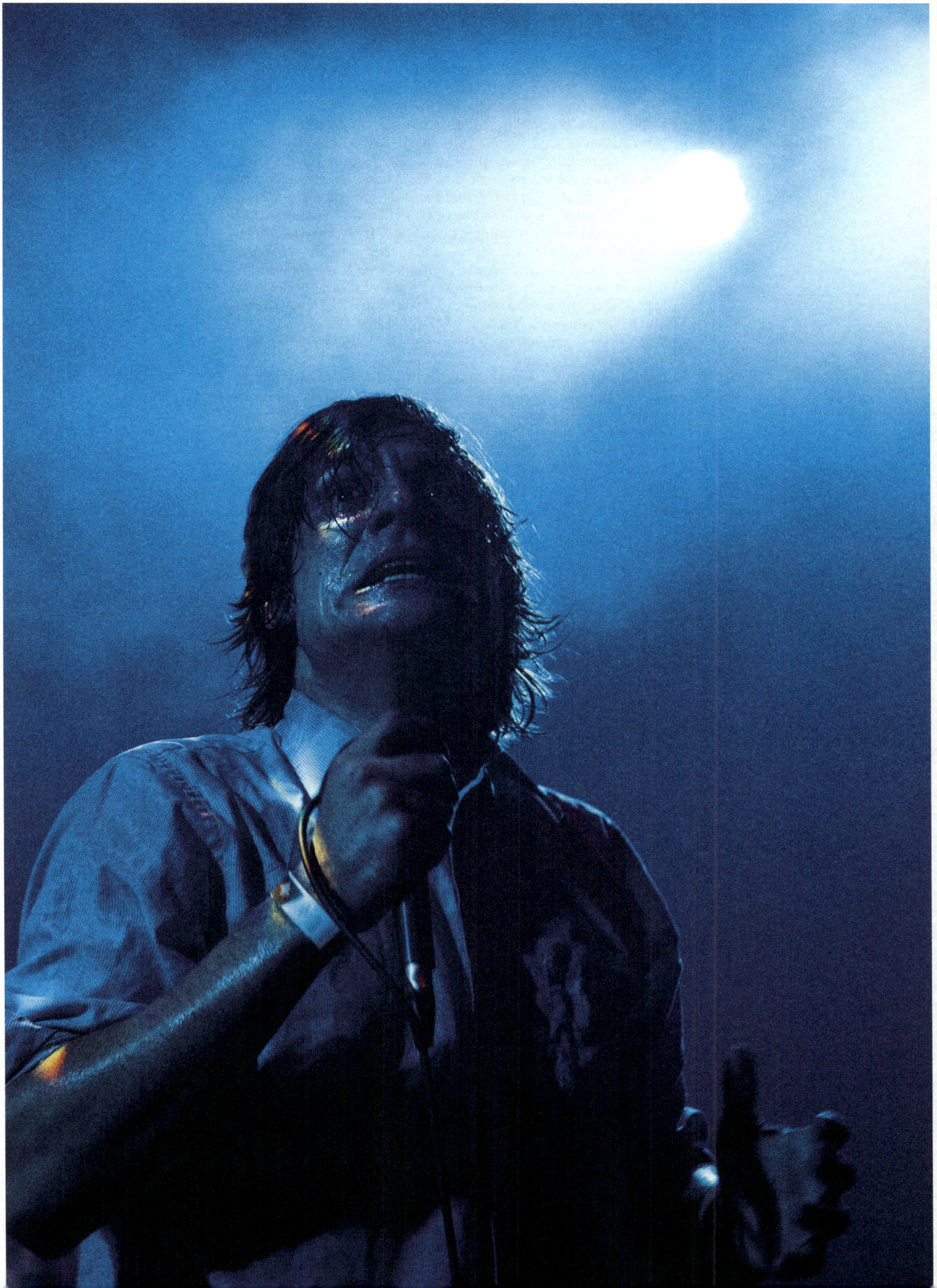

18th century. There's plenty of examples of this following through to breaking points, playing to the own melody of the thing itself.

HJ I understand the inclusion of a band as a way of negotiating the way the form is read. After touring this record, what could a further response be to the inclusion of the band?

JM Hypothetically speaking, the response would attempt to feel the tension of that form again. With the band, the ideal thing would be mobilizing the physics of the thing itself. So you don't only have the hysterical body on stage enraptured around a naked singularity, but around that there is torsion of physical materiality mobilized as only dedicated instrumental performers using this equipment could do. It comes out of precisely this thing that fascinated me—that post-war popular music is essentially a misuse of World War II equipment. It's a form of acceleration; scramblers, vocoders, mixing desks, tape desks, missiles, artillery, destruction. And then you had all these teenagers "misusing" them—I like that idea.

HJ What does it mean to you to engage with a live audience again after six years?

JM It's become more explicit in light of what we were talking about—the heaviness of the new album as opposed to an innocence of the previous album, the way that time seems to be accelerating and technocratic ideology seems to hold its way as a kind of terminate irreconcilability. Engaging with an audience has become more consciously exorcistic, like an exorcism of sorts—at least in my mind. More than it was in 2012, more urgent. "The Combine," the opening track of the new album, is very "John the Baptist," "locusts and honey," and "the kingdom is at hand." I don't like that it's sort of an association that has already been made, this evangelical thing, but it is a reading that has already happened. When I see the faces of the audience members now, lit up by looking down at their phones, it reminds me of the way mystic scholastic theology ontologizes evil as "uncreated light." But of course they aren't looking at their screens but at the text, the image of it all. It's the whole Silicon Valley ideology. Technology itself is beneath good and evil but it's the ideology that frames it, specifically this whole gnostic technocratic mindfulness, oneness, and progression when they talk about intelligence and evolution. The fact that this is becoming more and more the ideology fostered in me a more important irreconcilability.

HJ The lyrics of the new album again possess a recognizable immediacy. Reciting the lyrics to "The Combine" now in my mind, there must not be more than two repeated lines: "I see the combine coming, it's gonna dust us all to nothing." Do you see the lyrics functioning like mantras?

JM The wager that I make about the lyrics in general is that lyrics are the worst thing that's ever happened to music. This existence of verse in popular consciousness as being synonymous with music, it really is utterly foreign to music. So the words that remain are much more idioms. There are so many examples of language becoming a phonetic assault on meaning—language is set in a specific way of acoustic materiality. So in a way I'm again trying to push the lyrics through to their maxim. With some of them on the new record, I almost thought it would be too on-the-nose: "standing on the edge of forever," "your pets are gonna die." There must be some unconscious parallels with the current politics in which I wrote these lyrics, with the American elections having happened so recently. In a way, I'd hoped it had come out in correspondence of what my soil was while writing, and I thought that the apocalyptic would resonate. And then there are the lyrics on "Bombs Away" at the end of the album which are arguably the most philosophical verses on the album, talking directly about what it actually means to mobilize. And it's the furthest thing from the chronological time that the technocrats suggest, where moving forward always means progress, as if mobilization is always coming closer to perfection. But even when trying to push these idioms, I'm amused to see that the reviews write something like, "Oh damn, it's eighties retro man back in town with his hypnagogic pop-retro-synth-cold-wave-synthesizer album, with songs about farm machinery." I'm telling you, from now on my thing will just be to say: "It's chill, I'm chill."

HJ And being chill is always true.

JM (Laughing) Indeed, nobody wants to see a festering wound that screams on stage, or a blinding light—they just want to know it's chill, and wear Ninja Turtle shirts, and have a few yucks.

Interview Renick Bell

CODE POTENTIAL
RENICK BELL

Interview:
Mathis Neuhaus
Photography:
Martin Delaney

Renick Bell is a computer musician—not the kind of computer musician that a lot of people are these days, but someone who uses the machine and its inherent potentialities for writing music. By using code and algorithms to compose sounds, he frees himself from elaborate user interfaces. No Ableton needed, not in the studio and not on stage. The results of this can be heard most recently on the EP *Empty Lake* (UIQ, 2016), and they can also be seen, thanks to a website[1] accompanying the release which streams music via code from Bell's system.

Besides producing and performing electronic music, the Texas native is also a graduate of the doctoral program at Tama Art University in Tokyo, Japan, where he's been living since 2006.

The following conversation with Mathis Neuhaus took place in a small Indian restaurant in Tokyo's Kanda district. It touches on everything from the perception of algorithms to live coding as a demystifying strategy to the difference between performing and producing electronic music.

[1] empty-lake.u-i-q.org

Mathis Neuhaus: I want to start out this conversation by introducing my own perspective on algorithms in music. It is very different to your vantage point on this, but we'll talk about that later. I went to New York two years ago to research a story called *The Taste Machine,* which deals with the question of whether algorithms are able to make taste.

Renick Bell: And what is your conclusion?

MH Taste, of course, is a very vague term, but platforms like Spotify are definitely changing the ways people are listening to music. Playlists and therefore the algorithms working behind these playlists are doing what back in the days was the sole purpose of someone on the radio or in the record store: to recommend new music you've never heard before. And, at least in the mainstream, this is playing a very important role by now. I know people who completely rely on their Spotify recommendations for discovering new music. You still have the selectors, diggers and music nerds, but that is not most people—and Spotify as a platform is scaled for most people, not for the niche. So my perspective on algorithms focuses on analyzing their cultural impact while you think from the other side of the screen, so to speak.

RB I mean, there is obviously a wide variety, with many types of algorithms that apply to many different things. But in the end, they all require programming to implement.

MH How did you end up using algorithms for making music? Could you walk me through your history of composing and producing sounds? Were you interested in the potential of the machine from the very beginning, or were you also involved with conventional music?

RB As a very young child I sang in boys' choirs, and at nine I started to play the piano. During high school, I also started to play drums. I picked up guitar and did a lot of things. The first time I got into music done by a machine was with a Yamaha PortaSound PSS-560 synthesizer from 1990 that had this very simple synthesis section where you could adjust some parameters of the voice. It also had a drum machine, again very rudimentary, but you could boost the tempo to 260 bpm or something and get other strange things out of it. As a university student, I just wanted to do music and was looking for the right voice, but couldn't really find it. I wanted to do all these things I mentioned at the same time. The closest I got to that was playing in bands. Back in Texas I was in hardcore and screamo bands and played all the instruments in different contexts, but bands are hard to manage. Meanwhile, I was building up a studio with a friend and we were doing production work for hip hop groups. Furthermore, we started doing our own techno and trying to make things like what we were listening to at the time, which for me was releases on Mo'Wax and drum'n'bass. I stuck with that for a long time, doing drum'n'bass tracks and sending them to BBC 1Xtra and labels and trying to get them on 12", but I also really wanted to perform electronic music live. But if I am in the studio, dragging snare samples around, that is about as far from live as you can get. So I asked myself: "how can I do the things I am doing live?"

MH When was this?

RB That was before Ableton, in the mid-1990s. In college I was studying electronic music, so I knew about and had experience with tools like CSound and Max/MSP and thought that I could maybe use these tools to perform my music live. In my master's degree I built a piece of generative music software with a graphical user interface in SuperCollider. It worked fine, but after all it was all buttons and sliders, and I had to manipulate everything with the mouse. It was like playing guitar with one finger. It wasn't really satisfying. I thought at the time that maybe it was a factor of working with the wrong tools, like the wrong graphical user interface toolkit, so I started looking at other programming languages in depth. Along the way, in 2004, I read an article

Renick Bell ist ein Computermusiker. Nicht so, wie heutzutage viele mit dem Computer Musik machen, sondern wie jemand, der die inhärenten Möglichkeiten der Maschine zur Musikkomposition verwendet. Bell nutzt Algorithmen und Code für seine Arbeit und befreit sich dadurch von aufwendigen, meist grafischen Schnittstellen. Es geht auch ohne Ableton – im Studio und auf der Bühne. Die Ergebnisse seiner Arbeit konnte man zuletzt auf der EP Empty Lake (UIQ, 2016) hören; und auch sehen, dank einer das Release begleitenden Website, die den Code aus Bells System zur Musik streamte[1].

Neben seiner Arbeit als Produzent und Performer elektronischer Musik war der Texaner Teil des Graduiertenprogramms der Tama Art University in Tokio, Japan, wo er seit 2006 lebt. Das nachstehende Gespräch mit Mathis Neuhaus fand in einem kleinen Südindischen Restaurant in Kanda, Tokio statt und berührt Fragen der Wahrnehmung von Algorithmen in der Gesellschaft, coding als demystifizierende Strategie und die Unterschiede zwischen der Produktion und der Performance elektronischer Musik.

by Alex McLean called *Hacking Perl In Nightclubs*. He was doing this live coding stuff long before me, in 2004 already. I read the article at the time and thought, well, this is really cool, and it also seemed really ridiculous to me at the same time. Like, why would you ever do that? I didn't get the point. But around 2006, I was doing all this programming in Haskell – the language which is still my main language at the moment – and testing things. I realized: "oh, wait. I'm making sounds here, directly in code, without a graphical user interface, and it's kind of working." Then it clicked for me what Alex McLean was talking about in his article. I gave up on trying to build a graphical interface and pursued using the code directly.

MH You cut out the middle man.

RB Right, and it actually worked and was the outlet I had been looking for. When I played piano, I was never really good at letting my two hands work independently. With my drum technique, I managed to play a trap set but I could never really do the amazing things. Guitar was the same. My technical skills were always lacking. But all that time I was programming, also. My dad had a TI-994a computer at the house already when I was five, so I had been using them forever. I can type pretty well, you know, and I realized I have this technical skill that I am pretty good at, and by using this to make music directly, it all fell into place. From that point on, I followed this path and started to make my own tools for live coding.
I decided that I didn't want to sit and drag around snare samples and put the snare samples in exactly the right place because I don't have the time to do that. I want to generate the music, not specify each detail by hand, but exactly in that moment – though composing with algorithms does require exact specification in the code of each musical event, in some manner. Even a randomly-generated detail is precisely specified as random. The composer is ultimately responsible for nearly all of the details.

MH You said that you wanted to perform. Did you see the potential of writing music directly into code also for producing?

RB I was aiming at performing. That was my whole goal, but along the way I realized that I could use these generative tools to produce, too. And it's true: I can produce so much more than I could have ever done before. The computer can generate all those details that I spent six months creating in the studio. I can get the machine to do that for me in a second. I saw that benefit, but the original purpose was to use this for performing. And this was in line with what Alex McLean and Nick Collins were doing from the early 2000s on. They are the true originators of this thing called "algorave," where people are live coding on stage and other people are dancing to the music that is produced in realtime while being able to follow the coding process by watching a projection of what is on the screens.

MH Would you therefore consider yourself more as a performer then a producer?

RB No, because before I found this outlet of live coding I was heavily involved as a producer of electronic music.
I was performing before I was producing, but as an electronic musician I was producing before I was performing.

MH The process of live coding resembles jazz a lot, I find.

RB Definitely. Improvisation is a very important part. The process shares a lot of similarities with jazz. With my software, I can't produce the same song twice. Even if I wanted to I couldn't. The feature is not built in. I am trying to change that a bit, but right now I cannot reproduce the same song. And the way I am doing things and the way my setup is designed, I cannot completely foresee how things are going to come out. I hear it for the first time at the same time the audience hears it. And if I don't like it, then I change it. That is how I navigate a performance: letting things come

Mathis Neuhaus: Ich möchte unser Gespräch gerne beginnen, indem ich von meiner eigenen Perspektive auf Algorithmen in der Musik erzähle. Diese unterscheidet sich, soweit mir bekannt ist, recht deutlich von deiner; aber dazu später dann mehr. Vor zwei Jahren war ich in New York, um für eine Reportage mit dem Titel *The Taste Machine* zu recherchieren, die sich mit der Frage auseinandersetzt, ob Algorithmen fähig sind, Geschmack zu bilden oder zu beeinflussen.

Renick Bell: Und zu welchem Schluss bist du gekommen?

MN: Geschmack ist natürlich ein recht vager Begriff, aber Plattformen wie Spotify verändern definitiv die Art und Weise, wie Menschen Musik hören. Playlists und die Algorithmen, die im Verborgenen hinter diesen arbeiten, machen das, was früher eines der Alleinstellungsmerkmale von Radiosendern oder Plattenläden war: neue, überraschende und unbekannte Musik zu empfehlen. Und hier spielt Spotify mittlerweile eine sehr wichtige Rolle. Ich kenne Menschen, die sich für das Entdecken neuer Musik ausschliesslich auf die algorithmischen Empfehlungen der Plattform verlassen. Es gibt natürlich noch immer die, welche sich selber auf die Suche machen – aber das sind Ausnahmen. Meine Perspektive auf Algorithmen ist also die Analyse ihres kulturellen Einflusses, während du sozusagen von der anderen Seite des Bildschirms her denkst. RB: Es gibt natürlich eine Vielzahl unterschiedlicher Algorithmen, die in einer ebenso grossen Vielzahl verschiedener Gebiete ihre Anwendung finden. Aber letztendlich können sie alle nur mit Programmierfähigkeiten implementiert werden.

MN: Wie kamst du zu der Entscheidung, Algorithmen für die Musikproduktion zu nutzen? Warst du von Anfang an interessiert am Potential der Maschine oder auch involviert in konventioneller Musik? Oder anders gefragt: Kannst du bitte deinen musikalischen Werdegang skizzieren?
RB: Als kleines Kind habe ich in Knabenchören gesungen und mit neun fing ich an, Klavier zu spielen. Während der High-School habe ich dann auch Schlagzeug und Gitarre gespielt. Mit Musik, die von einer Maschine gemacht wurde, kam ich zum ersten Mal durch den Yamaha PortaSound PSS-560 Synthesizer aus dem Jahre 1990 in Berührung. Der hatte zum Beispiel eine Funktion, die einige Parameter der Stimme veränderte oder einen rudimentären Drumcomputer, mit dem 260 bpm Stücke oder andere merkwürdige Geräusche produziert werden konnten. Als Universitätsstudent wollte ich einfach nur Musik machen und war auf der Suche nach dem richtigen Outlet, ohne es jemals wirklich zu finden. Ich wollte all die Instrumente, die ich vorhin erwähnt habe, gleichzeitig nutzen. Naheliegend war auch, dass ich in Bands spielte. In Hardcore- und Screamo-Bands spielte ich alle Instrumente in unterschiedlichen Kontexten – aber Bands sind auf Dauer schwer zu managen. Zeitgleich begann ich, gemeinsam mit einem Freund ein Studio einzurichten und wir produzierten Beats für Hip-Hop-Gruppen sowie unsere eigenen Techno-Tracks. Wir versuchten Musik zu machen, die wie das klang, was wir zur damaligen Zeit gerne hörten: für mich waren das Veröffentlichungen auf Mo'Wax und Drum'n'Bass. Ich produzierte dann lange solche Sachen und schickte die Stücke an BBC 1Xtra und an Labels, um auf irgendwelchen 12-Inches zu landen. Ich wollte aber auch unbedingt elektronische Musik live auf der Bühne spielen. Im Studio Snare Samples von A nach B zu ziehen ist natürlich so weit weg von live, wie nur irgendwie möglich. Also stellte ich mir die Frage, wie ich die Dinge, die ich machte, auf der Bühne umsetzen könnte.

MN: Wann war das? RB: Noch vor Ableton, Mitte der 1990er Jahre. Im College studierte ich elektronische Musik, deswegen waren mir Werkzeuge wie CSound oder Max/MSP nicht fremd und ich dachte, dass ich diese möglicherweise für meine Performances nutzen könnte. Im Masterstudium habe ich dann letztendlich mit SuperCollider eine generative Musiksoftware mit grafischer Benutzeroberfläche gebaut. Das hat ganz gut funktioniert, aber man verliess sich doch immer noch auf Knöpfe und Regler und musste alles mit der Maus machen. Es war wie Gitarre mit nur einem Finger zu spielen: nicht wirklich zufriedenstellend. Ich dachte, dass ich vielleicht die falschen Werkzeuge nutze—das heisst, grafische Benutzeroberflächen—und schaute mir deswegen auch Programmiersprachen genauer an. Während meiner Recherche stiess ich 2004 auf den Artikel *Hacking Perl In Nightclubs* von Alex McLean. Ich las den Artikel, in dem es um Live-Codieren in Klubs ging, und dachte, dass das eine coole Idee sei, die sich aber gleichzeitig total absurd anhörte. Warum sollte man das machen? Ich erkannte den Kern der Sache nicht. Um 2006 programmierte ich viel in Haskell, der Programmiersprache, die ich auch heute noch hauptsächlich benutze, und merkte, dass ich Sounds direkt im Code produzieren konnte, ohne überhaupt eine grafische Benutzeroberfläche nutzen zu müssen. Das war der Moment, an dem ich verstand was Alex McLean in seinem Artikel sagen wollte. Ich gab auf, eine Benutzeroberfläche bauen zu wollen und begann, direkt im Code zu komponieren.

MN: Du verzichtest auf den Mittelsmann. RB: Genau. Und es funktionierte tatsächlich und war genau die Möglichkeit, nach der ich lange gesucht hatte. Als ich Klavier spielte, war ich nie wirklich gut darin, meine beiden Hände unabhängig voneinander arbeiten zu lassen. Mein Können am Schlagzeug reichte für ein Trap-Set, aber nicht mehr. An der Gitarre war es ähnlich. Meine technischen Fähigkeiten waren immer begrenzt. Aber parallel dazu programmierte ich immer. Mein Vater hatte schon als ich fünf war einen TI-994a Computer zu Hause. Ich konnte entsprechend gut tippen und realisierte endlich, dass ich diese technische Fähigkeit direkt nutzen konnte, um Musik zu machen. Es ergab Sinn. Ich entschied mich dazu, nicht jedes einzelne Sample hin- und herziehen und es an genau der richtigen Stelle fallen lassen zu müssen. Dafür habe ich keine Zeit. Ich will Musik generieren und nicht jedes Detail spezifizieren müssen. Obwohl das Komponieren mit Hilfe von Code natürlich exakte Spezifikationen jedes musikalischen Ereignisses verlangt—ein zufällig generiertes Detail ist präzise spezifiziert als zufällig. Der Komponist ist letztendlich für alle Details verantwortlich.

MN: Du erwähntest, dass du die Perfomance im Kopf hattest. Hast du das Potential des Komponierens im Code dafür auch sofort erkannt? RB: Mein Ziel war die Bühne, aber auf dem Weg dorthin realisierte ich, dass ich diese generativen Werkzeuge auch zum Komponieren nutzen kann. Ich kann so viel mehr Musik produzieren als jemals zuvor. Der Computer kann all die Details generieren, für die ich früher sechs Monate im Studio verbracht habe. Ich kann die Maschine dazu bringen, das in einer Sekunde zu erledigen. Ich erkannte diesen Vorteil—aber der ursprüngliche Grund war, den Code für die Perfomance zu nutzen. Das war auch im Sinne dessen, was Alex McLean und Nick Collins seit den frühen 2000er Jahren machen. Sie sind die Schöpfer der *Algoraves*, bei denen Menschen live auf der Bühne Code schreiben und andere zu der in Echtzeit produzierten Musik tanzen. Die Tanzenden können den Prozess nachverfolgen, indem ein Stream der Bildschirme an die Wand projiziert wird.

MN: Würdest du dich also eher als Performer denn als Produzent bezeichnen?

out, and if they are cool and surprising, I let them play, and if not, I change to the next thing as quickly as possible.

MH This is very debatable now, but I like to talk about failure as something to strive for or as a creative possibility. What is your stance on this? By doing things like you are doing them, can there be any failure in your performance?

RB I was part of this live coding conference recently, and Shelly Knotts, who is part of this duo called Algobabez, was one of the keynote speakers. One section of her keynote speech dealt with failure and emphasized that it is a principle and accepted part of live coding. The live coding community particularly is fine with that, I think. Depending on the system you are using, it can always be hit-and-miss. It's possible to shut everything down by accident, for example. That can happen because you used all your RAM or stuff like that. There is technical danger, but people are cool with that and don't really mind. I've tried to design my system so that it is robust against that kind of technical failure, but sometimes, from a musical perspective, I of course get things that are weird or that I'm not into at all. But while I'm changing it, I sometimes find elements that I actually want to keep playing for a little bit longer. At those times, maybe what I tried failed my initial intention, but it worked in other ways.

MH Is this approach very different to when you are producing music? Do you give yourself more time, for example, or do you lay out sketches?

RB After all, dance music is formulaic, to a certain extent. But there is one big difference for me between performing and producing: when I produce, I will usually have one sample set and one rhythm for a track, because I like that distinct sample set and distinct rhythm at that time, and then I will sit and improvise with it for an hour or so, and hopefully things I like will come out of that process. I will, say, let just the drums play, then just the synth parts, then just the melody, and I will record them one by one and come back to them and edit them together so that it makes sense. So I distill the hour-long process into three or four minutes. On the other hand, when I play live, I seldom let anything play for longer than a minute before I make changes to it. I try to move very quickly. That's a big difference for me between performing live and producing a track.

MH As I understand it, the visual element of live coding is as important as the music itself.

RB Yes. There is usually a projection behind the performer where you can see what he or she is doing at that very moment. It's about exposing the process.

MH It becomes transparent and lifts the curtain.

RB Yes, and that's a very important issue for our community, also to make the process of coding more accessible. Another good example of people in the community trying to make our approach more accessible is the work of Shelly Knotts, who I mentioned before, and also Joanne Armitage. They are doing these workshops for women on how to use the tools of live coding. After a couple of days, the participants are all producing music, and it shows that what we are doing is maybe not extremely simple but also not that difficult. People like Shelly and Joanne are helping a lot to demystify the whole process. Everybody can do this stuff.

MH Is the coding more important than the result?

RB I've heard some people complain that the process is emphasized to the result's detriment. Maybe sometimes that's true. I hope in my case that it isn't, because I'm very concerned with the final result. But the question has to be asked: what is the result? Just the audio? Because that is not the only and sole point of live coding. Most algorave performers want to have people dancing, and they want to make something that sounds cool, but they also want to show the process and build a community. It isn't like the process is more important, because there isn't a single important aim but rather a variety

RB: Nein, denn bevor ich anfing, Code zu nutzen, war ich stark als Produzent elektronischer Musik involviert. Ich performte mit Code, bevor ich damit produzierte, aber als elektronischer Musiker produzierte ich, bevor ich performte.

MN: Der Prozess des Live-Codings erinnert mich an Jazz. RB: Auf jeden Fall. Improvisation spielt eine wichtige Rolle. Es teilt viele Gemeinsamkeiten mit Jazz. In meiner Software kann ich das gleiche Stück nie zweimal produzieren, selbst wenn ich wollte. Dieses Feature existiert nicht. Ich versuche das zu ändern, aber momentan kann ich kein Stück reproduzieren. Die Art und Weise wie ich Code nutze und wie mein Setup aufgebaut ist, sorgt dafür, dass ich nie komplett sicher sein kann, wie das Ergebnis genau klingen wird. Das Publikum und ich hören alles gemeinsam zum ersten Mal. Wenn es mir nicht gefällt, ändere ich es. So navigiere ich meine Performance: ich versuche Dinge und wenn diese cool und überraschend sind, lasse ich sie laufen und wenn nicht, wechsle ich so schnell wie möglich zu etwas anderem.

MN: Ich möchte gerne über das Scheitern sprechen: Wie kann in deinem Modus überhaupt irgendetwas scheitern? Gibts es dafür überhaupt ein Potential? RB: Ich war vor kurzem auf einer Konferenz, bei der Shelly Knotts, die Teil des Duos Algobabez ist, eine Keynote hielt. In einem Teil ihrer Präsentation setzte sie sich genau mit dieser Frage des Scheiterns auseinander und betonte, dass es ein Prinzip und akzeptierter Part des Live-Codings ist. Die Community hat kein Problem damit. Das System, das man nutzt, kann manchmal für Probleme sorgen. Es kommt vor, dass alles runterfährt, weil man all seinen RAM verbraucht hat. Es gibt eine technische Gefahr, aber die Leute kümmert das nicht wirklich. Ich versuche zwar, mein System so zu gestalten, dass es immun ist gegen solch technische Fehler, aber aus musikalischer Perspektive gibt es auch immer mal wieder Dinge, die seltsam klingen oder die mir gar nicht gefallen. Aber während ich sie ändere, finde ich manchmal Elemente, die ich doch noch ein bisschen laufen lassen möchte. Wenn das passiert, bin ich vielleicht mit meiner ursprünglichen Idee gescheitert, habe sie aber auf andere Art und Weise nutzen können.

MN: Inwiefern unterscheidet sich deine Herangehensweise von der herkömmlichen Komposition von Musik? Gibst du dir mehr Zeit oder arbeitest du mit Skizzen? RB: Dancemusic ist bis zu einem gewissen Grad schablonenhaft. Aber es gibt für mich einen grossen Unterschied zwischen dem Komponieren und der Perfomance: Wenn ich produziere, habe ich für ein Stück meist ein Sampleset und einen Rhythmus, weil mir zu dem Zeitpunkt ein bestimmtes Sampleset und ein bestimmter Rhythmus besonders gefallen. Damit improvisiere ich dann für eine gewisse Zeit und hoffentlich ergeben sich aus diesem Prozess Dinge, die ich mag. Ich lasse zum Beispiel nur die Drums laufen, dann nur die Synthesizer-Parts und dann nur die Melodie. Ich nehme diese Teile einzeln auf und editiere sie anschliessend zusammen, sodass es Sinn ergibt. Ich destilliere aus einem Prozess, der eine Stunde oder länger dauert, ein Ergebnis, das drei oder vier Minuten lang ist. Wenn ich hingegen auf der Bühne bin, lasse ich selten etwas länger als eine Minute laufen, bevor ich Dinge verändere. Ich versuche mich schnell zu bewegen.

MN: So wie ich das verstehe, ist das visuelle Element beim Live-Codings genauso wichtig wie die Musik selbst? RB: Das stimmt. Eine Projektion hinter dem Perfomer zeigt, was er oder sie in genau dem Moment macht. Es geht darum, den Prozess offenzulegen.

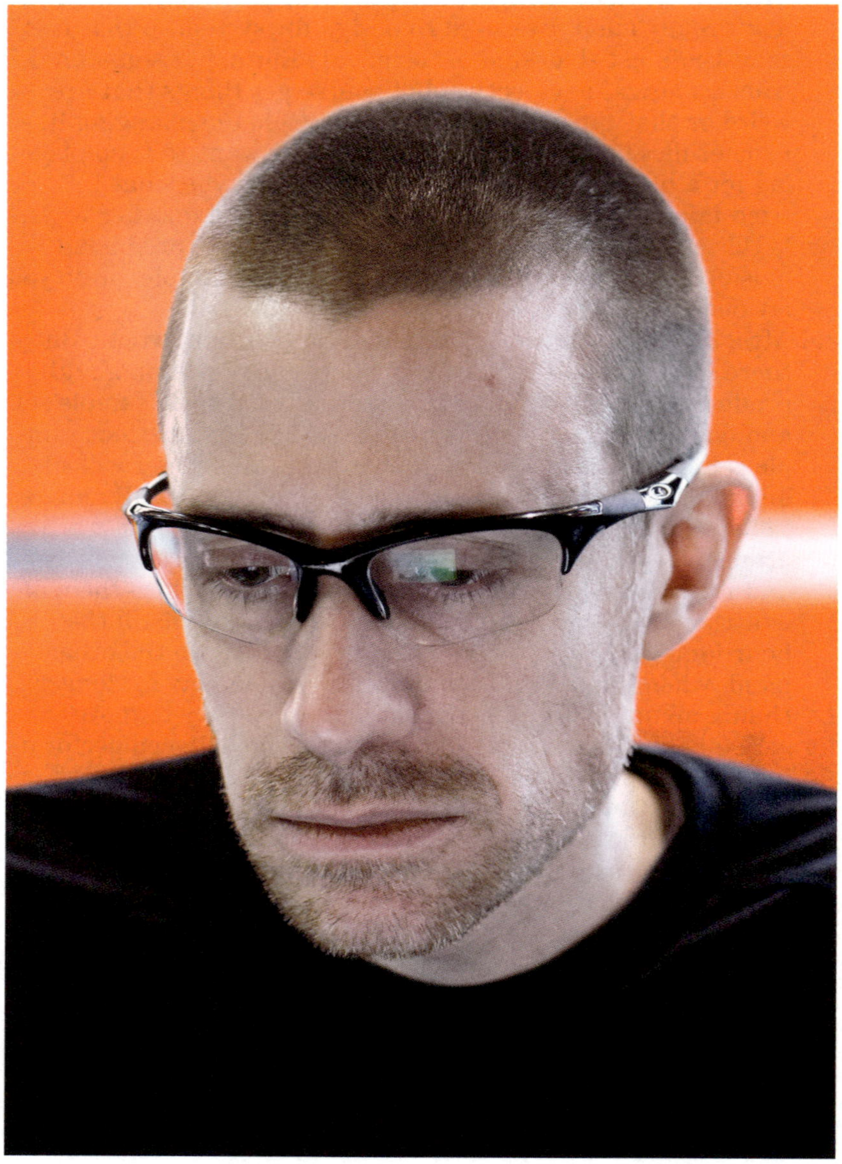

MN: Es wird transparenter und der Schleier wird gelüftet. RB: Ja, und das ist eine sehr wichtige Sache für die Community: den Prozess des Codens zugänglicher zu machen. Ein gutes Beispiel dafür sind Shelly Knotts, die ich schon erwähnt habe, und Joanne Armitage. Sie organisieren Workshops für Frauen, die die Werkzeuge des Live-Codings kennenlernen möchten. Nach ein paar Tagen sind alle Teilnehmerinnen in der Lage, Musik zu produzieren und es zeigt, dass das, was wir machen, vielleicht nicht extrem simpel, aber auch nicht unglaublich schwierig ist. Personen wie Shelly und Joanne helfen sehr dabei, den Prozess zu entmystifizieren. Jeder kann dieses Zeug.

MN: Ist der Code wichtiger als das Ergebnis? RB: Ich kenne das Argument mancher, die sagen, dass der Prozess zu sehr und zum Nachteil des Ergebnisses in den Mittelpunkt gerückt wird. Vielleicht stimmt das in einigen Fällen. Ich hoffe nicht in meinem, denn mir ist das Ergebnis äusserst wichtig. Aber es muss die Frage danach gestellt werden, was das Ergebnis ist. Ist es nur die Musik? Das ist nicht der einzige und wichtigste Punkt beim Live-Codieren. Die meisten Teilnehmer eines *Algoraves* wollen, dass die Leute tanzen und sie wollen etwas produzieren, das cool klingt. Aber sie wollen auch ihren Prozess offenlegen und eine Community aufbauen. Der Prozess ist nicht alleine entscheidend, weil es kein singuläres Ziel gibt, sondern viele verschiedene. Und wegen limitierter Fähigkeiten oder situativer oder anderer Gründe werden manchmal einige Ziele eher erreicht als andere.

MN: Die *Algorave* Community scheint grossen Wert auf Inklusion zu legen und einen antikommerziellen Zugang zu verfolgen. Algorithmen spielen natürlich eine grosse Rolle und mich würde interessieren, ob du der Beobachtung zustimmst, dass es eine Dialektik zwischen diesem Zugang und der Tatsache gibt, dass Algorithmen mehr und mehr zu sehr kommerziellen Zwecken genutzt werden? RB: Algorithmen sind lediglich Werkzeuge und jeder kann diese für jeden selbstgewählten Zweck nutzen. Falls jemand sie nutzen möchte, um elektronische Musik zu kreieren, ist das eine Sache und falls jemand die gleichen Werkzeuge für kommerzielle Zwecke nutzen möchte, eine andere. Es gibt unzählige Algorithmen, die einfach nur Befehlssätze sind. Aber wir können diese nutzen und ihre Aufgabe ändern. Zum Beispiel ist ein Algorithmus, den ich zur Komposition von Rhythmen nutze, ursprünglich geschrieben worden, um das Wachstum von Pflanzen zu beschreiben. Ich habe dieses sogenannte *Lindenmayer-System* genommen und dessen Aufgabe geändert, sodass es nichts mehr mit der ursprünglichen Idee zu tun hatte. Andersherum könnte auch jemand von uns geschriebenen Code für kommerzielle Zwecke nutzen. Eines meiner grössten Anliegen ist die Paranoia, die Algorithmen umgibt. Falls Menschen besser darüber informiert wären, wie und wo Algorithmen überall zur Anwendung kommen, würden sie möglicherweise anders urteilen. Es gibt das Missverständnis, dass Dinge ausser Kontrolle geraten, sobald Algorithmen involviert sind. Aber schlussendlich sind es Menschen, die die kommerziellen Entscheidungen treffen. Meine Sorge ist, dass diese Tatsache aus dem Blick gerät und Algorithmen als grundsätzlich abzulehnen eingestuft werden. Ich möchte der Meinung vorbeugen, sie seien etwas Böses, dem nicht vertraut werden kann. Der Diskurs sollte nuancierter sein und ich hoffe, dass *Algoraves* und Live-Codings Initiativen sind, die einen nuancierteren Blick fördern.

of them. And for skill or situational or other reasons, sometimes some aims are more successfully achieved than others.

MH The algorave community seems to be very inclusive and anti-commercial and obviously algorithms play a big role in this whole thing. I was wondering if you'd agree that there is a certain dialectic between this and the fact that algorithms more and more are getting used for very commercial purposes?

RB Algorithms are just tools, and anybody can use any tool for any purpose. If somebody chooses to use the tools for electronic music creation, that's one thing, and if someone else chooses to use the tools for commercial purposes, that's another thing. There are so many algorithms, and they are just sets of instructions. But we can take algorithms and change their purposes. For example, one of the algorithms I use for rhythm patterns was originally designed to describe the growth of plants, called the Lindenmayer systems. I have taken this and am using it to produce rhythms, so it isn't connected to its original purpose anymore at all. The other way around, if we publish something, there's nothing that stops someone from taking our code and turning it into some kind of commercial tool. One of my main concerns at the moment is this paranoia that surrounds the use of algorithms. If people are more aware of algorithms and of where they are being employed and how they are being employed, they might judge differently. There is this misunderstanding or feeling that once algorithms are involved, it gets out of control. But, after all, it's people making the commercially-driven choices. My concern is that this is not put into consideration enough and that algorithms get rejected completely. I want to prevent the belief that algorithms are some evil thing that can't be trusted. I would like the discourse to be more nuanced, and I hope that algoraves and live coding are things that give people that view.

ANNA HOMLER

"BUT I CAN GIVE YOU A FEELING?"

Interview:
Remo Bitzi
Photography:
Susan Einstein,
Randy Tischler

It's shortly after 10 o'clock in the morning on a cloudy autumn day, inside the Chez Marion bistro in Zurich Niederdorf. A few regulars are engrossed in their newspapers while other pairs or small groups chat about daily news and banalities in muted voices. Moments later, the idyll is interrupted by the appearance of a quirky American named Anna Homler, who has spent a few weeks in a hotel across the street. She immediately greets one of the employees with "Hi darling" and orders an extensive breakfast.

Homler is a performance and improv artist whose early work as *Breadwoman* was re-released on an eponymous album by the New York label RVNG Intl. in 2016. On the record, Homler sings in a strange language, accompanied by the sounds of composer Steve Moshier. The album, which originally appeared as a cassette on Homler's label, Pharmacia Poetica, in 1985, documents a performance piece she developed and performed in the mid-eighties. In the piece, Homler became "Breadwoman," a mysterious being who carries bread all over her body.

Remo Bitzi awaits Homler in the Zurich bistro where she regularly breakfasts during her stays. What follows is a conversation about Homler's current practice: her vocals, her diverse collaborators, and the toys and objects she uses during concerts. The meeting took place one day after the artist performed at Moods Zurich with bassist Christian Weber upon the invitation of Maria Micciche (aka Iokoi).

D E Anna Homler D

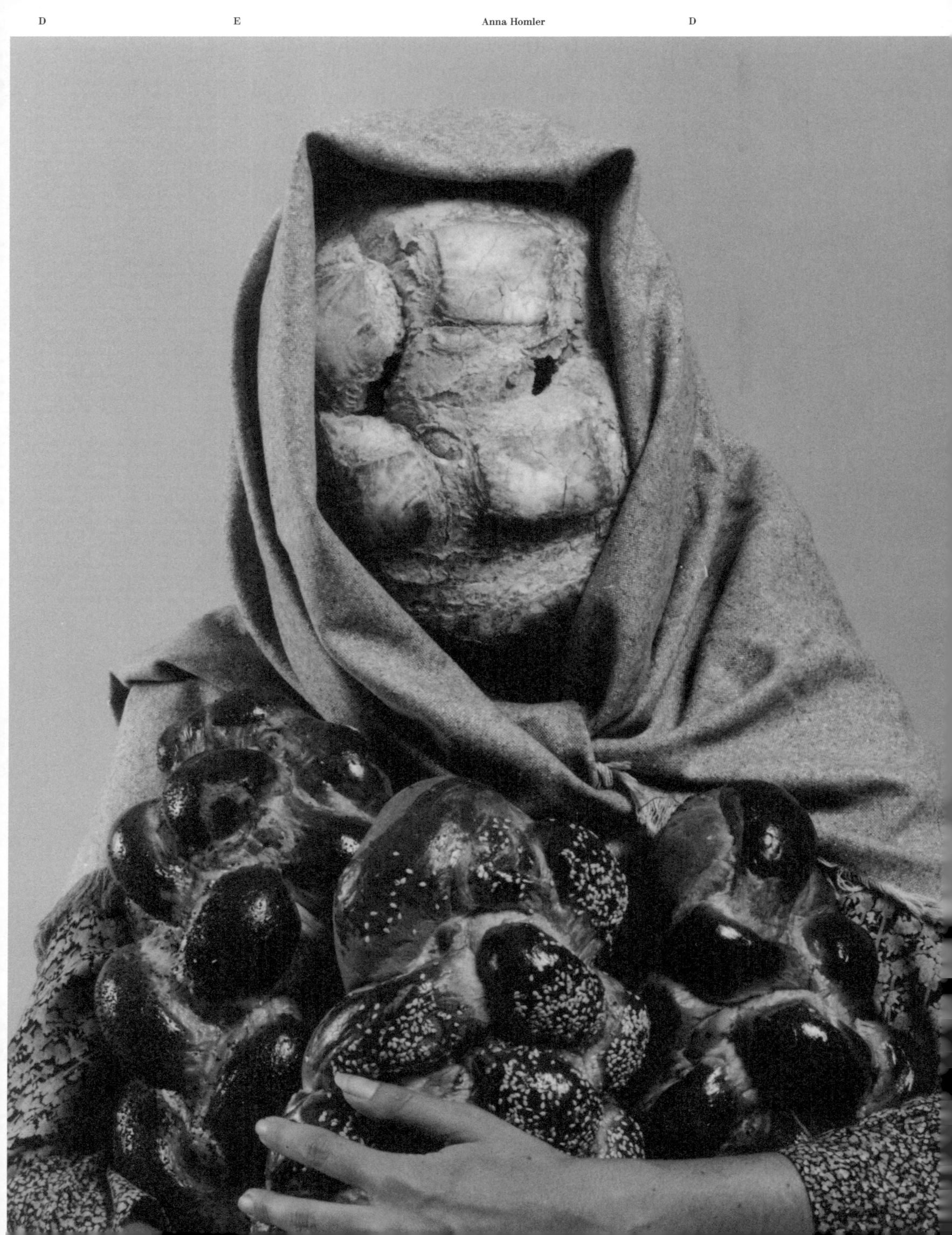

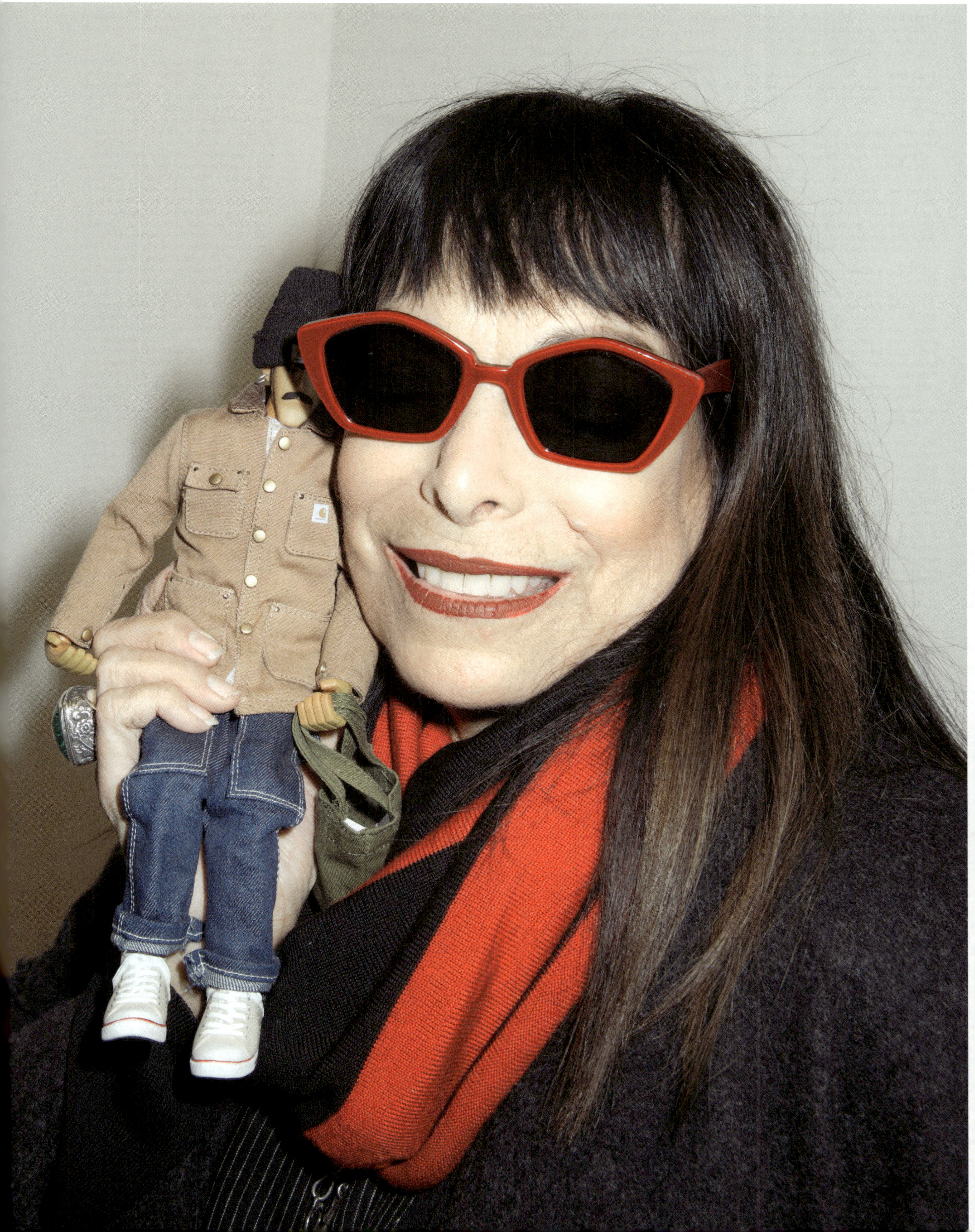

Remo Bitzi You arrived in Europe three weeks ago and Zurich has been your base since. Why Zurich?

Anna Homler I have been coming to Zurich through the years for different projects... But not often enough.

RB In recent interviews you have been talking about musical and linguistic influences,[1] but not much about the influences from (performance) art. I was wondering if Dada might be a reason for choosing Zurich as a base—after all Cabaret Voltaire is just around the corner.

AH I know. I finally got there. Somehow, Zurich is my spiritual home.

RB So was Dada one of your influences?—I'm thinking of the language you are using, but also the way you performed in the early days.

AH A bit. But mainly the way this language came to me was from a completely different route. It came more from the interior and more spontaneously. It didn't have an intellectual component. Later I would find an intellectual component; I did research afterwards. Actually, Surrealism was a big influence and inspiration on my early work.

RB Did it take a long time till the language made sense from an intellectual perspective?

AH No, it was so intimate and authentic, I trusted it. It came as chants and melodies. I recorded them on cassettes and soon I had drawers full of tapes with song fragments in this language. Later, I met a composer, Steve Moshier, who placed them with an electronic background, and producer/musician Ethan James, who did instrumentation for them. I recorded as I was driving in my car.

RB Did you try to make sense out of the recordings at one point?

AH With some of the melodies I could see images. For instance, in "Karu Karu," I could see a white walled city in the desert where women were dancing in a line. That's on my first CD, *Do Ya Sa'di Do*. "Karu Karu" is also a Maori song, but that is completely different from what I am singing. Only the name is the same. Ethan James did the instrumentation for my version. He had a studio called Radio Tokyo in Venice where all the LA punk bands and poets recorded.

RB Is the language that you are using based on something?

AH The language is a bit like Hawaiian. It has twelve syllables or letters. It's not a large language. And it's spontaneous.

RB Do you speak Hawaiian?

AH No, but I was in Hawaii and I knew a bit of the language, I knew that the alphabet only had twelve letters. Do you speak Hawaiian?

RB Not at all. I think that is interesting: You say the language is something that came spontaneously and from the interior, yet it is related to something that is out there in the world.

AH Oh yes...

RB How comes?

AH This may be a more philosophical answer to your question. Everyone has a different process. In my opinion you need to go down inside yourself to go out, a bit like the letter "L." Jungian psychology appeals to me. What's inside is reflected outside. Outside is a big mirror. After all, everything is connected on the quantum level.

RB In today's world people have problems understanding each other. It seems as if they don't speak the same language—even if they actually do. Now you've introduced this new language—back in the 80s—which you still use today. Don't you think it would be better—as an artist, but also as a human being—to reduce the amount of languages instead of adding another one?

AH There is something Enzo Minarelli said to me years ago. He is a poet and was the organizer of a sound poetry festival I participated in. He said: "Don't perform in English. English is the language of the rulers of the world, it's the language of Nixon. Stick to the 'chika chika'." I always remember that. So I think my language is on another level, I think it's bio-

[English – Interview]

logical. It's cellular. I cannot give you an analysis in my language, but I can give you a feeling. It's really a different brain hemisphere. I did one performance piece with Steve Moshier that was called *Deliquium in C*. It was about the dissolution of language and stages of alchemy. We called it an underwater sound poem. I'd like to present it again with a dancer.

RB You mentioned the Surrealists as an influence and inspiration for your early work. Does some part of that remain in your work today?

AH This is most obvious in my Pharmacia Poetica, which is an ongoing installation/performance project. The prescriptions are poetic: images, sounds, colors, and stories. These are perceptual shifts from the literal to the lyrical. It's a manicure for the mind. A big part of the Pharmacia is a library of glass bottles containing an assortment of objects floating in liquid. The Pharmacia started as a radio play and then evolved into a storefront installation that travelled throughout the US and Europe. Right now it's in my living room in Los Angeles and in my friend's cellar in Cologne. Most recently the Pharmacia has found a new life as a film by Will Saunders and Hans Diernberger and will be presented at a conference on sound called "Fluidity" in San Diego. Kyn Taniya [aka Luis Quintanilla] is a poet I just discovered. I read some of his texts in the performance with Christian yesterday. He was a Mexican surrealist, who started writing after translating avant-garde poetry into Spanish. In the past, I've bottled poems and will definitely bottle some of his. Eventually, all the words dissolve in the liquid and only the essence is left.

RB You said in an interview that you don't do solo performances anymore, because you don't have time.[2]

AH I didn't have the time and the space to develop something new until now. I prefer to play with another person on stage. I like interacting with another person's sounds and energy. It's the magic of another person.

RB You work with a lot of different people. Among those collaborators there's a huge variety in instrumentations and styles. How do you find those people, how do you select them?

AH It's mostly by *Zufall*.

RB Yesterday you played with Christian Weber. How did you get in touch with him?

AH We were introduced by a friend in Zurich about four years ago.

RB Was it the first time you were on stage together?

AH Yes, four years later.

RB How did you go about that performance? Did you just go on stage and start improvising?

AH Oh, we have played together before; I didn't just get on stage with Christian and play. We spent a whole afternoon in Zurich jamming together. Christian had access to a big studio where we could play. It seemed like we would work well together. I used to play with Peter Kowald, who died more than ten years ago. Since then I've been looking for a stand-up bass or cello player to work with. I really love the sound of the human voice with those deep strings. I was hoping it could be a possibility to work with Christian so I was happy to have a chance to play at Moods, thanks to Mara.

RB Is that the reason why there is always a new collaborator: Because you are always looking for new possibilities?

AH I like the energy of collaboration. It's more interesting for me and new things come out of it.

RB Did you know Steven Warwick [aka Heatsick; see zweikommasieben #13] before you collaborated with him? How did you get in touch with him?

AH I didn't know his music before I played with him. The label that re-released *Breadwoman*, RVNG Intl., put us together. He is a road warrior and an art star. He's really great to tour with and I've learned a lot from him.

RB You worked on existing material with him. When was the last time that you developed something new, apart from the improvisations on stage?

[Deutsch]

Kontakt gekommen? AH: Ein gemeinsamer Freund stellte uns vor etwa vier Jahren in Zürich vor.

RB: Gestern seid ihr das erste Mal zusammen aufgetreten, ja? AH: Ja, vier Jahre später.

RB: Wie seid ihr vorgegangen? Seid ihr einfach auf die Bühne gegangen und habt angefangen zu improvisieren? AH: Oh, wir hatten vor dem Auftritt gestern schon zusammengespielt; wir sind nicht einfach auf die Bühne gegangen und haben angefangen. Wir verbrachten einen ganzen Nachmittag in Zürich und jammten. Christian hatte Zugang zu einem grossen Studio, wo wir spielen konnten. Es schien, als ob es mit uns gut funktionieren würde. Früher spielte ich mit [dem Bassisten] Peter Kowald; er verstarb vor mehr als zehn Jahren. Seither bin ich auf der Suche nach einem Stand-up-Bassisten oder -Cellisten. Ich liebe den Sound der menschlichen Stimme kombiniert mit jenem dieser tiefen Saiten. Ich hoffte, dass Christian eine Option wäre; entsprechend glücklich war ich, als sich die Möglichkeit ergab, mit ihm im Moods zu spielen—dank Mara.

RB: Ist das ein Grund dafür, warum immer jemand neues ins Spiel kommt: Weil du stets auf der Suche nach neuen Möglichkeiten bist? AH: Ich mag die Energie von Kollaborationen. Das ist für mich interessanter und es entstehen dabei neue Sachen.

RB: Kanntest du Steven Warwick [aka Heatsick; siehe zweikommasieben #13], bevor du mit ihm zusammenarbeitet hast? Wie bist du mit ihm in Kontakt gekommen? AH: Ich kannte seine Musik nicht, bevor wir zusammenarbeiteten. Das Label, das *Breadwoman* wiederveröffentlichte, RVNG Intl., brachte uns zusammen. Steven ist ein Tausendsassa und ein Kunst-Star. Mit ihm zu touren ist wirklich grossartig und ich konnte vieles von ihm lernen.

RB: Mit ihm hast du an bestehendem Material gearbeitet. Wann hast du das letzte Mal an etwas komplett Neuem gearbeitet—abgesehen von den Improvisationen auf der Bühne? AH: Steven und ich haben nicht bestehendes Material für *Breadwoman* benutzt. Wir improvisierten und fanden dabei einige Muster, die wir mochten. Davon abgesehen gibt es einige unveröffentlichte Projekte, die nun bald erscheinen—unter anderem in Grossbritannien. Es gibt ein Sprichwort: «Aus alt mach neu.» Unglücklicherweise fehlt mir in Los Angeles Zeit und Raum, um Neues zu kreieren. Früher war das anders. Ich sollte an einem Residenz-Programm teilnehmen.

RB: Warum ist dem so? AH: Mein Vater verstarb und das brachte eine Menge komplizierter administrativer Auflagen mit sich. Mein Leben in LA ist eher administrativ als poetisch. Um neue Sachen kreieren zu können, muss ich in Europa sein. All die Leute, mit denen ich zusammenarbeite, sind hier. Zudem kann ich—wie wohl alle—ohne all die täglichen Verantwortlichkeiten eher träumen. Im vergangenen Jahr konnte ich aber eine Arbeit, die noch nicht abgeschlossen ist, mit dem London Improvisers Orchestra präsentieren. Sie heisst *Probate Codes: An Exorcism*. Die Arbeit kombiniert Schichten von englischen Texten: gesetzliche Bestimmungen aus einem Nachlassverfahren, sowie poetische Auszüge aus *Bleak House* und *The Godfather*. Adam Bohman und Sue Lynch brummten die Bestimmungen vor sich hin. Steve Beresford dirigierte das Orchester und ich las den Text. Das war sehr erfüllend.

RB: Lass uns über die Objekte reden, die du bei deinen Auftritten einsetzt: Ich fragte mich, was das Verhältnis zwischen den Objekten und deinem Gesang ist? AH: Vorab muss ich sagen, dass ich eine Sammlerin bin. Ich sammle Sounds, Wörter und Bilder. Ich bin stets auf der Suche nach klingenden Objekten, die visuell interessant sind. Zum Beispiel liebe ich Holzteufel—dieses Spielzeug, das einen sehr trockenen, knarrenden Sound erzeugt. Das ist ein Instrument, das ich immer bei mir habe. Und weil die nicht sehr lange leben, muss ich immer eins finden, egal in welchem Land ich grad bin. Wie auch immer, ich kenne meine Spielsachen, meine Objekte. Das sieht zwar wie Krimskrams auf dem Tisch aus, unorganisiert noch dazu, aber ich habe eine Beziehung zu jedem einzelnen Objekt. Wo jemand anderes eine Einstellung auf einem Gerät ändern würde, habe ich ein Objekt, das genau den Sound macht, den ich liebe. Das gefällt mir, obwohl das Schleppen mühsam ist.

RB: Die meisten dieser Objekte sind sehr gewöhnlich, man findet sie überall... AH: Wie das Klebeband?

RB: Ja genau, das ist ein gutes Beispiel. Diese Objekte sind einfach erhältlich; gleichzeitig ist da dein Gesang, der sehr speziell ist—nur du kannst in dieser Sprache singen. Ich fragte mich, ob diese beiden Sachen als Kontrast gemeint sind? AH: Ich setzte die Spielsachen hauptsächlich ein, damit ich mit anderen Leuten zusammenspielen kann. Sie erlauben es mir, mich sozusagen einzubringen. Manchmal lässt sich keine Verbindung zwischen den Vocals und dem Sound herstellen. Den Spielzeugen gelingt das aber immer.

RB: Warum ist dem so? AH: Weil ich eine Nischensängerin bin, die in einer anderen Sprache singt.

RB: Du meintest, du seist eine Sammlerin. Hast du einen Raum zu Hause, wo du alles aufbewahrst? Gibt es eine Ordnung, die es dir erlaubt, die Sammlung im Griff zu behalten? AH: Ja, es gibt einen Raum in meinem Haus, der gefüllt ist mit Spielsachen und Objekten, die Sound erzeugen. Die meisten Spielsachen und Objekte befinden sich in Regalen, versorgt in farbcodierten Plastikboxen. Grössere Stücke sind in Schrankkoffern verstaut, kleinere in Schubladen und Körben. Sie sind nach «Familien» geordnet. Zudem sind die Dinge, die ich ständig benutze, in einem Koffer verstaut, der vor jedem Trip umgepackt wird.

RB: Und wie gehst du da vor—wie wählst du die Objekte aus? AH: Nun, einige Sachen kommen immer mit. Zum Beispiel nehme ich einige wunderschöne französische Vogelpfeifen immer mit auf Reisen. Die sind stets mit dabei, weil sie einfach transportierbar sind. Ich habe einige grossartige Sounds zu Hause, die aber unmöglich zu transportieren sind—beispielsweise ein Uhrengehäuse. Dieses sieht wunderschön und geheimnisvoll aus, aber es ist zu sperrig. Ich besitze einige wirklich grosse Objekte, die ich nur in LA einsetzten kann. Mein Spielzeug-Koffer ist ohnehin schon schwer und teuer genug—ich muss jeweils fast hundert Euro für Übergepäck bezahlen.

RB: Hast du dir jemals überlegt, die Sounds aufzunehmen und sie als Samples mit auf Tour zu bringen? AH: Ich liebe den visuellen Aspekt der Spielsachen. Einen Computer anzuschauen, ist für mich nicht wirklich interessant. Und es geht um Zeit. Wann sollte ich all die Sounds meiner Spielsachen und Objekte aufnehmen?

ALPENFLAGE SEASON 6
LOCAL SPOTLIGHT SWITZERLAND
WWW.REDBULLRADIO.COM

References

1. e.g. Jones, M. I. (2016, February 9). Breadwoman rises: The making of a modern mystic. Retrieved from http://www.factmag.com/2016/02/09/breadwoman-interview/ or

   Arnott, B. (2016, February 9). Breadwoman–Speaking in Tongues. Retrieved from https://www.junodownload.com/plus/2016/02/09/breadwoman-speaking-in-tongues/

2. Jones 2016

AH Steven and I didn't use existing material for *Breadwoman*. We improvised and found some patterns we liked. I have some unreleased projects that are now just starting to be released in the UK. There's a saying: "What's old is new again." Sadly, I don't have the quality of time and space that I used to have to create new work in LA. I probably need to go on a residency.

RB Why is that?

AH My father died and there was a lot of complicated administration. My life in LA is more administrative than poetic. To create new things, I need to be in Europe. All the people I work with are here. Also, like everyone, my mind is more free to dream without day-to-day responsibilities.

RB Isn't that frustrating?

AH Yes, it is. [Laughs] *Natürlich*. [Laughs]
Last year I was able to perform a work in progress with the London Improvisers Orchestra called *Probate Codes: An Exorcism*. It combined layers of text in English: probate codes, poetic extractions from *Bleak House* and *The Godfather*. Adam Bohman and Sue Lynch read the codes, droning on and on. Steve Beresford conducted the orchestra and I read the text. It was very fulfilling.

RB Let's talk about the objects you're using when performing: I wondered what the relationship is between your vocals and those objects?

AH I'm a collector, first of all. I collect sounds, words, and images. I look for sonic objects that are visually interesting. For instance, I love wood devils—it's this toy that makes a very dry, creaking sound. It's an instrument that I always have with me. And because they don't live very long I have to find one, no matter what country I am in. Anyway, I really know my toys, my objects. It looks like *Krimskrams* on the *Tisch*, not so organized, but I have a relationship with each one. Where somebody else might do a different setting on a device, I have an object that makes that one sound that I love. I like it like that, even though it's hard to *schlepp*.

RB Most objects are very common, one could get them everywhere…

AH Like the *Klebeband?*

RB Yeah exactly, that's a perfect example. It's easy to get those objects. On the other hand, your vocals are very special—only you can sing in that language. I wondered if you have these two elements for contrast?

AH I have the toys so I can play with other people—they allow me to relate, sound-wise. Sometimes it is not possible to connect with the vocals to the sound. The toys can always do it.

RB Why is that?

AH Because I am a niche singer in another language.

RB You said you're a collector. Do you have a room at home where you store everything? Is there an order or a way that allows you to keep track of your collection?

AH Yes, I have a room in my house entirely filled with toys and sound-making objects. Mostly the toys and objects are on shelves and in color-coded plastic tubs. Larger items are in trunks and smaller items are in drawers and baskets. They are grouped together by "families." The things I use all the time are in a suitcase that gets re-packed before a trip.

RB And how do you choose between those objects?

AH Well some things come with me, always. I travel with some beautiful French bird whistles for example. Those always come, because they are portable. I have really great sounds at home, but it's impossible to bring them, like a clock case, for instance. It looks beautiful and mysterious—but it's too bulky. I have really large things that I could only use in LA. My toy suitcase is already really heavy and expensive—it's always an extra EUR 100 to bring it.

RB Have you ever thought of recording the sounds and bringing them as samples?

AH I love the visual aspect of the toys. Looking at a computer isn't really interesting for me. It's about time as well. When would I record all those sounds my toys and objects are making?

DIAL MM
FOR MMODEMM

Portrait:
Kevin Goonewardena
Photography:
Mihaly Podobni

Since 2015, Mmodemm has been releasing music by artists such as Felix Kubin, Nika Son, The Thing, Hypnobeat, Container, Wilted Woman, Nick Klein, Yung Prado, dane//close, Machine Woman, As Longitude, and Palmbome II. The Frankfurt-based label has garnered attention not only for its compelling selection (one, mind you, that lines up uncannily with our own tastes: see zweikommasieben #3, #10, #12, #13, #16...) but also for its preferred release format: tracks of up to 5 minutes are recorded onto five different monochrome cassettes, all of which are housed in a transparent box. The boxes, which are each marked with a different letter of the alphabet, come with a short epigraph containing the most important information. MModemm is also known for its mostly "secret" or "fun" events, which take place at regular intervals in a variety of different contexts and venues. In hopes of learning more about the label's work and events and about the scene in Frankfurt, Kevin Goonewardena spoke with the three operators, Benni Bascom, Toben Piel and Charlotte Simon, for zweikommasieben.

Frankfurt phenomena abound: gray concrete, rough jargon, glass façades, handkerchiefs, brooches, the skyline along the Main, apple wine, "Krankfurt," as they say. Dorian Gray, Moses P., Omen. Amen. "I find Frankfurt very unpretentious. Take, for example, the area around the main train station. You see people walking with their briefcases to their banking jobs and one street further there's the crack scene. Everything is more interwoven here, and in my view this also applies to the scenes. There's none of the elitism here that you find in other places," says Benni Bascom, a freelance sound designer, graphic designer, creative coder, and tutor who runs the Frankfurt label MModemm together with Toben Piel and Charlotte Simon. During our conversation, the three of them try to find words to describe not only the concept of their label, but also the city of Frankfurt and its significance. The days of UFO 361, Omen or Dorian Gray are long-gone; it's already been a while since *Frontpage* relocated to Berlin; Talla 2XLC is only a household name among people in the scene and in Frankfurt's cultural aristocracy. Has the former "Weltstadt des Techno" ["World City of Techno" according to Frankfurter Rundschau], home of the first club for electronic music in Germany—the Technoclub, founded in 1984—completely lost its relevance today?

There's also the financial center and the cliché of the snobby banker who earns his bundles of money in the city and carries it all back to the surrounding Main-Taunus area. Main-Taunus is a different place altogether from the neighborhood around the train station, whose crack scene, hustlers, and rappers (e.g. Schwesta Ewa) equally personify Frankfurt. If you think of electronic music from this metropolis on the river Main, you think of a faded scene and its founders and leftovers—Sven Väth, for example–, none of whom are exactly popular figures.

Do it Yourself!

Toben, Benni, and Charlotte run MModemm with the same openness they feel is offered by the city. Modemm operates more as a kind of multi-layered platform than as a simple means to release recordings. The term "platform" is usually associated with the promotion of exchange, networking, and creativity as it's often manifested in DIY collectives—and that fits Modemm well. As Toben describes, though, the label's working methods have emerged more out of necessity than out of the desire to follow a certain ethos. But Charlotte, Toben and Benni are no strangers to punk, hardcore, and noise–scenes with which the term "DIY" particularly resonates.

"Eight years ago we were putting on concerts at Excess, a legendary punk shop in Frankfurt's Bockenheim district" says Charlotte, who studied art with Judith Hopf at the Städelschule [Academy of Fine Arts] in Frankfurt. She describes the early days of the label, which is based in Fechenheim, one of the neighborhoods furthest to the East: "We've always been addicted to organizing events and concerts, bringing together bands and artists, and releasing things. We are late-nineties children who come from a post-rock scene and only later started becoming interested in electronic music, and our activities have reflected that... Both MModemm and our involvement with it have developed very organically, but that doesn't mean that things just happened by themselves or that we didn't think about anything or plan anything. For a long time we've been interested in releasing the electronic and experimental projects, B-sides, and demos of our friends and acquaintances. But before we started the label, we drank a lot of beer for about a year, all got the same haircut, and thought about how best to go about it."

Whereas many label owners have a specific recording format in mind from the start, the three MModemm organizers weighed the pros and cons of various possibilities, from 3D objects to USB sticks to Flexidiscs. "Physicality was never a particular priority for us; we've also considered the option of just publishing things digitally," explains Toben, who works as a nurse. "What was more important to us was to be able to do track-based releases—i.e., things that stand on their own and aren't tied to a context like an album. One of the first ideas we discussed was to do singles. But cassettes provide a similar physical value as vinyl. They're also cheaper and easier, and can be produced and reproduced faster. Most importantly, you can make them yourself, even if dubbing the blank tapes is a lot of work," continues Toben.

Fetish Alphabet

However, despite the description "Frankfurt Based Tape Label" on the Modemm website, the three organizers don't really think of themselves as a cassette label. The fact that they've used the medium almost exclusively for publications is ultimately a result of an interest in the format itself. It's also due to an engagement with electronic dance music and an exploration of their individual interests within the genre. At the same time, though, the format isn't set in stone—they're actually already in the process of searching for a suitable new medium, simply because the cassette boxes they've used until now are no longer being produced. The Modemm founders aren't picky about the stylistic specifications of their music, nor do they care about the prominence or previous productivity of their artists. Yung Prado, for example, a Barcelona-based teenager who has two releases on the label, has only 60 likes on Facebook and similarly few followers on Soundcloud. One of his two releases, *Low Budget High Life*, was put out on cassette. As a four-track EP, though, it represents an outlier in the label catalogue.

Toben summarizes the requirements for a release on Modemm in a short sentence: "The pieces have to be between 4:20 and 4:50 minutes long, and the music should be danceable in the broadest sense—that's it." Despite the serious deliberations about release formats ahead of founding the label, the recording medium is still of secondary importance. MModemm releases always appear in editions of 80, and there are hardly ever re-pressings. With limited editions like these, it's much easier to avoid the usual production and promotional cycles than with editions of 500 or 1000. Aside from some activity on the internet, they also do not next to no promotion—their slogan is "We just knock things out." Another one of MModemm's particularities: with a few exceptions, such as the releases of Rolande Garros, Danse Musique Rhône-Alpes, or the previously-mentioned EP by Yung Prado, Modemm never releases albums, EPs, or singles by individual artists. The cassettes, which are catalogued alphabetically, all assemble pieces by several different artists, and in this way are more like samplers or compilations. "Musically, we've always taken up the outsider positions. The word 'B-sides' describes it pretty well," says Charlotte, adding, "The B-sides usually have the songs that aren't as catchy—they don't attract the mainstream but they're often total pearls. We release some pretty crude music, but ultimately it's all dance music, in the broadest sense."

From the very beginning, the MModemm creators have been supported by people following similar concepts and, in some cases, who knew them from times when they were still playing in bands themselves. "Examples would be Nikae and Phuong Dan from the Golden Pudel or dane//close and the Sameheads people in Berlin," says Charlotte. "It's often people who also come from the DIY scene, who organize similar events in which the social aspect plays an important role."

The Night Offered More Than the Evening Had Promised

Whereas other labels rarely organize events outside of label showcases for their own promotion, Toben, Benni, and Charlotte often book artists who aren't on their roster. It's also important to them to go beyond pure party events or club nights– their *MModemm Nights* series likewise includes live performances by bands. And the focus isn't only on satisfying different tastes–it's mostly about defying expectations, according to Toben. "We recently threw a party featuring both Ryoma Sasaki from Transit and Alessandro Adriani from Mannequin. Ryoma played almost deep house and Adriani came after that. Some people were pretty shocked. It didn't fit together at all, but it was a great evening." According to Toben the form of a party would be conceived from the outside anyway. People come to events with ideas about what a party is. You can choose to fulfill those expectations, or "you can provoke people, in a good way. I find that much more interesting."

MModemm events take place in different locations. According to Charlotte, there are three kinds of contexts in Frankfurt that suit a project like MModemm: "A university environment like the Städelschule, clubs like Tanzhaus West or Robert Johnson where it's possible to slip in occasionally, and off-locations, which–given the size of the city–are plentiful." The MModemm creators are particularly interested in the temporary locations that keep popping up, because they're not yet occupied (in any sense of the word) they don't yet have a context and can therefore still be filled with content. "With its 700,000 inhabitants, Frankfurt is very small compared to Berlin or Hamburg. Still, though, there are always new places for us to use," says Toben, who makes music under the pseudonym Rolande Garros. "The situation is usually precarious and the places are often gone after a few weeks, but there are always new ones. There aren't really any cool neighborhoods where things are concentrated, as there are in Hamburg or Berlin. In Frankfurt, everything is spread out all over the city."

Frankfurt After the Rush

Are there connections between high culture, which has legacy and importance in Frankfurt, and the scene for electronic music? There is indeed a bit of crossover, says Charlotte. "Museums like Schirn and MMK are beginning to host DJ evenings more frequently. We ourselves are in contact with the Mousonturm, because Toben and I are also doing events with Les Trucs. And we and other groups also receive support from the city's cultural council." But that's all peanuts compared to the MOMEM (Museum of Modern Electronic Music), which is the first museum in Germany to deal with electronic music and club culture. Its formal establishment—initially it's a pop-up museum temporarily housed at the Frankfurt Hauptwache—can be understood not only as a large-scale documentative effort, but also as an urban-political achievement in the commercially-minded hope of resurrecting the city's long-faded relevance. The metropolis on the Main no longer plays the role (or anything even close to the role) it played in the national and international scenes from the eighties to the late nineties—not even if you were to generously consider Robert Johnson, which is located in neighboring Offenbach, as belonging to Frankfurt.

Meanwhile, as it moves into the future, MModemm will uphold certain constants, such as the two cornerstones of publications and events, according to Charlotte. But there will also be some changes, like the new, yet-to-be-determined format. 2018 will bring various new projects—for one, Charlotte, Toben and Benni are thinking of offering studio residencies in Künstlerhaus Mousonturm. The idea is to enable artists to record music that will later appear on the label. With MModemm, things will continue to be as they always were: open, DIY, Frankfurt-based.

Seit 2015 veröffentlicht !Modemm Musik von Künstlerinnen wie Felix Kubin, Nika Son, Das Ding, Hypnobeat, Container, Wilted Woman, Nick Klein, As Longitude, Yung Prado, dane//close, Machine Woman, Palmbomen II und mehr. Dabei fällt das Frankfurter Label nicht nur durch eine bestechende Auswahl auf, die sich über weite Strecken mit der unseren deckt (siehe zweikommasieben #8, #10, #12, #13, #16…), sondern auch durch das bevorzugt gewählte Format: In transparenten Boxen werden jeweils fünf monochrome Kassetten mit je einem Track à maximal 5 Minuten veröffentlicht. Begleitet werden die Boxen, denen jeweils ein Buchstabe des Alphabets zugeordnet ist, durch eine kleine Legende mit den nötigsten Informationen drauf. Ansonsten steht !Modemm für mehr oder weniger «geheime» und/oder «lustige» Veranstaltungen in unterschiedlichen Kontexten und an unterschiedlichen Orten, die in regelmässigen Abständen stattfinden. Um mehr über die Label-Arbeit, die Veranstaltungen und Frankfurt zu erfahren, hat sich Kevin Goonewardena für zweikommasieben mit den drei Betreibern Benni Bascom, Toben Piel und Charlotte Simon unterhalten.

MModemm

Grauer Beton, rauer Jargon, gläserne Fassaden, Einstecktücher, Anstecknadeln, Skyline am Main, Apfelwein, Krankfurt. Startbahn West, Schwester S, Häuserkampf, Joschka Fischer Turnschuhminister, EZB, ole ole. Frankfurter Würstchen, Frankfurter Schule, Bahnhofsviertel, Rödelheim, Dorian Gray, Moses P., Omen. Amen. «Ich finde Frankfurt sehr unprätentiös. Sinnbild dafür ist das Bahnhofsviertel, wo man Leute sieht, die mit ihren Aktenkoffern zu ihren Bankjobs laufen und eine Strasse weiter findet man die Crack-Szene. Hier ist alles verwobener und meiner Wahrnehmung nach trifft das auch auf die Szenen zu. Es gibt hier keinen krassen Elitarismus, wie anderswo», so Benni Bascom, ein freier Sound- und Grafikdesigner, Creative Coder und Tutor, der zusammen mit Toben Piel und Charlotte Simon das in der Stadt ansässige Label MModemm führt. Beim Gespräch versuchen die drei nicht nur das Konzept ihres Labels, sondern auch die Stadt Frankfurt und deren Bedeutung in Worte zu fassen. Die Tage von UFO 361, Omen oder Dorian Gray sind längst gezählt, die *Frontpage* ist sowieso schon früher nach Berlin umgezogen und Talla 2XLC ist allenfalls Szeneleuten und dem Frankfurter Kulturadel noch ein Begriff. Hat die ehemalige «Weltstadt des Techno» (Frankfurter Rundschau), die mit dem 1984 eröffneten Technoclub den ersten Klub Deutschlands beherbergte, in dem ausschliesslich elektronische Musik gespielt wurde, also heutzutage komplett an Relevanz verloren?

Der Finanzplatz, das Klischee des versnobten Bankers, der sein Geld in der Stadt verdient und mit beiden Händen in den umliegenden Main-Taunus-Kreis trägt. Als Gegensatz das Bahnhofsviertel, Crack, Stricher, Rapper wie Schwesta Ewa, die Frankfurt auch personifizieren. Wenn man an elektronische Musik aus der Mainmetropole denkt, dann an eine aus einer längst verblassten Zeit und deren Begründer und Überbleibsel wie Sven Väth auch nicht gerade als Sympathieträger gelten.

Macht es selbst!

So offen wie Toben, Benni und Charlotte die Stadt empfinden, so offen gestalten sie ihr Label MModemm, das eher einer vielschichtigen Plattform gleicht, als einem Mittel zum Zweck, um Tonträger herauszubringen. Beim Begriff Plattform schwingt ja auch immer eine verbindende, den Austausch und die Kreativität fördernde Komponente mit, wie man sie von DIY-Kollektiven kennt—und das passt zu MModemm. Die Arbeitsweise sei allerdings aus der Not geboren, ihr läge kein Ethos zu Grunde, erzählt Toben. Dennoch sind Verbindungen zu den Punk-, Hardcore- und Noise-Szenen—bei denen DIY immer mitschwingt—in der Vergangenheit von Charlotte, Toben und Benni zu finden. «Noch vor acht Jahren haben wir Konzerte im Exzess—einem legendären Punk-Laden in Frankfurt Bockenheim—veranstaltet», berichtet Charlotte, die Kunst bei Judith Hopf an der Städelschule Frankfurt [der Hochschule für Bildende Künste] studiert hat. «Wir waren schon immer süchtig danach, Veranstaltungen und Konzerte zu organisieren, Bands und Künstlerinnen zusammenzubringen und Sachen zu veröffentlichen. Als Kinder der End-Neunziger, die aus einer Postrock-Ecke kommen und erst später begannen, sich für elektronische Musik zu interessieren, haben wir das Ganze dann einfach logisch weitergeführt», beschreibt sie die Anfänge des im Stadtteil Fechenheim—im äussersten Osten der Stadt—beheimateten Labels. «Wie wir uns und wie MModemm sich entwickelt hat, ergab sich wie von selbst. Das heisst aber nicht, dass alles einfach so passiert ist und wir nichts durchdacht, nichts geplant hätten. Das Interesse, die Projekte, die B-Seiten, die Demos experimenteller und elektronischer Natur unserer Freundinnen und Bekannten zu veröffentlichen, war schon länger da. Bevor wir aber mit dem Label anfingen, haben wir zuerst einmal ein Jahr lang viel Bier getrunken, uns alle die gleiche Frisur zugelegt und uns überlegt, wie wir am besten ein Label aufziehen.» Während für andere das Format ihrer Veröffentlichungen von Anfang an klar ist, diskutierten die drei Labelmacherinnen von MModemm vorab die Vor- und Nachteile diverser Möglichkeiten—von 3D-Objekten über USB-Sticks bis hin zu Flexidiscs. «Dabei stand noch nicht einmal das physische Format an sich im Vordergrund; wir haben uns durchaus auch überlegt, die Sachen nur digital zu veröffentlichen», erläutert Toben, der als Krankenpfleger arbeitet. «Wichtiger war uns, dass wir trackbasierte Veröffentlichungen machen können—also solche, die für sich alleine stehen und nicht an einen Kontext wie etwa ein Album gekoppelt sind. Eine der ersten Ideen, die wir diskutiert haben, war entsprechend, Singles zu machen. Kassetten bieten jedoch nicht nur einen ähnlichen physischen Mehrwert wie Vinyl, sie sind auch günstiger, einfacher und schneller zu produzieren und zu reproduzieren. Vor allem kann man das selbst machen—auch wenn es viel Arbeit bedeutet, die Blanko-Tapes zu überspielen», so Toben weiter.

Fetisch Alphabet

Nichtsdestotrotz – und entgegen dem Gruss, der den Besucher auf der Website von MModemm erwartet («Frankfurt Based Tape Label»)—versteht man sich doch nicht als Kassettenlabel. Dass bisher fast ausschliesslich dieses Medium

für Veröffentlichungen genutzt wurde, hat sich schlussendlich nicht nur aus der Auseinandersetzung mit dem Format an sich, sondern auch aus der persönlichen Beschäftigung mit elektronischer Tanzmusik und der Ergründung dessen, was die drei an diesem Genre interessiert, ergeben. Gleichzeitig ist das Format nicht in Stein gemeisselt. Die Suche nach einem neuen, geeigneten Medium ist gar bereits in vollem Gange; ganz einfach, weil die bisher verwendeten Kassettenboxen nicht mehr produziert werden.
Stilistische Vorgaben gibt es dabei nicht, auch die Bekanntheit einer Künstlerin oder die Anzahl der bisherigen Veröffentlichungen stellen für MModemm irrelevante Grössen dar. So kommt etwa die Facebook-Seite von Yung Prado gerade einmal auf 60 Likes. Auch auf Soundcloud hat der in Barcelona beheimatete Jugendliche kaum mehr Follower. Trotzdem hat er gleich zwei Mal auf MModemm veröffentlicht. Unter den beiden Releases findet sich *Low Budget High Life*—natürlich auf Tape erschienen, und dennoch eine Ausnahme im Labelkatalog, da es sich um eine vier Tracks starke EP handelt.

Was es braucht, um auf MModemm seine Musik herauszubringen, fasst Toben in einem knappen Satz zusammen: «Die Stücke müssen zwischen 4:20 und 4:50 Minuten dauern und die Musik soll im weitesten Sinne tanzbar sein—das war's.» Der Tonträger, auf dem die Stücke dann erscheinen, bleibe trotz der Gedankenspiele im Vorfeld der Labelgründung immer noch zweitrangig: MModemm-Veröffentlichungen erscheinen immer in einer Auflage von 80 Stück, Re-Presses gibt es kaum. Ein Label, das seine Musik in solch geringen Auflagen herausbringt, kann sich noch mehr den gängigen Produktions- und Promotionszirklen entziehen, als es bei Stückzahlen von 500 bis 1000 Einheiten der Fall wäre. Promotion findet, ausser im Internet, folglich auch nicht statt: «Wir hauen die Sachen einfach raus», lautet die Devise. Eine weitere Besonderheit von MModemm: Bis auf wenige Ausnahmen, wie etwa die Releases von Rolande Garros, Danse Musique Rhône-Alpes oder die schon erwähnte EP von Yung Prado, bringt MModemm keine Alben, EPs oder Singles einzelner Künstlerinnen heraus. Die Tapes, die alphabetisch katalogisiert werden, versammeln mehrere Stücke von verschiedenen Künstlern, sind also eher als Sampler oder Compilations zu verstehen. «Musikalisch griffen wir immer schon Aussenseiterpositionen auf. Das Wort B-Seiten beschreibt es ganz gut», findet Charlotte und führt aus: «Auf B-Seiten finden sich eher nicht eingängige Stücke—nicht jene, die die Masse anziehen, aber dennoch oftmals richtige Perlen sind. Wir bringen zwar etwas krude Musik heraus, schlussendlich handelt es sich aber im weitesten Sinne immer um Tanzmusik.» Unterstützung haben die MModemm-Macherinnen dabei von Anfang an von Leuten erfahren, die ähnliche Konzepte verfolgen und die sie teilweise noch aus Zeiten kannten, als sie noch selbst in Bands spielten. «Ich denke an Nikae und Phuong Dan vom Golden Pudel oder dane//close und die Sameheads-Leute aus Berlin», erzählt Charlotte. «Oft sind es Leute, die auch aus der DIY-Ecke kommen, die ähnliche Events machen und bei denen die soziale Komponente ebenfalls eine wichtige Rolle spielt.»

Die Nacht hielt mehr, als der Abend versprochen hatte

Wo andere Labels im Rahmen von Veranstaltungen oftmals nicht über eine reine Labelshow zur eigenen Promotion hinausgehen, buchen Toben, Benni und Charlotte nicht nur Künstler aus ihrem Roster. Zudem sei es ihnen wichtig, über reine Partyveranstaltungen hinauszugehen. Live-Auftritte von Bands im Rahmen ihrer *MModemm Nights*-Reihe sind deswegen keine Ausnahme. Dabei geht es nicht nur darum, verschiedenen Geschmäckern gerecht zu werden, sondern vor allem auch Erwartungen zu brechen, erklärt Toben: «Wir schmissen neulich eine Party, bei der zuerst Ryoma

Sasaki von Transit spielte und danach Alessandro Adriani von Mannequin. Ryoma legte fast schon Deep House auf und im Anschluss lief dann die Musik von Adriani—die Leute waren teilweise schockiert. Es hat überhaupt nicht zusammengepasst, aber es war ein super Abend.» Die Form, sagt Toben, werde sowieso nur von aussen erdacht, die Leute kämen mit ihrer Vorstellung von einer Party zu einer Veranstaltung, die man zwar auch erfüllen könne, «aber man kann die Leute auch vor den Kopf stossen—im positiven Sinne. Das finde ich viel spannender.» MModemm-Veranstaltungen finden an verschiedenen Orten statt. In Frankfurt selbst gebe es, so Charlotte, drei Gattungen von Kontexten, in denen ein Projekt wie MModemm umgesetzt werden könne: «Eine universitäre Umgebung, wie jene der Städelschule, in Klubs wie dem Tanzhaus West oder dem Robert Johnson, wo man ab und zu reinrutschen kann, sowie in Off-Locations, die es—gemessen an der Grösse der Stadt—in einer Vielzahl gibt.» Diese temporären Orte, die immer wieder aufpoppen, wären besonders interessant, da sie noch nicht besetzt sind—im übertragenen Sinne—und sich damit noch in keinem Kontext befinden, also noch mit Inhalten gefüllt werden können. «Frankfurt ist mit seinen 700 000 Einwohnern im Vergleich zu Berlin oder Hamburg sehr klein. Trotzdem gibt es regelmässig neue Orte, die man nutzen kann», weiss Toben, der hinter dem Pseudonym Rolande Garros steckt. «Deren Situation ist zwar prekär und oft sind die nach ein paar Wochen schon wieder weg, aber es kommen stets neue dazu. Es gibt hier auch nicht wie in Hamburg oder Berlin so etwas wie coole Stadtteile, wo sich dann viel konzentriert. In Frankfurt ist eigentlich alles über die ganze Stadt verteilt.»

Frankfurt nach dem Rausch

Ob Hochkultur, die in Frankfurt Tradition und Gewicht hat, und die Szene für elektronische Musik in irgendeiner Weise verknüpft sind? Annäherungsversuche gäbe es tatsächlich, so Charlotte. «Museen wie die Schirn und das MMK veranstalten vermehrt DJ-Abende; wir selbst stehen mit dem Mousonturm in Kontakt, weil Toben und ich da auch mit Les Trucs Veranstaltungen machen. Zudem bekommen wir und andere Gruppen Unterstützung vom Kulturamt der Stadt.» Dabei handelt es sich jedoch um Peanuts, verglichen mit der Operation MOMEM (Museum of Modern Electronic Music), dem just in Frankfurt eröffneten, deutschlandweit ersten Museum, das sich mit elektronischer Musik und Klubkultur auseinandersetzt. Dabei kann die Einrichtung des Museums—es ist zuerst dem Pop Up-Konzept folgend temporär an der Frankfurter Hauptwache untergebracht—getrost als eine stadtpolitisch hofierte und natürlich neben dokumentarischen Zielen auch durch kommerzielle Gedankenspiele angetriebene Reanimation einer längst verblichenen Relevanz gesehen werden: Die Mainmetropole spielt weder in der nationalen, noch internationalen Szene auch nur annähernd die Rolle, die sie von den Achtzigern bis Ende der Neunziger einmal gespielt hatte. Selbst dann nicht, wenn man die im benachbarten Offenbach gelegene Institution Robert Johnson grosszügig zur grössten Stadt Hessens zählen würde. Die Zukunft von MModemm indes wird Konstanten beibehalten—wie die Eckpfeiler «Veröffentlichungen» und «Veranstaltungen», zwei feste Grössen, so Charlotte. Aber auch Veränderungen stehen an—wie das neue, noch zu bestimmende Format. Innerhalb dieses Rahmens werden 2018 verschiedene Projekte umgesetzt. Es sei etwa angedacht, so erzählen Charlotte, Toben und Benni, im Künstlerhaus Mousonturm Studio-Residenzen anzubieten—ausgehend von MModemm. Dort sollen Künstlerinnen Musik aufnehmen können, die später auf dem Label erscheint. Mit MModemm geht es also weiter wie bisher: offen, mit den Mitteln des DIY, von Frankfurt aus.

SOLIDIFY OSSIA

Interview:
Guy Schweger,
Remo Bitzi
Photography:
Lendita Kasthanjeva

Daniel Davis, who grew up in Bristol, runs RWDFWD, a central music node in the world's second dubstep capital. Along with an online shop and distribution company, Davis and partner Alex Digard run a bunch of labels—Peng Sound, Hotline Recordings, NoConer, FuckPunk, Lavalava(...)—all the while developing other projects indirectly through RWDFWD. In his own music as Ossia, Davis blends diverse influences using dub techniques and their inherent focus on the mixing desk. His music has found an outlet via labels such as Blackest Ever Black and Berceuse Heroique. A central figure in contact with all of Bristol's hitmakers, Davis is also part of the Young Echo crew.

In December 2017, Ossia played at the *Bold* series in a basement club in Zurich, co-hosted by zweikommasieben. Remo Bitzi and Guy Schwegler met up with the producer to explore his tangle of musical connections and influences, and to hear about his current life as a Berlin-based DJ, producer, and label head. Lendita Kasthanjeva joined in to photograph Davis in the Zurich club's labyrinthine rooms.

Der mitunter in Bristol aufgewachsene Daniel Davis betreibt mit RWDFWD einen zentralen Knotenpunkt im musikalischen Netzwerk der zweiten Dubstep-Hauptstadt. Verbunden mit dem Online-Shop und Vertrieb sind unzählige Labels, wovon einige von Davis selbst und seinem Geschäftspartner Alex Digard betrieben werden—Peng Sound, Hotline Recordings, NoConer, FuckPunk, Lavalava, (...)—, während andere und weitere Projekte eher indirekt mit RWDFWD zusammenhängen. In seiner eigenen Musik lässt Davis diverseste Einflüsse via Dub-Techniken und deren Fokus auf die Arbeit am Mischpult verschmelzen. Diese wird dann auf Labels wie Blackest Ever Black oder Berceuse Heroique unter dem Ossia-Alias veröffentlicht. Neben alledem ist Davis auch Teil der Young Echo-Crew und zudem mit gefühlt sämtlichen Exportschlagern aus Bristol befreundet.

Im Dezember 2017 spielt Ossia an der von zweikommasieben mitveranstalteten *Bold* Reihe in einem Kellerklub in Zürich. Vor Davis' Auftritt versuchten Remo Bitzi und Guy Schwegler in einem Gespräch dieses Knäuel von Verbindungen, Einflüssen und Arbeitsbereichen des mittlerweile in Berlin lebenden DJs, Produzenten und Labelbetreibers zu entwirren. Und Lendita Kasthanjeva fotografierte Davis in den labyrinthartigen Kellerräumlichkeiten.

Remo Bitzi: You run a network of labels. To what extend is everything planned and orderly or chaotically and happening by chance? And how do you decide if and when a new label is founded? For instance, you recently started Lavalava...

Daniel Davis: Yeah, it's been a year since the first record with Lavalava. I've always felt an urge to push this kind of strange and maybe more electronic side of dancehall. I've always come to electronic music from a reggae and dancehall angle anyway, so that's something I've always felt close to. But I think it was probably inspired by the first Lurka record on Hotline, *Full Clip/BR Greaze*. At the time, I felt dubstep was kind of dead, or at least going into a new phase, towards what it is now. And I felt that this could be the next sort of thing. Lurka didn't really continue doing similar stuff, although we did a few kinds of dancehall tunes together that never got released. Also, Lurka and I have this project called Two Lava, so the label name is derived from that. But where the chaos comes in: I got side-tracked and at some point I got those Alterecho and E3 tunes, and just started with that. And I guess I got a bit precious with the tunes by Lurka and me — I enjoyed having them unreleased—and I want to make more stuff with him. But coming back to why we need a new label for this—I don't know. I think it's nice to have a loose theme behind a label, kind of for sanity reasons and maybe also to help people digest it a bit more easily. Some labels pull it off to be super eclectic, to have it all under one banner, and that's really cool. But Alex [Digard] and I have always been a bit more inclined to start something new, to bring a whole aesthetic with it that people can follow. And that can also be a reason for making a new label, rather than doing something on the same one. Because it opens up a new avenue.

RB And you keep going with all the other projects as well? The labels? So the amount of work always gets bigger?

DD Yeah... not sure if it's necessarily a smart move in that sense. On the other hand, if we had released six records on one label, then, well, six records would be out at the same time, for example. Doing six releases on one label would probably confuse people more than doing six releases on six labels at the same time.

Guy Schwegler And do you think people kind of know this? Do they think, "oh, it's that Ossia guy doing another label again"? Maybe they don't really care if the stuff is on a different label.

DD Originally, when we started the [Lavalava] label, an interview made it public that I was involved in it. Before that interview we hadn't really announced that we were the ones behind the label, and maybe we did see the benefit of doing so afterwards, a bit. For instance, making it a proud factor that these labels are a RWDFWD thing helped tie RWDFWD together as well, and made it less disparate. But this wasn't a thought first, that people would recognise our output under the RWDFWD umbrella, or as coming from Ossia or Tape Echo.

GS I didn't know until recently that you were behind Lavalava.

RB Same for me with Hotline.

DD For Hotline specifically, we really made an effort to keep it indefinite. I kind of regret that it came out [that we were behind it]. The idea with this phone line was always that it should be kind of incognito and that no one should really know what Hotline is. But the beans got spilled.

RB And what's the motivation behind staying incognito?

DD Just romanticising this idea of a mysterious hotline. It's inspired by this kind of free-party-rave-scene[1], the mystery of who's organising it—but you still can take part by calling the hotline. It's about staying off the grid, keeping this mystery. Initially the idea was just a 12" with the [phone] number on it—no further info. You'd have to call to hear which tracks are on there. And then Alex got the idea to do some more design-oriented stuff, so it changed.

RB: Was ist die Motivation dahinter—warum wollt ihr inkognito bleiben?
DD: Das ist einfach eine Romantisierung dieser mysteriösen Telefonnummer, inspiriert von den Free Party Raves[1]. Die Organisation bleibt ein Mysterium—aber indem man anruft, kann man trotzdem Teil des Ganzen sein. Die ursprüngliche Idee war eigentlich, nur 12-Inches mit der Nummer drauf zu veröffentlichen—ohne weitere Infos. Du hättest also anrufen müssen, wenn du die Informationen zur Platte haben wolltest. Aber Alex hatte dann mehr Ideen fürs Design, also hat sich das noch geändert.

GS: Inwiefern unterscheiden sich die Labels deiner Meinung nach? Oder was wäre der Mehrwert aus der Unterscheidung? DD: Jeder muss sich dazu selber etwas überlegen. Wir haben natürlich gewisse Ideen, aber hoffen auch, dass die Labels für sich selber sprechen: Über die Musik, das Aussehen von Platten und Tapes, aber eben auch wie das Label geführt wird—Hotline ist ein spezielles Beispiel dafür.

GS: Die Frage nach Distinktion stellt sich für mich in einigen Bereichen deiner musikalischen Tätigkeit, zum Beispiel auch bei Young Echo. Da sind einige recht verschiedene Leute involviert und man könnte sich fragen, was der Gedanke dahinter ist, oder aber auch inwiefern sich die Mitglieder unterscheiden…
DD: Rund um diese Frage gab es in den letzten Jahren einige Diskussionen bei Young Echo. Als diese Gruppe entstand—also noch bevor ich ein Mitglied war—, bewegten die Leute sich ganz natürlich in ähnlichen Gefilden; die Mitglieder waren jung und vielleicht auch noch nicht so weitläufig in einem musikalischen Sinne. Man dachte also nicht weiter über diese Frage nach. Jetzt sieht man aber deutlich verschiedene Ansätze in Young Echo und es gab Momente, in denen das Projekt fast beendet wurde—nicht wegen einem Streit oder so, sondern einfach aufgrund der Tatsache, dass jeder seinen eigenen Weg ging und einige der Mitglieder als Solokünstler sehr beschäftigt waren. Schlussendlich einigte man sich aber in einer grossen Diskussion darauf, dass es keine uniforme Mentalität braucht, sondern dass man gerade mit den Differenzen gemeinsam unterwegs sein kann. Sei das nun Kahn und Neeks Grime oder Chester Giles und Vessels seltsam Electronica oder… Diese Gleichzeitigkeit von individuellen Ansätzen und das gemeinsame Wertschätzen ist doch etwas sehr Schönes. Ein ähnlicher Prozess hat auch bei dem im Februar erschienenen Album stattgefunden: Den ersten Entwurf der Trackliste lehnten wir aus dem Grund ab, dass er zu einheitlich war. Das Album sollte Ecken und Kanten haben, denn es gibt einfach keinen Young Echo-Sound per se.

RB: Und was wäre dann der gemeinsame Nenner von Young Echo? Lediglich die geografische Referenz—also Bristol? DD: Manonmars, einer der Vocalists, und Vessel leben mittlerweile in London; ich lebe in Berlin. Es ist also nicht mehr ein reines Bristol-Ding, obwohl unsere Veranstaltungen dann doch wieder dort stattfinden. Die Gemeinsamkeit ist aber wohl allein die Tatsache, dass wir alle Freunde sind, die gemeinsam zu einem Soundpool beitragen, davon lernen und diesen teilen.

GS: Einen geographischen Punkt als Gemeinsamkeit und zwecks Gruppenidentität zu haben,[2] ist ja auch schon fast ein Privileg heutzutage und für viele nicht möglich, weil man auch nicht immer an selben Ort leben kann.
RB: NON wäre ein Beispiel für den genau umgekehrten Ansatz. Bei ihnen geht es wohl mehr darum, eine Verbindung wiederaufzunehmen, und zwar unbedingt in einem ästhetischen Sinne.
DD: Es ist auch tatsächlich eine Herausforderung, die Unterschiede zusammenzubringen—und zwar mehr die musikalischen als die geographischen.

GS Are there specific ways in which your different projects, the labels, are distinct?
DD It's for everyone to make up their own mind about that. We probably have some ideas of what makes each distinct, but they also kind of speak for themselves when you listen to the music and see the records and tapes and the way each label is handled—as with Hotline, for example.
GS The question of distinction is related to some areas of your musical activity, I think, including Young Echo. There are quite a few people involved in that project. What creates its group spirit? Do the different members each leave their respective mark on the project?
DD This has actually been a bit of a talking point in Young Echo over the last couple of years. We didn't really think about it at first. When it started—before I was a member—people were naturally working in a similar field, were younger, and maybe not yet as broad in musical sense. But now there are definitely different minds in Young Echo and there were points when the project almost ended. Not in a kind of arguing way, but rather like, okay, everyone is taking different paths and certain people have really gotten busy as solo artists. But in the end, what got everyone back together was just a big discussion in which everyone agreed that there doesn't have to be a uniform group mind-set, and that the great thing is that you can still work together with those differences. Embracing all the different angles, whether it's Kahn and Neek's grime side or the weird electronics of Chester Giles and Vessel. I think it's just about letting everyone be an individual, but appreciating it together. And I think this is a really nice thing. Also, with the Young Echo album, there were drafts of the tracklist and it sounded a bit uniform. But then we were like "no, it has to be angular, there have to be differences, it's just not one Young Echo sound, there have to be edges, it has to be a bit messy." Then again, all the tracks are just listed as Young Echo, which makes it easier to read, but also harder to distinguish the sounds.
RB And what's the common ground with Young Echo? Geography? People from Bristol?
DD Actually, Manonmars, one of the lyricists, lives in London, but he used to live in a small town near Bristol with Amos Childs from Jabu, so that's the connection to the West Country, at least. Vessel lives in London now, and I live in Berlin. So it's actually not fully Bristol anymore, but it's still there—also with the nights and stuff. So, common ground… I think it's just the fact that we are all friends, that we each feel like we can contribute to and learn from the pool of sounds we create, and that we all have something to share: the music.
GS I think it's almost a luxury situation to think of a geographical point of origin as a common denominator for group identity.[2] Living in one place all the time isn't possible for many people anymore…
RB Yes, if you take NON Worldwide for example, it's the opposite approach. More like re-connecting—but not really in an aesthetic way.
DD I think this is also kind of the challenge for Young Echo—to pull together not so much the geographical but the musical differences. For example, when we do an event, there is the idea to put all of these sounds into one night. And that's a challenge—but a fun one. I don't think it can necessarily go down in every club or city in the world, but I think there's a certain time and place where people really appreciate it. In Bristol, it was still a very small-scale kind of thing, but Young Echo definitely were known for, you know, never knowing what the next record might be. And I think people appreciated that. That makes it worth sticking together.
GS The idea of mixing different stuff together is very present in your work, and in articles or interview introductions about you. The writers point out a mixture of dub, punk, techno,

Gerade wenn wir eine Nacht lang spielen, ist es auch das Ziel, all die Sounds zu spielen. Das ist natürlich eine Herausforderung—aber eine, die Spass macht. Ich denke aber auch, dass das überall funktionieren kann. Es braucht den richtigen Ort und die richtige Zeit dafür—und auch in Bristol fand das Ganze ja nur in einem kleinen Rahmen statt. Aber diese Nächte waren bekannt dafür, dass man nie wusste, was als nächstes gespielt werden wird. Das haben einige Gäste wohl sehr geschätzt und nur schon dafür lohnt es sich, zusammen weiterzumachen.

GS: Die Idee, verschiedene Stile und Sounds zusammenzubringen, ist sehr präsent in deiner Arbeit. Auch Journalistinnen und Reviewer verweisen gerne auf eine Mischung von Punk, Dub, Techno und was-auch-immer in deinen Produktionen. Dieser sehr offene Ansatz fand insbesondere in den letzten Jahren weite Verbreitung und ist meiner Meinung nach sehr wichtig. Aber ich frage mich auch: Wann müssen wir damit aufhören und uns wieder voll auf etwas konzentrieren, um das dann weiterzuentwickeln? DD: Darauf habe ich (noch) keine wirklich schlaue Antwort; ich habe mir aber schon viele Gedanken dazu gemacht. Gerade wenn ich auflege, versuche ich viele verschiedene Stile zusammenzubringen. Das funktioniert zum Teil, aber dann habe ich manchmal wieder das Gefühl, es wäre produktiver, sich auf eine Sache zu konzentrieren und die Leute für eine Stunde im selben musikalischen Vibe aufgehen zu lassen. Das ist natürlich stimmungsabhängig und ich glaube nicht, dass man das forcieren kann. Gleichzeitig ist es schon eine Frage, ob jemals wieder eine wirkliche Szene entsteht. Die letzte, an die ich mich erinnern kann, war Dubstep. Sogar UK Funky war ziemlich kurzlebig. Ich weiss nicht, ob etwas Ähnliches je wieder so passieren wird—also ein Genre und eine Gemeinschaft darum herum. Die heutige Gesellschaft und insbesondere deren Informationsverarbeitung mit dem Internet machen das ziemlich schwierig… Gleichzeitig gibt es ja Beispiele für aktuelle Szenen rund um einen Sound: Die Príncipe Crew in Lissabon etwa oder Gqom aus Südafrika.

RB: Príncipe ist ein sehr gutes Beispiel dafür, was passiert, wenn man immer weiter an etwas Bestimmten arbeitet—aber genau das könnte man auch bezüglich RWDFWD sagen. Zumindest ist dies meine naive Perspektive: Trotz der Tatsache, dass es eine Mischung ist, schafft es etwas Spezifisches und man weiss ein wenig, was man erwarten kann. DD: Mhh, ja, das Ganze verfestigt sich doch langsam. Vielleicht habe ich da einen etwas kritischeren Blick darauf, weil ich mich nicht so stark persönlich involviert fühle, obwohl doch die meisten Leute aus diesem Umfeld zu meinen Freunden zählen. Ich verspüre irgendwie nicht dieselbe Aufregung, die ich bei Dubstep-Nächten in Bristol hatte. Damals war das eine wirkliche Entdeckung für mich.

GS: Retrospektiv und aus meiner Sicht betrachtet, wurde der ganze Bristol-Sound immer experimenteller. Denkst du das stimmt? DD: Ja, ich glaub schon. Es kommt jedoch noch ein wenig darauf an, worüber man spricht. Oft dreht sich die Diskussion ja um Labels wie Timedance und Livity Sound. Und die sind im Vergleich zu UK Garage, Funk oder auch Grime—deren eigentliche Vorgänger—unglaublich reduziert. Die Produktionen von Lurka, Batu und Kinlaw sind so mutig. Sie sind auf das nötigste reduziert, sind speziell und trotzdem funktional. Peder Mannerfelt, der zwar nicht aus Bristol ist, wäre auch ein Beispiel dafür.[3] Daneben gibt es aber eine eigentliche DIY- und experimentelle Szene in Bristol, die mindestens ebenso lebendig ist—vielleicht nicht, wenn man sich konkrete Besucherzahlen und ähnliches anschaut, aber es passieren da sehr spannende Sachen. Ein Freund von mir, Max, der auch Teil von Bad Tracking⁴ ist, macht zusammen mit einigen anderen die Slack Alice Abende. Die sind schon sehr toll und haben insofern eine Ähnlichkeit mit Young Echo, als dass es reguläre Zeiten für Sets und ähnliches nicht gibt. Es passiert also auch einiges in einer eher experimentellen Szene per se.

RB: Glaubst du, dass du irgendwann die ganze Dancemusic hinter dir lässt und nur noch experimentelle Sachen machst?
DD: Das ist etwas, das mich stark beschäftigt. Denn ich produziere und spiele wirklich sehr gerne experimentelle Sachen. Aber dann erlebe ich Momente, in denen ich einfach nur ein Rave-Set spielen will. Daher: Ich weiss es nicht. Das wird sich mit der Zeit zeigen. Vielleicht bin ich irgendwann zu alt, um zu raven. Zurzeit gefällt es mir sehr gut zwischen den beiden Bereichen hin und her zu wechseln.

GS: Du hast im Laufe der Jahre einiges an Wissen bezüglich Musikdistribution angehäuft und auch einige Institutionen aufgebaut. Auch hast du mit diesem Wissen bereits anderen ausgeholfen—zuletzt etwa Cera Khin mit ihrem Lazy-Tapes-Label. Trotzdem wollte ich fragen, wo du Möglichkeiten siehst, wie du dein Wissen oder auch die aufgebauten Strukturen vermitteln und weitergeben könntest? DD: Vor kurzem habe ich ein Interview mit Batu im *Crack Magazine*⁵ gelesen. Und das hat mich sehr daran erinnert, wie inspirierend es für mich war, Peverelist—jemanden den ich persönlich kenne—und dessen Livity Sound-Label zu sehen. Damals entstanden einige Labels, weil Platten in tieferen Auflagen verkauft und daher auch produziert werden konnten—es wurde möglich, ein Label zu machen und Geld für die Pressungen aufzutreiben, ohne grosse Finanzierungspläne und Deals. Livity Sound inspirierte mich Peng Sound zu machen, das erste Label. Und Batu hat eben im *Crack Magazine* erzählt, dass unsere Arbeit mit RWDFWD und den Labels wiederum ihn inspiriert hat. Das ist innerhalb von drei Jahren passiert. Das zeigt, was möglich ist, ohne direkt zu vermitteln—einfach schon deshalb, weil wir ganz normale Leute sind.

E Interview Ossia

etc. And I think this approach was and still is really relevant in general, especially in the last few years. But at what point might one have to stop with that and really focus again on a specific thing in order to develop it further?

DD I don't really have a good answer for that, but it's definitely something I do think about. For example, when I'm DJing, I love so much different music and sometimes I pull off bringing a lot of different sounds together. But other times, I do think "wow, I should focus a bit more on one kind of thing, one sound and one kind of headspace for an hour." It really depends on the mood, and I don't think you can control all these things or actively put an end to mixing different styles. But sometimes I do wonder whether there will ever be a proper scene again. The last one I remember was dubstep. Even UK funky was really short-lived. I wonder whether there will ever be a proper focus on a genre and a community around it—partly because of society now, the Internet, and the way the consumption of information is organised. I wonder whether it will happen in the same way ever again. But you have the Príncipe crew, or stuff in South Africa with Gqom, so...

RB I think Príncipe is a really good example of what can happen if you stick to your thing and just keep pushing there—but you could say the same thing about what is happening in Bristol or with RWDFWD, I guess. At least that's my very naive perspective on it. It's very specific, in a way—although it is mixed. You kind of know what you can expect.

DD Yeah, you're right. It is sort of solidifying a bit, isn't it? Maybe it is just because I don't feel as involved in that personally, even though a lot of them are friends. For me it doesn't have the same kind of excitement that dubstep had when I was going to nights in Bristol in the earlier days, when there was this kind of feeling of discovery.

GS In retrospect, and from my point of view, the Bristol sound has gotten more and more experimental over time. Do you think this is true?

DD Yes, I think so. Maybe it depends a bit on what people or journalists talk about. They mostly seem to be talking about Timedance and Livity Sound. I'd even say that the Livity Sound or Timedance stuff is more stripped back than UK garage, grime, or funky; their early incarnations. It is so much more stripped back, dub—the reduction has taken place. I feel like people became quite bold with their productions. Lurka, Batu, Kinlaw—they do it really well. The tracks are so stripped back and really weird, but somehow still kind of catchy. Peder Mannerfelt—though not really from Bristol³—would also be an example for this kind of approach.

In addition, I'd say the DIY and experimental scene in Bristol is equally healthy, even healthier, though not necessarily in numbers. If you go to gigs there's maybe 50 people there, but still, it is happening and there's some really interesting stuff being done. My friend Max, who's also part of Bad Tracking⁴, has been doing this night called *Slack Alice* with a few friends in Bristol. It's a really cool thing, a bit like Young Echo in the way it refrains from smoothened set times or anything like that. So there are interesting things going on in that kind of more underground electronic side.

RB Do you think you'll have to leave the whole dance music thing behind at some point and just do experimental stuff?

DD That's something I find myself torn with as well, because I really enjoy making really experimental stuff. And also playing it. But I do also have moments where I just want to rave and make people dance. I don't know—time will tell. And at the moment I'm happy to try and straddle them. Maybe that will change when I'm too old to rave.

GS You've accumulated a lot of industry knowledge and helped other people out with their projects (recently Cera Khin with the LazyTapes label). Do you see more ways in which you could pass on your knowledge or also the musical framework that you've built?

DD That's actually really interesting. I read a recent interview with Batu in *Crack Magazine*[5], and it reminded me of myself being interviewed years ago, when I was asked: "How did you get inspired to make a label?" And one of the inspiring things for me was seeing Peverelist (someone who I actually knew personally) and the Livity Sound label develop. It was a time when a lot of labels were appearing, because records were sold in lesser amounts, so it became easier in general to manage a label without big deals and without big money to back the pressings. So Livity Sound was an inspiration to start Peng Sound, which was my first label. And yeah, in the *Crack Magazine* interview, Batu was saying that what we were doing was an inspiration for him in starting Timedance. This happened within three years. Even if we didn't directly teach them, it kind of showed people that it can be done—by regular people.

References

1   Regarding Free Partys, see the interview with Ekman in zweikommasieben #14.

    Siehe bezüglich Free Partys auch das Interview mit Ekman in zweikommasieben #14.

2   Regarding geographical points and their relevance, see the snapshot-camera column with DJ Overdose in zweikommasien #12.

    Siehe bezüglich geographischen Referenzpunkten die Einwegkamera-Kolumne mit DJ Overdose in zweikommasieben #12.

3   Together with Bristol based Hodge, Peter Mannerfelt produced the EP *All My Love* (Peder Mannerfelt, 2017).

    Peder Mannerfelt hat mit dem in Bristol lebenden Hodge die EP *All My Love* produziert (Peder Mannerfelt, 2017).

4   See the EP *XP-3* from Bad Tracking, including a remix by Ossia (Mechanical Reproductions, 2017).

    Siehe auch die EP *XP-3* von Bad Tracking, inklusive Remix von Ossia (Mechanical Reproductions, 2017).

5   De Chroustchoff, Gwyn Thomas. 2017. "Batu is keeping innovation at the top of Bristol's agenda." *Crack Magazine*. https://crackmagazine.net/article/long-reads/batu-keeps-innovations-top-bristols-agenda/ (accessed 08.02.2018)

    De Chroustchoff, Gwyn Thomas. 2017. «Batu is keeping innovation at the top of Bristol's agenda». *Crack Magazine*. Online unter: https://crackmagazine.net/article/long-reads/batu-keeps-innovations-top-bristols-agenda/ (heruntergeladen 08.02.2018)

RAVE IS REVOLUTION
GABBER ELEGANZA

Interview:
Conor McTernan
Photography:
Paolo Stroppa,
Mauro Puccini

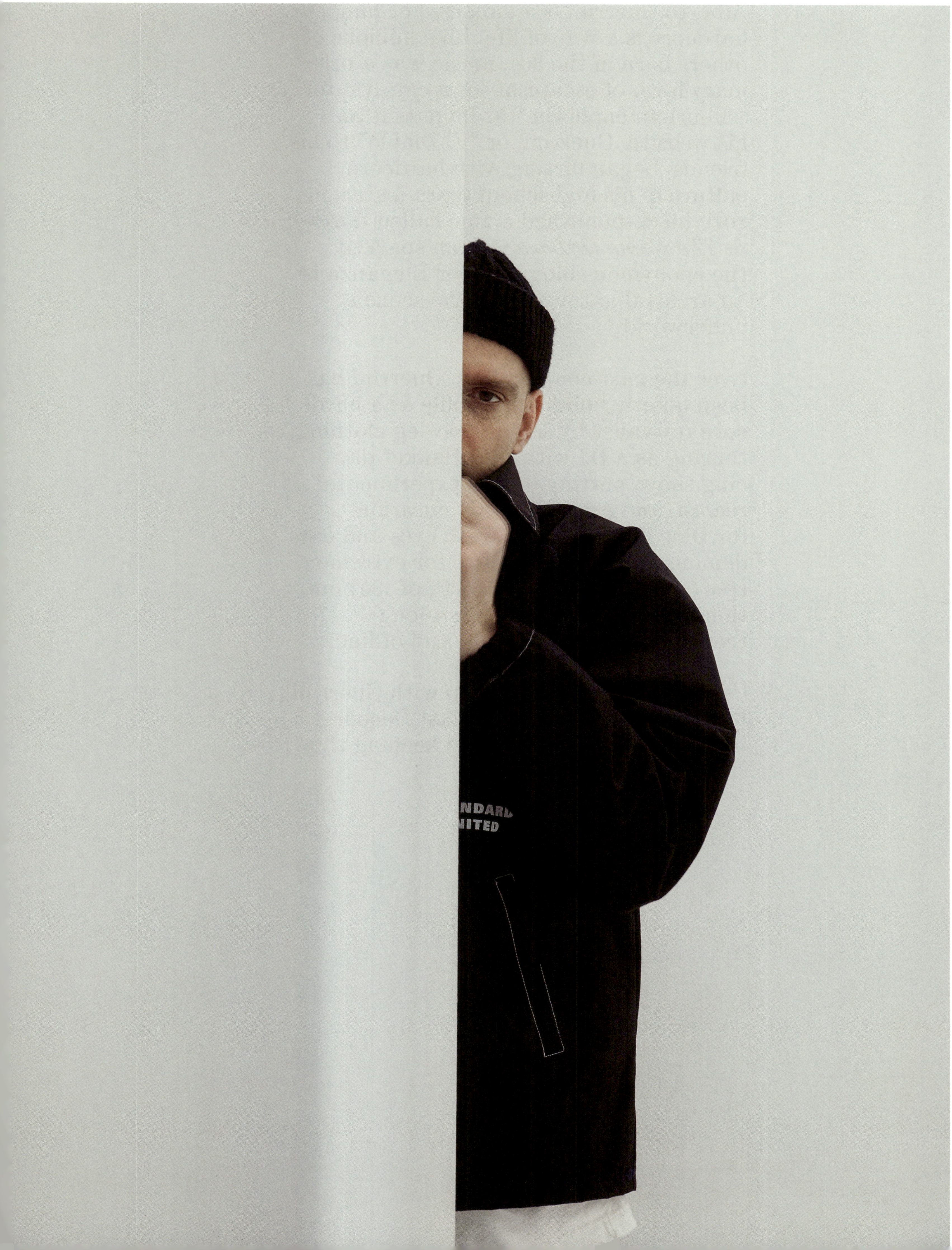

Alberto Guerrini is a gabber. For him, hardcore is a way of life. Like millions of others born in the 80s, music was a primary form of escapism—or a catalyst for "suburban euphoria," as he puts it on his website. Guerrini, or "El Diablo" to his friends, began flirting with hardcore culture in his highschool years. Later, in 2011, he co-published a zine called *Gabber In The Name Of Love*,[1] which sparked the eponymous blog; Gabber Eleganza is an archival gateway into the scene's underworld.

Over the past couple years, Guerrini has been quietly building a profile as a hardcore revivalist by selling bootleg clothing, touring as a DJ with the "Hakke" dancing show, putting out an experimental record, and even doing art curation for Dior Homme. With fresh eyes and ears demonstrating an appetite for extreme sportswear and sounds north of 180 bpm, there's renewed interest in a long-troubled culture—both on- and offline.

Conor McTernan caught up with Guerrini before a DJ set in London last December to talk about his role in keeping the spirit alive.

Alberto Guerrini ist ein Gabber. Für ihn ist Hardcore eine Lebensart. Wie für Millionen andere, die in den Achtzigern geboren wurden, war für ihn Musik hauptsächlich eine Form von Eskapismus—oder ein Katalysator für «Vorstadt Euphorie», wie er es auf seiner Website nennt. Guerrini, der von seinen Freunden «El Diablo» genannt wird, begann sich während seiner Zeit als Oberstufenschüler für Hardcore und die Kultur drum herum zu interessieren. Jahre später—anno 2011—gab er ein Fanzine namens *Gabber In The Name Of Love*[1] heraus, das auch die Initialzündung für den Blog *Gabber Eleganza* war. Heute ist der Blog ein archivarischer Zugang zur (Unter-)Welt besagter Szene.

Über die vergangenen Jahre hat sich Guerrini einen Namen als Hardcore-Revivalist gemacht, indem er Bootleg-Klamotten verkaufte, als DJ und mit seiner «Hakke»-Show tourt, eine experimentelle Platte veröffentlicht und auch für Dior Homme einen Art-Curation-Auftrag übernahm. Mit frischen Augen und Ohren fördert er einen Appetit für extreme Sportbekleidung und Sounds nördlich von 180 bpm, was dem neuaufkommenden Interesse—on- wie auch offline—an einer lange belächelten Kultur dient.

Conor McTernan traf Guerrini vor einem DJ-Gig in London im vergangenen Dezember um mit ihm über seine Rolle in der Szene zu reden.

Conor McTernan: Do you recall the first time you heard hardcore music?

Alberto Guerrini: It was at my hometown street market, which takes place every Wednesday. In the summer it was a meeting point for kids to buy illegal bootleg tapes. Circa 1996 to 1997 was the peak of the hardcore boom in Italy. Around the same time my cousin and some older friends were circulating hardcore tapes. We would listen to broadcasts on Radio Base 87.5. "Hey you are on Radio Base 87.5. This is from the number one discotheque, this is the Hardcore Warriors... bam bam bam bam!" It was quite strange as I was ten years old, so my daily routine aside from this was watching cartoons and listening to pop music... I wasn't just into hardcore as a kid. We were into Gigi D'Agostino, italo classics, hard dance stuff from Mauro Picotto, and also a lot of hip hop, which is still the music I listen to most in my car. My first ever CD was *X-Terror Files* from Simonetti, who was one of the most respected synthesizer artists in Europe. He was a member of The Goblins, a great krautrock / synth group.

CM What is it about gabber culture that appeals to you so much?

AG I discovered the music (hardcore) before I discovered the sub-culture. The first time I encountered gabber was when I was 14, in my school's study hall. There was a guy who was a couple of years older than me and also into hardcore. He told me about going to clubs and seeing the legends. He pointed out another guy in front of me and said, "he likes the music too." I said: "But he looks a bit different than me?" He responded: "Yeah... he's a gabberhead." I looked at the guy, who was bald and wearing a tracksuit. I thought: "shit... this is cool!" I've always loved clothes and sportswear, but I was never into shocking people. For me gabber is a really minimal and pragmatic style. As is the music; it's just a beat—it's really simple but also really iconic. It's not aggressive, like skinhead culture, but at the same times it's masculine and androgenic—the girls often dress like men. In the 90s, it was super simple. A white tracksuit with some texture, a bald head, maybe some rings. That's it... Simple.

CT Gabber fans have a striking physical appearance. You've faced problems in the past because of this. How do you react when people attack you for looking the way you do?

AG Obviously in the past some gabber fans have aligned to the right, but they are the minority. I'm a left leaning guy, so when someone compares my project to fascism it breaks my heart. But I know that there are people with prejudices who don't understand that my project is more than some bald guy dancing on stage—just like punk. When it arrived in Italy it was popular with the art kids, but people assumed they were fascists. I've met fascist gabber kids in the past. They are the ones who do stupid poses with pills in their mouths. These guys are less than 5% of the scene. In reality, Nazis hate gabber fans... they see the scene mainly as people who go to raves and listen to techno and black music. Lots of black people dance to hardcore too.

CM Let's talk about your merchandise. It's quite popular. Did you expect this?

AG [Laughs] No. I started with four t-shirts, which sold out in one day. I never expected things to sell so fast. I just posted a picture on Instagram and bought my Big Cartel upgrade for GBP 10 a month. I've started working with a couple of stores in Tokyo, Taipei, and now Milan. The money is a nice base to start a new project like a label, which I am in the process of doing. My friend Marco at Studio Temp helps me out with vectors for design, and there is a print studio that helps me with silk-screening. I've always been into creative processes—graphic design, creative direction, and the music especially. It's a 360-degree project.

CM In the last run, there is a "Total Football" t-shirt. Are you a football fan or is this more about the trend of sportswear in the rave scene?

Conor McTernan: Erinnerst du dich an das erste Mal, als du mit Hardcore-Musik in Kontakt kamst?

Alberto Guerrini: Das war auf dem Markt in meiner Heimatstadt, der jeden Mittwoch stattfand. Im Sommer war das ein Treffpunkt für Kids, um illegale Bootleg-Tapes zu kaufen. 1996 oder 1997 erlebte Hardcore einen Boom in Italien. Etwa zur gleichen Zeit zirkulierten unter meinem Cousin und einigen älteren Freunden Hardcore-Tapes. Wir hörten uns Sendungen auf Radio Base 87.5 an. «Hey, du hörst Radio Base 87.5. Direkt aus der besten Disco bringen wir die Hardcore Warriors zu dir... Bam bam bam bam!» Das war ziemlich seltsam—immerhin war ich erst zehn Jahre alt. Neben diesen Sendungen schaute ich mir Cartoons an und hörte Popmusik. Meine Kindheit bestand also nicht ausschliesslich aus Hardcore. Wir mochten Gigi D'Agostino, italienische Klassiker, Hard-Dance-Sachen von Mauro Picotto und auch jede Menge Hip-Hop. Letzteres ist übrigens jene Art von Musik, die ich nach wie vor am meisten höre, wenn ich mit dem Auto unterwegs bin. Meine erste CD überhaupt war *X-Terror Files* von Simonetti, einem der renommiertesten Künstler aus dem Feld der Synthesizer-Musik in Europa. Er war Teil von The Goblins, einer Krautrock- und Synth-Gruppe.

CM: Was an der Gabber-Kultur gefällt dir am meisten? **AG:** Ich entdeckte die Musik, bevor ich zur dazugehörigen Subkultur kam. Gabber lernte ich kennen, als ich 14 Jahre alt war. Das passierte an meiner Schule: Da gab es diesen Mitschüler – er war ein paar Jahre älter als ich –, der auf Hardcore stand. Er erzählte mir davon, wie er in Klubs gehen würde und von den Legenden, die er dort sah. Einmal zeigte er auf einen Typen, der auch grad da war und ebenfalls auf Gabber stehen würde. Der sah definitiv anders aus als ich—worauf mein Mitschüler meinte: «Ja, er ist ein Gabber». Ich schaute mir den Typ an—er hatte eine Glatze und trug einen Tracksuit—und ich dachte: «Shit... das ist ziemlich cool!» Ich mochte schon immer Kleidung und vor allem Sportsachen, aber ich war nie daran interessiert, Leute zu schockieren. Für mich ist Gabber ein minimaler und pragmatischer Stil. Wie der Beat in der Musik—der ist ziemlich einfach und gleichzeitig sehr ikonisch. Die Kultur ist nicht aggressiv—wie jene der Skinheads etwa. Gleichzeitig ist alles maskulin und androgyn: Die Frauen tragen oft dasselbe wie die Männer. In den Neunzigern war das sehr simpel: Ein weisser Tracksuit mit einem Muster, eine Glatze und vielleicht ein paar Ringe. Das war's. Ziemlich einfach.

CM: Gabbers haben ein spezifisches Erscheinungsbild. Aufgrund dessen hattest du in der Vergangenheit auch schon Probleme. Wie gehst du damit um? **AG:** In der Vergangenheit haben sich einige Gabbers offensichtlich mit Rechten verbündet; dabei handelt es sich aber um eine Minderheit. Ich selbst tendiere eher nach links. Vergleicht jemand also mein Projekt mit Faschismus, dann bricht mir dies das Herz. Aber ich weiss, dass es Leute gibt, die Vorurteile haben und nicht wissen, dass mehr hinter der Sache steckt, als dass eine Glatze auf der Bühne tanzt—so wie Punks. Als die Sache in Italien wiederaufkam, interessierten sich hauptsächlich Leute aus der Kunstszene dafür, aber viele Leute dachten, es handle sich um Faschisten. Ich bin auch schon faschistischen Gabber-Kids begegnet. Das sind auch jene, die etwa mit Pillen im Mund für Fotos posieren. Dabei handelt es sich aber um weniger als 5% der Leute. Tatsächlich hassen Nazis Gabbers... Es handelt sich hauptsächlich um Leute, die an Raves gehen und Techno und Black Musik mögen. Es gibt auch viele dunkelhäutige Leute, die zu Hardcore tanzen.

CM: Lass uns über deinen Merchandise sprechen. Die Produkte wurden ziemlich populär; hattest du das erwartet?
AG: [Lacht] Nein. Ich begann mit vier T-Shirts, die nach dem ersten Tag bereits ausverkauft waren. Ich erwartete nicht, dass das so schnell gehen würde. Ich hatte lediglich einen Post auf Instagram gemacht und besorgte mir ein Upgrade auf Big Cartel für zehn Pfund pro Monat. Später begann ich mit einigen Läden in Tokio, Taipei und Mailand zu arbeiten. Das Geld, das ich damit verdiene, ist eine tolle Ausgangslage für neue Projekte, wie dem Label, das ich zurzeit aufziehe. Mein Freund Marco von Studio Temp hilft mir mit den Vektoren bei der Gestaltung und es gibt eine Werkstatt, die mir beim Siebdrucken hilft. Ich möchte schon immer kreative Prozesse—Grafikdesign, Art Direction und vor allem die Musik. Gabber Eleganza ist ein 360-Grad-Projekt.

CM: Jüngst gab es ein T-Shirt mit dem Aufdruck «Total Football». Bist du ein Fussballfan oder geht es dabei eher um den Trend von Sportbekleidung in der Rave-Szene? AG: Ich bin ein Fussballfan. Ich respektiere die Kultur und mich interessiert die Folkloristik von Jugendkulturen wie jene der Ultras in Italien. Da ich aus Bergamo komme, fasziniert mich das wirklich. Ich mag das Phänomen und alles drum herum. «Ultra» ist ein Synonym für Hooligan. Aber es geht auch drum, zu sagen: «Ich als Fan bin mehr Ultra als du!» Es geht um Extremismus. «Total Football» ist der Name eines Tracks auf meiner letzten EP, Never Sleep #1. Es geht um die Demokratie in einem Fussballspiel und darum, dass alle Spieler ersetzt werden können. Der Song hat fünf Teile; wechselt man diese aus, dann ändert sich nichts—es geht also um dasselbe wie bei einer Fussballmannschaft. Dabei ist das Stück ein bisschen abstrakter, als man das erwarten könnte. Aber weil es auf einem experimentellen Label erscheint—auf Presto!? –, wollte ich, dass dem so ist. Die Grafik auf dem Rücken des Shirts beinhaltet verschiedene Sportmarken von italienischen Fussballmannschaften, etwa Kappa, Joma, Givova, Errea, Asics, Gola, Umbro, Nike... Der Ausdruck «Sportmarken Patriotismus» wird hier also ein bisschen auf die Schippe genommen.

CM: Dein «Never Sleep»-Emblem ist eine Version von Bayers Firmenlogo. Mit Kappas Logo gehst du bei deiner Reinterpretation für das «Gabba»-Shirt ähnlich um—diese spielvollen Interpretationen haben die Leute berührt. Woher kommen diese Bootlegs? AG: Das «Gabba»-Logo ist ein Bootleg von einem Bootleg. Ich glaube, das existierte bereits irgendwo, ich verwendete es schlicht für meine Zwecke. Ich möchte die Neunziger und den Rave-Boom in Europa schon immer. Ich mag es auch, mich durch alte Rave-Magazine zu kämpfen, und darin findet man viele Bootlegs. Der NASA-Rave-Flyer etwa war in Amerika besonders berühmt. Ich verstehe mich als Teil dieser Tradition. Der Name «Gabber Eleganza» ist ein bisschen sinnlos, es ist ein Paradox. Mein Merchandise ist ebenfalls ein bisschen ironisch, weil Gabber nicht ernst sein soll, sondern eher lustig. Das Projekt ist aber ernst gemeint.

CM: Gibt es denn keine Probleme mit diesen Marken bezüglich Copyright?
AG: Nein, ich ersetze ja alles. Schaut man sich etwa die Haare im «Gabba»-Logo an, sieht man, dass es anders ist als beim Kappa-Logo, oder beim Bayer-Logo ist der Kreis grösser und der Text fetter als bei meiner «Never Sleep»-Interpretation. Es handelt sich offensichtlich um einen Beschiss, aber ich beschiesse gut genug, um damit durchzukommen. Würden diese Unternehmen mir schreiben, würde ich sie fragen, ob sie mit mir zusammenarbeiten wollten. Und wenn sie das nicht wollen, dann würde ich einfach vorwärtsschauen und etwas Anderes machen.

AG I'm a football fan. I respect the culture and I'm really interested in the folklore of youth subcultures like the Italian Ultras. Coming from Bergamo it really fascinates me. I like the phenomena around it. "Ultra" is another name for hooligan. But it's also about: "As a fan, I'm more ULTRA than YOU!" It's about extremism.
"Total Football" is the name of one of my tunes from the recent *Never Sleep #1* EP. It's about the democracy of a football team, everybody has the same role, and everyone can be exchanged. You can divide this song into five parts, switch it around, and it won't change. It's kind of the same idea. It's a bit more abstract, and because it's out on an experimental label—Presto!?—I wanted to experiment.
The graphics on the back of the shirt feature all the premier sports brands from teams across the various regions of Italy, like Kappa, Joma, Givova, Errea, Asics, Gola, Umbro, Nike... So the term "Sportswear Patriotism" is a bit of ironic fun.

CM Your "Never Sleep" logo is a play on Bayer Pharmaceuticals, much like the "Gabba" reinterpretation of the Kappa logo—these playful renditions have struck a chord with people. Where did you come up with these bootlegs?

AG The "Gabba" logo is a bootleg of a bootleg. I believe it already existed elsewhere, I just put my own touch on it. I've always been a fan of the 90s and the European rave boom. I'm really into digging through old rave magazines, and in there you will find lots of bootlegged stuff. The NASA rave flyer in the USA was particularly famous. I come from that kind of heritage. The name "Gabber Eleganza" [translates to Gabber Elegance] is a bit nonsensical, it's a paradox. My merchandise is also a bit ironic, because gabber isn't supposed to be serious, rather a bit funny. The project, however, is serious.

CM Are there any brand copyright issues?

AG No, I change everything. If you look at the hair in the "Gabba" logo it's different and on the Bayer logo the circle is bigger and the text is bolder. It's clearly a rip off, but I've changed it enough. If they wrote to me I would ask them if they would like to collaborate, otherwise I would stop and move on to something new.

CM When or where do you think the cultures of gabber and high fashion collided?

AG I've never been into high fashion, but I like style and I'm curious about trends. Sportswear has blown up in the last two to three years, for instance the aesthetic of Gosha Rubchinskiy's tracksuits. Next year we'll probably see "Gabba" t-shirts in Topshop. If you look back, the early Raf Simons collections were always about music. There was the techno couture collection (2011), another one inspired by new wave, the Kraftwerk aesthetic (1998), and the 1999 to 2000 catwalk collection featured a hardcore soundtrack.[2]

CM You mentioned that Gabber Eleganza is slightly ironic. Have you had any reactions from other hardcore purists to the "gabber fashion" trend that you're a part of?

AG If you look at my blog archive, you will see that I always credit the photographers or artists. 95% of gabberheads in Italy gave me good feedback before I started the "Hakke" show. There are some who criticize my choice to take my work past the blog, as a DJ, because they want to protect the hardcore scene. Many articles were written in Italy after my Club To Club show last year. There are some hardcore heads that think that my project is a commercial push to make gabber become mainstream.

CM What is your response to people who feel that way?

AG Many people have a prejudice against gabber, and that's just part of the game. Through my blog I hope to re-evaluate gabber and extreme post-rave scenes and to bring them into the general public's eye. I get many kids writing to me saying that they've discovered gabber through me. Others write to me saying, "thank you for pushing gabber," with a respectful touch.

CM: Wann und wo, denkst du, kollidierte die Gabber-Kultur mit der Modeindustrie? AG: Mich hat High-Fashion nie wirklich interessiert, aber ich mochte Mode und ich interessiere mich für Trends. Während den vergangenen zwei bis drei Jahren waren Sportmarken ein grosses Thema, ersichtlich etwa in der Ästhetik von Gosha Rubchinskiys Entwürfen. Nächstes Jahr werden wir wahrscheinlich «Gabba»-T-Shirts im Topshop kaufen können. Schaut man ein bisschen zurück, erkennt man, dass Raf Simons' frühe Kollokationen immer von Musik handelten. Es gab Techno-Couture (2011), eine Kollektion war von New Wave inspiriert, es gab die Kraftwerk-Ästhetik (1998) und von 1999 bis 2000 wurde der Catwalk von Hardcore dominiert.[2]

CM: Du sagst, Gabber Eleganza ist ein bisschen ironisch gemeint. Gab es darauf Reaktionen von Hardcore-Puristinnen? Schlussendlich bist du ein sogenannter «Mode-Gabber»... AG: Schaut man sich meinen Blog an, sieht man, dass alle Fotografinnen und Künstler in den Credits erwähnt werden. Als ich Leuten aus der italienischen Gabber-Szene von meiner «Hakke»-Show erzählte, waren die Rückmeldungen zu 95 Prozent positiv. Manche kritisieren mich, weil ich mich vom Blogger hin zum DJ entwickelt habe – sie wollen die Hardcore-Szene beschützen. Nach meinem Auftritt im Rahmen von Club To Club im letzten Jahr gab es viele Artikel in Italien. Es gibt einige Hardcore-Heads, die denken, dass mein Projekt Gabber kommerzialisiert und in den Mainstream drängt.

CM: Wie antwortest du jenen Leuten? AG: Viele Leute haben gegenüber Gabber Vorurteile, aber das gehört einfach dazu. Meine Mission mit dem Blog ist es, die Gabber- und Extreme-Post-Rave-Szene zu reevaluieren und als einen Teil des generellen Interesses zu etablieren. Es gibt viele Kids, die mir schreiben und die mir sagen, sie hätten Gabber durch mich entdeckt. Andere schreiben Sachen wie: «Danke, dass du Gabber pushst», mit einem respektvollen Unterton.

CM: Du sammelst Gabber Memorabilien und hast ein eigenes Fanzine gemacht: Gabber In The Name Of Love (Automatic Books, 2009). AG: Ja, das machte ich zusammen mit Marco Fusoloni von Studio Temp—ein guter Freund von mir. Wir entschieden uns dazu, ein Gabber-Fanzine zu machen. Wir machten während Raves Bilder und kreierten eigene Collagen. Wir veröffentlichten 100 Stück über Automatic Books, ein Verlag aus Venedig; zudem machten wir eine Veranstaltung während der Biennale. Die Fanzines waren innert Kürze ausverkauft und die Veranstaltung hat Spass gemacht! Das war mein erstes Projekt, das von Gabber handelte, und das veranlasste mich dazu, den Blog zu lancieren.

CM: Gab es in den Neunzigern einen heiligen Gral unter den Gabber-Fanzines? AG: Thunder. Das wurde von ID&T gemacht, den holländischen Veranstaltern hinter Thunderdome. Sie veröffentlichten 35 Ausgaben verteilt auf ein paar Jahre – und ich kaufte mir alle für ein paar Euro. Dann gab es noch Strobe, ein Hochglanzmagazin. Das bestand aus einem Mix aus Techno und Hardcore.

CM: Wo findest du solche Sachen in der Regel? AG: Normalerweise im Internet. Ich bin ein Nerd.

CM: Was ist die ultimative Destination für Hardcore-Rave? AG: Nochmals: Thunderdome war bei weitem das grösste. ID&T waren Marketinggenies, deshalb konnten sie die bedeutendste Hardcore-Marke der Welt etablieren. In den Neunzigern war ich nie da, aber im letzten Jahr gab es eine Ausgabe, die 40 000 Leute anzog. Ich war bei jener davor dabei – das war im Jahr 2012.

HARDCORE
HAPPINESS

CM You collect gabber memorabilia and have also create a zine of your own: *Gabber In The Name Of Love* (Automatic Books, 2009).

AG Yes, I created it with Marco Fusoloni at Studio Temp, who is one of my best friends. We decided to make a fanzine together about gabber. We started taking pictures at raves and creating our own artwork collages. We printed 100 editions with Automatic Books, a publisher from Venice, and did an event during the Venice Biennale. They sold out really fast and it was nice! That was my first project with gabber, and it's what gave me the energy to start the blog.

CM Was there a holy grail of gabber fanzines in the 90s?

AG *Thunder*. It was produced by ID&T, the Dutch promoters behind *Thunderdome*. They produced thirty-five issues over a couple of years, and I bought all of them for about two euro each. There was another one called *Strobe*, which was a glossy magazine. It was a mix of techno and hardcore.

CM Where do you generally look to find these things today?

AG Usually on the internet. I'm a nerd.

CM How about the ultimate hardcore rave destination?

AG Again, *Thunderdome* was the biggest by far. ID&T were huge marketing heads, so they created the most important hardcore brand in the world. I never visited in the 90s, but they did one last year which attracted 40 000 people. I went to the one before that, in 2012. It was all about nostalgia. *Digital* and *Razorblade* were some other big ones. In Holland, the gabber revival is about pop culture. It's one of the biggest sub-cultures they have. Holland is like the Jamaica of Europe—all their music is top quality. They are the kings of trance, their EDM artists are the best at EDM. Maybe not as much techno, but the weirder stuff there like Clone, Rush Hour, Dekmantel are all fucking huge… Dutch power.

CM There's another collective from Paris, Casual Gabbers.[3] Do you have a relationship with them?

AG Yes, we are friends. I met Paul Ozoni, one of the guys, in 2013. He wrote to me on Tumblr to say he liked my blog, and he wanted to put on an event together in Paris. Two weeks later he took a bus from Paris and came to stay at my house. I've since visited and played a couple of times with them in Paris.

CM "Suburban Euphoria" is a keyword on your website. Can you explain that idea or how it relates to the context of your home in Bergamo, Lombardy?

AG I come from a tiny town named Calco. It's a flat place with highways and cows—a mix of working class areas, countryside farms, and deep depression. It's a boring place to live but at the same time it's a comfort zone because nothing happens… It's the perfect place to die on drugs.
Bergamo is a big countryside city, and a wealthy place. "Suburban Euphoria" is about escapism. When I started the blog with the "digital folk" aesthetic it became about more than just gabber. It's a similar feeling to the suburbs of England or Scotland. People listen to different music, but it's the same attitude or style, it's a kind of romanticism.

CM When was the moment you realized that this project was something you could do for a living?

AG When I started receiving ten e-mails every day about some form of collaboration, a gig, or someone's merchandise order that had not arrived on time. After last summer, I decided this was my work, and I wanted to evolve it because I love it and enjoy it.

CM What work or career did you have previously?

AG My father is a baker, so I worked in his bakery for several years. Listening to hardcore on my headphones, selling bread to old ladies. [Laughs] I was also a dog-sitter for two years. Meanwhile I started promoting nights and DJing in Bergamo. I opened an independent store and an event agency with my wife. We sold clothes and vinyl, and ran music and cultural events such as artisanal fairs in Bergamo. It was open for seven years and closed three years ago.

CM You've been touring your "Hakke" show this year. Where did you recruit all the dancers in your crew?

AG They are all ex-gabberheads. The first three shows were with close friends, and I asked a young gabber couple—aged 18 and 19—to join-in to bring some new energy. My friend Mino is the one who waves the giant flag. He's a traditional tattoo artist by trade. Originally an outsider to gabber, he's become a hardcore head through the project. He's a great motivator and the bridge between the dancers and the crowd.

CM What does it mean to you being a gabberhead?

AG The meaning of gabber is "friend," like your partner in crime.[4] The raver has changed, but I think the electronic music scene needs something like gabber, not for the sound, but for the energy of the music. It's like dirty punk, it keeps the energy alive through the spirit of rave… And rave is revolution.

References

1 http://www.madeintemp.com/2013/gabber-in-the-name-of-love/

2 Simons' Spring/Summer 2000 "Summa Cum Laude" collection, features a famous oversized MA-1 bomber jacket, with the pyramid logo of the Rotterdam Terror Corps on the back.

Simons' Spring/Summer 2000 "Summa Cum Laude" Kollektion beinhaltete eine legendäre oversized MA-1 Bomberjacke, mit dem Pyramiden-Logo des Rotterdam Terror Corps auf dem Rücken.

3 See the Interview with Casual Gabbers in zweikommasieben #16

Siehe das Interview mit Casual Gabbers in zweikommasieben #16

4 Gabber derives from the Yiddish term "khaver," which means friend.

Gabber kommt vom jiddischen Ausdruck «khaver», der soviel wie «Freund heisst».

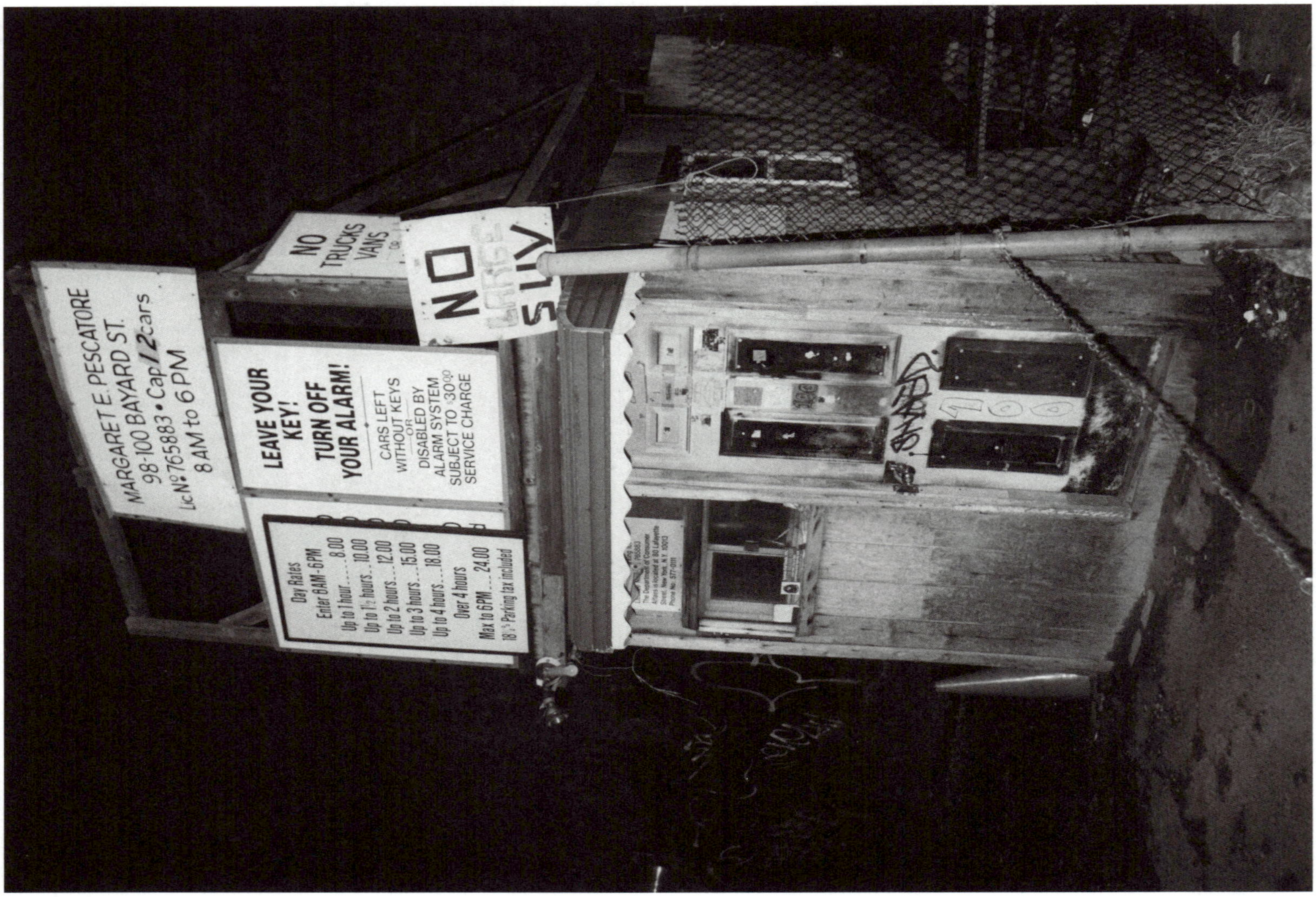
MARGARET E. PESCATORE
98-100 BAYARD ST.
Lic No 765883 • Cap 12 cars
8 AM to 6 PM
NO TRUCKS VANS
NO LARGE SUV
LEAVE YOUR KEY!
TURN OFF YOUR ALARM!
CARS LEFT WITHOUT KEYS OR DISABLED BY ALARM SYSTEM SUBJECT TO $30.00 SERVICE CHARGE
Day Rates
Enter 8AM - 6PM
Up to 1 hour......8.00
Up to 1½ hours......10.00
Up to 2 hours......12.00
Up to 3 hours......15.00
Up to 4 hours......18.00
Over 4 hours
Max to 6PM......24.00
18⅜% Parking tax included

RAW

ENDLESS NOW

Photography:
Georg Gatsas
Featuring:
DJ Lag
Tebogo Ribane [Dear Ribane]
Jamal Nxedlana [Bubblegum Club]

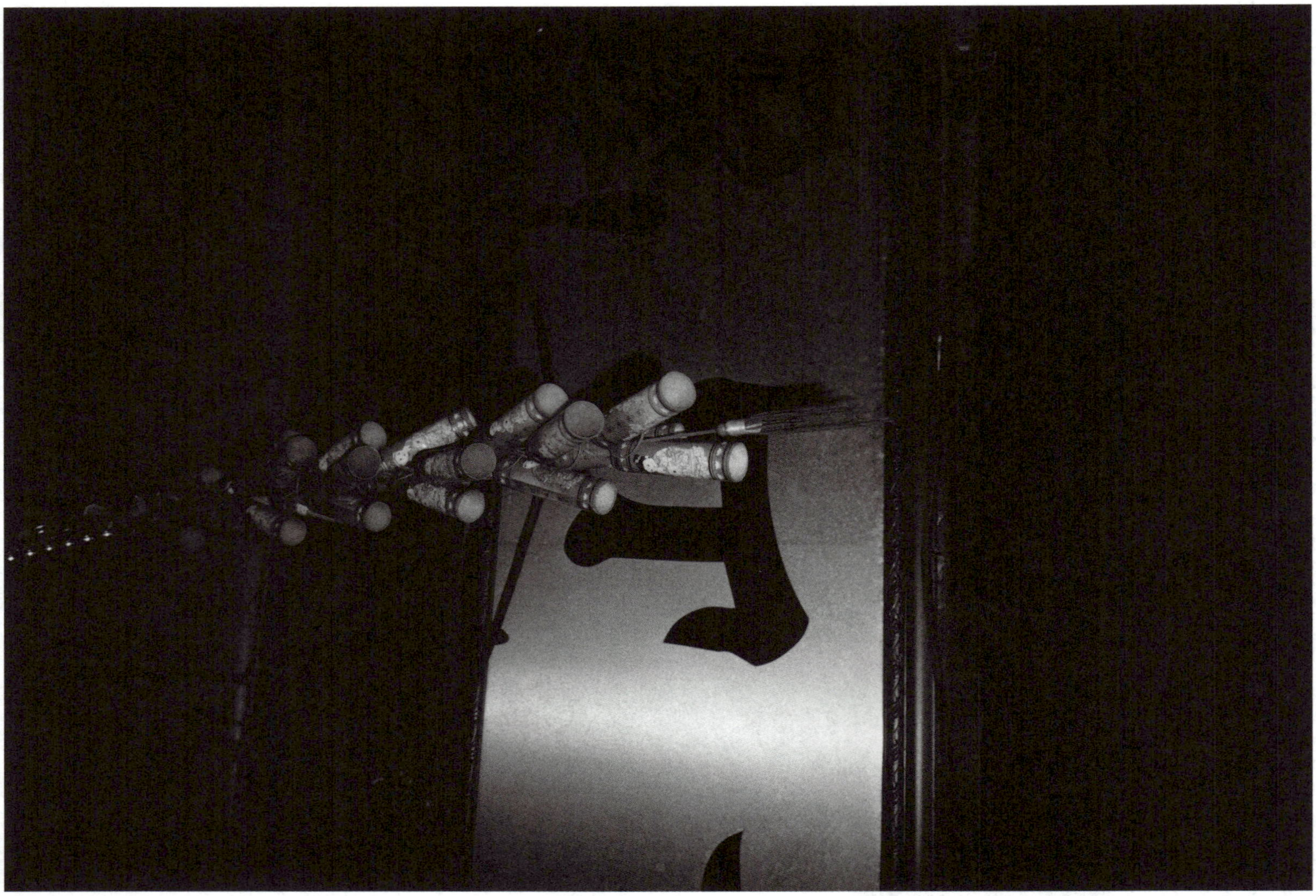

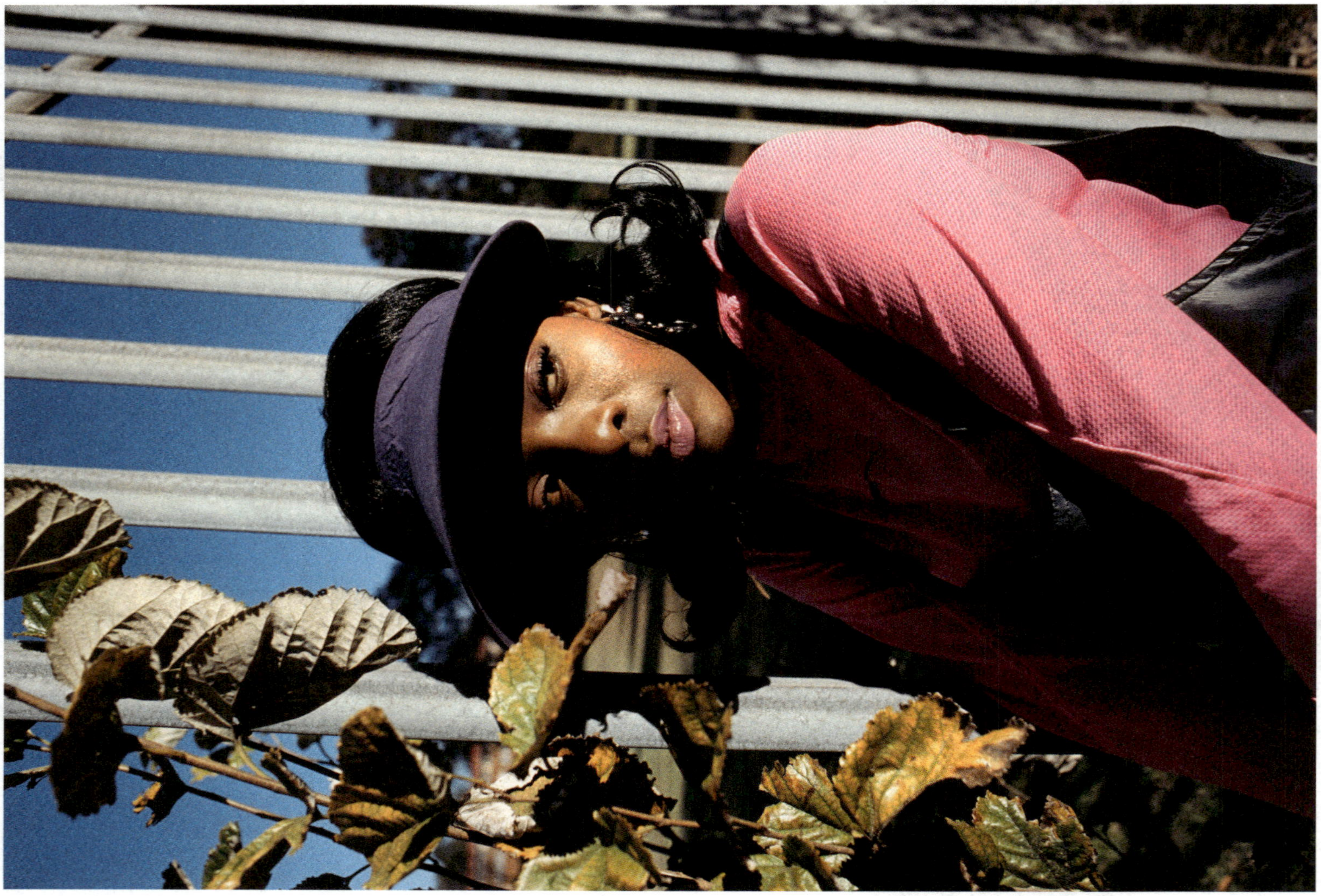

Column   We Are Time

CARRYING FORWARD
ALESSANDRO CORTINI

Interview & photography:
Alexandra Baumgartner

Alessandro Cortini stimmt die letzten Töne an: «Finire»—beenden, heisst das Stück. Es ist das Ende einer aufwühlenden Reise durch fremde und eigene Erinnerungen. Schliesst man die Augen, flimmern die Bilder noch eine Weile nach. Fliessende Aufnahmen, weiche Farben, grinsende Kindergesichter, eine verschneite Einfahrt, Schnitt ins blühende Rosenbeet. Ein paar Stunden Videomaterial aus dem Familienarchiv stellten die Ausgangslage für Avanti, das aktuelle Album Cortinis. Während der Tour- und Studiomusiker von Nine Inch Nails (NIN) für dieses Album seinen analogen Gerätschaften treu bleibt, kommt der Sound Avantis erst in der Live-Performance zu seiner Vollständigkeit. Dann nämlich bringt er die Archivaufnahmen und seine Stücke zusammen.

Seitdem Avanti 2016 erstmals am Atonal Festival in Berlin aufgeführt wurde, ist Cortini damit auf vielen verschiedenen Bühnen aufgetreten—unter anderem auch im Südpol Luzern, wo Alexandra Baumgartner den mittlerweile in Berlin lebenden Musiker zum Gespräch getroffen hat.

Alessandro Cortini plays the last notes of a piece called "Finire," i.e., "to finish." It's the close of a stirring journey through foreign and private memories. If you close your eyes, the images continue shimmering in the mind—flowing shots, soft colors, children's faces smiling, a snowy driveway, a blooming bed of roses. A few hours of video footage from the family archive were the starting point for *Avanti*, Cortini's latest album. A tour and studio musician for Nine Inch Nails (NIN), Cortini remains faithful to his analogue equipment for the album, but *Avanti* comes to fruition in the live performance—it's then that he brings the video archive and his music together.

Since performing *Avanti* for the first time at the *Atonal* Festival in Berlin in 2016, Cortini has brought it to many other venues, including Lucerne's Südpol. It was here that Alexandra Baumgartner met to speak with the musician, who now lives in Berlin.

Alexandra Baumgartner: Du hast jetzt *Avanti* doch schon einige Male live vorgetragen. Was für ein Gefühl wecken die Videoaufnahmen in dir? Ich nehme an, dass du dich nicht an alle Szenen erinnern kannst, zumal du in einigen Aufnahmen als Kleinkind zu sehen bist, während dem andere gedreht wurden, als du noch nicht geboren warst.

Alessandro Cortini: Ich kann mich an keine der Szenen erinnern. Woran ich mich allerdings gut erinnere, ist die Umgebung. Die Videos wurden mehrheitlich von meinem Grossvater auf Ausflügen oder während Ferien gedreht, teilweise war da auch meine Mutter noch ein Kind. Viele der Szenen sind bei meinen Grosseltern in Argenta in Italien gedreht worden, wo ich aufgewachsen bin. Das Videomaterial repräsentiert meine Familie, zeigt Orte an denen ich viele Jahre verbracht habe. Es ist immer noch sehr... Es verändert sich. Als ich anfing, *Avanti* aufzuführen, stellte ich die Leinwand hinter meinem Rücken auf. Der Fokus lag für mich so automatisch stärker auf der Musik. Mit der Zeit begann ich jedoch die Leinwand anders aufzustellen—seitwärts, wie heute Abend zum Beispiel. Ich merkte, dass ich auf diese Weise musikalisch stärker auf das Filmmaterial eingehen kann. Dabei realisierte ich auch, dass ich jeden einzelnen Abend meine Familie und Ereignisse aus meiner Kindheit zu sehen bekomme. Emotional macht das einiges mit dir. Letztlich gehören diese Erinnerungen jedoch der Vergangenheit an. Das Einzige was du tun kannst, ist diese Erinnerungen als das anzusehen, was sie sind, nämlich schöne Erinnerungen. Und dennoch erfüllen sie einen Zweck, bringen etwas voran.

AB: Das ist ein interessanter Punkt: Wer schaut sich jeden Tag Familienfotos an? Kaum jemand setzt sich auf diese Weise seiner Erinnerung aus, wie du es bei deinen Liveshows tust. Es geht ja nicht bloss um vergilbte Bilder einer vergangenen Kindheit, sondern um die Konfrontation mit dem eigenen Familiennarrativ, das man womöglich nie hinterfragt hat. Was hat das für Auswirkungen auf dich und den Sound den du spielst? AC: Es gibt Szenen wo man meine Mutter sieht, wie sie als Kind Weihnachtsgeschenke auspackt... Sie wurde später in ihrem Leben krank und es stimmt mich immer wieder nachdenklich, wenn ich dieses glückliche Kind sehe und dann daran denke, was Jahre danach passierte. Alles in allem kommt es sehr darauf an, worauf ich mich konzentriere—ob ich mich von den schönen oder von den traurigen Erinnerungen festhalten lasse. Ich werde oft gefragt, ob es nicht seltsam sei, diese privaten Aufnahmen mit fremden Leuten zu teilen. Aber ich erlebe oft, dass die Leute nicht wirklich mich oder meine Familie sehen, sondern ihre eigenen Erinnerungen und Wahrnehmungen in die Bilder hineinprojizieren. Diejenigen, die wie ich in den 1970er oder 80er Jahren aufgewachsen sind, teilen wohl ähnliche Erinnerungen. Oftmals sind es dann auch die Leute, die nach den Auftritten mit Tränen in den Augen zu mir kommen. Aber es ist eine gute Art zu weinen! Es ist befreiend, nicht schlecht—zumindest hoffe ich das.

AB: Neben Video und Musik besteht *Avanti* aus einem dritten Element: Field-Recordings. Die Audioaufnahmen beinhalten italienische Dialoge. Man hört im Hintergrund Gelächter, das Klirren von Geschirr, Kindergeschrei—ein Einblick in ein Familienfest im Garten? AC: Die Stimmen hat ebenfalls mein Grossvater auf zwei C90 Kassetten an zwei Anlässen aufgenommen: Einmal an Ferragosto und das andere Mal an Ostern. Mein Grossvater legte jeweils seinen Walkman auf den Tisch, liess das Tape laufen und fing die Atmosphäre ein. Naja, du kannst dir vorstellen, was dabei herausgekommen ist; eine italienische Familie, ein- bis eineinhalb Stunden Geplauder und

Gespräche, auch während des Essens. Und sie sprechen über alles Mögliche; die Kopfschmerzen meiner Mutter, man hört wie sich meine Grosseltern zanken und wie jemand das Telefon im Haus beantwortet. Es ist ein bisschen was von allem dabei.

AB: Du benutzt diese Audioaufnahmen nur in ganz bestimmten Momenten und scheinst sehr darauf zu achten, dass es zu keiner Vermischung oder Überlagerung zwischen den eigentlichen Stücken von *Avanti* und den Dialogen kommt. Wie begründest du deine Entscheidung, in diesem Fall so strikt vorzugehen? AC: *Avanti* wurde als Performance entwickelt und weil die Performance auf dem Grundsatz eines Kassettenrecorders entstanden ist, habe ich begonnen den Dialog als Trennung zwischen den Stücken zu verwenden. Dadurch weiss ich genau, wann ich das eine Stück beenden muss, um mit dem nächsten zu beginnen. Auf der Rückseite der Kassette sind Aufnahmen von einer Probe der Live-Performance von *Avanti*. Bis anhin habe ich diese Aufnahme nie gebraucht, aber sie liegt bereit, wenn ich auf der Bühne irgendwelche technischen Schwierigkeiten habe. Falls mit den Kassetten also irgendetwas schiefgeht, bringe ich mein Backup-Tape ins Spiel. Die Idee hinter dem Ganzen ist, dass ich mir so Zeit verschaffen kann, um das Problem zu beheben. Weisst du, die Kassetten sind ziemlich anfällig und wenn man viel unterwegs ist, muss man einfach damit rechnen, dass sie beschädigt werden und nicht mehr richtig laufen. Dann kannst du nicht mehr auf Play drücken, aber die Visuals laufen immer noch und am Ende stehst du einfach blöd da. Was mich total verrückt macht, ist die Vorstellung, dass Leute zu meinen Konzerten kommen, sich Karten kaufen und ich auf der Bühne mit technischen Problemen zu kämpfen habe. Dann stehe ich dort, versuche alles wiederherzurichten, entschuldige mich und verschwende eine halbe Stunde. Das ist pure Verantwortungslosigkeit! Diese Haltung lässt sich natürlich aus den vielen Jahren ablesen, die ich mit NIN verbracht habe und der Paranoia die er stets hatten. Dinge gehen einfach schief. Das tun sie nun Mal [klopft aufs Holz]—das ist der Grund, weshalb ich bei meinen live Performances versuche Redundanzen zu schaffen.

AB: Das Filmmaterial, das du für die Live-Performance von *Avanti* verwendest, besteht aus konvertierten Super-8-Filmen. Der Transfer in die verschiedenen Formate, sowie die Eigenheiten des ursprünglichen Formats, haben auf dem Filmmaterial ihre Spuren hinterlassen. Man sieht kleine Hicks, Bildrauschen, Farbfehler oder Staubflecken. Was du hiermit visuell greifbar machst, ist ein Thema wofür du dich schon seit längerem interessierst: Die Widerspenstigkeit und Unzulänglichkeit von Geräten. AC: Ich glaube, dass sich hier der Einfluss von William Basinski deutlich ablesen lässt. Seine Arbeit war meine erste bewusste Erfahrung oder Auseinandersetzung mit der Verwendung technischen Zerfalls auf eine kreative Art und Weise. Was mich etwa bei *Disintegration Loops* besonders faszinierte, war, wie er die Mängel einer Technologie als Ausdrucksform nutzt. Das halte ich für eine ziemlich originäre Arbeitsweise. Was mich betrifft, so bin ich für *Avanti* anders vorgegangen. Meine Arbeitsweise unterscheidet sich insofern, dass für einen wie mich, der mit dem Walkman aufgewachsen ist, klar war, dass dieses konstante fffffffss-Geräusch, das man von Kassetten kennt, Teil der Aufnahme ist und aus diesem Grund mit auf das Album muss. Ich finde, dass die Unvollkommenheit oder Mängel von Geräten im Allgemeinen einen grossen Teil zum persönlichen Charakter der Musik beisteuern. Heutzutage geht es oftmals darum, Perfektion zu erreichen. Sogar in der neuen Analog-Renaissance, die wir gerade miterleben, verfolgt man eher den Ansatz, Ungenauigkeiten zu unterbinden. Die

Alexandra Baumgartner: You've performed *Avanti* live several times now. What kinds of feelings does the footage evoke in you? I'd imagine you don't remember everything—in some parts you were a small child, and in others you weren't in the picture at all because the footage is much older.

Alessandro Cortini: I don't remember any of the scenes, although I remember the environment very well. The footage was mostly filmed by my grandfather during outings or vacations. A lot of it is shot at my grandparent's place in Argenta, where I grew up. The footage represents my family and so it's still very... you know, it changes. I have to say that I started playing the *Avanti* show with the visuals behind me, so it was more about the music. And then slowly I started setting up the screen to the side, like I did tonight, so I can react more directly to the visuals. And I realized that I get to see my family and events of my young life every night, and it can get emotional. At the end of the day tough, all that has passed, and the only thing you can do is look forward and take them for what they are, which is beautiful memories. The only thing they have left to do is keep on going forward, which is also the reason for the name of the record.

AB: That's an interesting point—who actually looks at family photos every day? Very few people face their own memories in the way you do in your live shows each evening. It's not just about yellowed photos of a past childhood, but rather about a confrontation with a family narrative—what the family is or used to be. What does this do to you and to the sound experienced live?

AC There are some scenes where you see my mother as a child opening Christmas presents—you know, my mother got sick later on in her life, and it makes you think about seeing this child being happy, and then about what happened later. How I feel really depends on the night. Sometimes I'm just concentrated on my mom being happy and then I'm happy—other times I think about what happened after. I get asked a lot if I feel weird about the fact that everybody gets to see my personal life, but from what I've heard and from what I see, I don't think people really see me or my family that much. I feel like there's a common ground somewhere, especially with people who have similar memories to mine, or who grew up in the 70s or 80s. Usually those people are the ones that cry during the show, too. They come to see me after the show, and they're all crying. It's good crying, though—it's liberating, it's not evil. Or at least I hope it isn't!

AB The third core component of *Avanti* consists of audio recordings of dialogues in Italian—laughter, clattering dishes, children yelling—a glimpse of a family gathering in the garden?

AC The voices come from two C90 cassette tapes that my grandpa recorded on two occasions. One was Ferragosto, which is August 15th, and the other one was Easter. My grandpa used to put his Walkman on the table. And you can imagine an Italian family—it would be an hour and a half of a lot of chatting, a lot of talking, even though we were eating. They talk about everything! They talk about my mom's headaches; you can hear my grandpa and my grandma bickering; somebody calls the house and you can hear my grandpa answering the phone... it's a little bit of everything.

AB You use the dialogue at very specific moments. They never interfere with the main pieces of *Avanti* and you don't seem to allow them to overlap. Why this strict approach?

AC Since *Avanti* was born as a performance, and since it's a cassette-based piece, I originally used the dialogue to get an idea when I had to fade one piece out and start the second one—it's a reference to change the cassette, since I use a four-track recorder for the live show. The second side, which I never really had to use, is the live recording from a rehearsal of *Avanti*, so if anything goes wrong technology-wise I can bring that in, troubleshoot, and figure out what's wrong with the cassettes. When you travel, sometimes the cassettes get

alten analogen Geräte sind aber nun mal so perfekt wie sie 1979 oder 1980 sein konnten. Sie mit unseren heutigen Standards zu messen ist Schwachsinn. Ich denke die Schönheit elektronischer Musik und ihrer Präzision, bedeutet nicht zwangsläufig, dass sich diese Musik nicht menschlich anfühlen oder eine Seele haben darf.

AB: Gibt es andere Bereiche, in denen du momentan die Idee der Unvollkommenheit weiter erforschst? AC: Im Moment tendiere ich dazu, Unvollkommenheit mit der ersten Idee gleichzusetzen. Ich bin auf der Suche nach einer echten, unveränderten und rohen Form von Kreativität und versuche stets die ersten Ideen festzuhalten. Ich glaube jedoch, dass ich an einem Punkt angelangt bin, an dem ich, bevor ich den Aufnahmeknopf drücke, die Geräte schon so eingestellt habe, dass es nicht mehr ganz die echte erste Idee ist... Ich habe ein gewisses Vertrauen in meine Arbeit entwickelt, sodass ich weiss, dass wann immer ich aufnehme, bereits ein bestimmter Schwellenwert erreicht ist. Es ist so, wie wenn man sich als Kind zu Weihnachten ein bestimmtes Spielzeug wünscht, es bekommt und auspackt und damit spielt—doch wie lange? Vielleicht zwei, drei Stunden... Und dann ist die Aufregung dahin! Es gibt dieses sehr enge Zeitfenster; das ist der Moment des Auspackens, den ich auszuspielen und festzuhalten versuche. Wenn man es schafft, diesen Moment aufzunehmen und er zum Kernstück einer Komposition wird, so hat man eine ziemlich pure, unberührte Idee, mit der man weiterarbeiten kann. Ich denke, Musik tendiert dazu, ihre Magie immer mehr zu verlieren, je länger man daran arbeitet. Das ist eine sehr persönliche Ansicht. Ich kenne eine Menge Leute deren Meisterwerke auf der Grundlage von unendlich vielen Verfeinerungs- und Überarbeitungsschritten beruht. Und das ist total in Ordnung, denn für sie ist es eine wunderbare Herausforderung. Aber so funktioniere ich einfach nicht.

AB: Deine Alben *Sono* und *Risveglio* sind aus Schlafliedern entstanden, die du dir um besser einschlafen zu können, auf Tour selber vorgespielt hast. Was mich daran beeindruckt, ist, dass diese Stücke, bevor es irgendeinen anderen Plan gab, aus einem sehr persönlichen und konkreten Bedürfnis für Musik entstanden sind. War es ähnlich für *Avanti*? AC: Ja, es ist immer gleich. Für diese Werke ist meine Herangehensweise ganz anders als beim Songwriting. Alles begann mit *Force*. Es ging einfach darum, sich beim Musikmachen gut zu fühlen—im Gegensatz zur Studio-Umgebung, die dir konstant das Gefühl vermittelt, dass du ein neues Album machen musst. Es gab keine Idee zu einem neuen Album. Ich hatte genügend Material für drei Doppelalben aufgenommen, aber hatte nicht die Absicht, es zu veröffentlichen. Das gleiche gilt für *Sonno*. Ich nahm das auf-wobei aufgenommen schon fast zuviel gesagt ist, weil ich bloss meinen Synthesizer im Hotelzimmer aufgestellt habe—und ich hatte genau denselben Recorder [zeigt auf das Aufnahmegerät auf den Tisch]. Ich ging damit im Zimmer hin und her und nahm Sequenzen vom Synthesizer aus verschiedenen Winkeln auf. Es war aufregend! Ich ging ins Badezimmer, drehte den Hahn auf und war so: «Oh shit, wenn ich das von hier aus aufnehme, dann höre ich den Wasserstrahl, aber im Hintergrund höre ich immer noch die Sequenz aus dem anderen Zimmer!» Es machte einfach Spass. Ich war wie ein Kind, glücklich mit seinen Spielzeugen. Ich hatte keine Ahnung, dass *Sonno* ein Album sein könnte, bis Dominick Fernow von Hospital Productions zu mir kam und sagte, dass er es rausbringen wolle. «Was rausbringen?», fragte ich, «das ist Zeug wozu ich einschlafe.» Es dauerte eine Weile, bis ich begriff, dass wenn ich Musik für einen bestimmten therapeutischen Zweck mache—für *Sonno* war es, um einzuschlafen und für *Avanti* ist es, um mich an meine Familie zu erinnern und melancholisch zu sein–und es für mich funktioniert, es höchstwahrscheinlich auch für andere Leute funktionieren würde.

AB: Siehst du das Ganze auch als Antwort auf die NIN-Welt in der du eine viel kommerziellere Art und Weise des Musikmachens erfahren hast? AC: Ich glaube, es war eher eine allgemeine Reaktion auf die Welt des traditionellen Songwritings. Als ich in die USA kam, wollte ich dort mit meiner Band durchstarten. Ich wollte von meiner Musik und den Songs, die ich schreibe, leben. Und es machte Spass! Irgendwann gelangte ich aber an einen Punkt, an dem ich begriff, dass mich das System in dem ich steckte, extrem einengte. Jede Nacht für eine Band im Vorprogramm aufzutreten, dasselbe auf die gleiche Art und Weise zu spielen, zerstörte für mich die Magie, die aufkommt, wenn man im Studio an den Songs arbeitet. Das war zu der Zeit, als ich begann, Musik für *Force* zu machen. Es fühlte sich einfach total anders an. Ich hörte auf mich und spielte simple Sequenzen ein. Dann liess ich die Musik laufen, legte mich hin und fühlte mich einfach gut dabei. Ich war immer davon ausgegangen, dass die Arbeit darin bestehe, die Songs wieder und wieder zu bearbeiten; zurück ins Studio zu gehen, um hier oder da noch etwas zu verändern, Teile erneut aufzunehmen—es korrekt zu machen, im Takt und mit einem Metronom... Ich hatte verrückte Vorstellungen! Aber wofür? Damit alles genau aufeinander abgestimmt ist und mit dem Grid der Software übereinstimmt? Warum? Weil ich dann zu einem späteren Zeitpunkt noch etwas hinzufügen kann? Aber vielleicht will ich überhaupt nichts hinzufügen! Es brauchte Zeit, bis ich begriff, dass es unterschiedliche Arten gibt, Musik zu machen. Für meine Musik gibt es keine Regeln. Wenn ich bei jedem neuen Album sage, ich hätte keine Ahnung, was es eigentlich sei, bis es irgendwann steht, dann stimmt das wirklich! Je glücklicher ich damit bin, desto glücklicher sind die Leute in der Regel mit der Veröffentlichung. Und ich will nicht, dass sich das jetzt super spirituell anhört, weil ich eigentlich überhaupt nicht der Typ dazu bin, aber ich glaube, dass in der Musik immer ein emotionaler Gehalt steckt. Wenn ein Künstler diesen emotionalen Gehalt in seine Arbeit hineingibt, werden andere Leute darauf eingehen können. Aber es ist nicht wirklich greifbar. Es ist nichts, das man studieren könnte, wenn man sich für ein paar Stunden hinsetzt.

AB: Hört sich so an, als hättest du einen Weg zur Erleuchtung gefunden! AC: Ich weiss nicht, das sind grosse Worte. Aber ja, in musikalischer Hinsicht schon. Ich muss gestehen, dass ich speziell in letzter Zeit ein wenig damit überfordert bin, dass mittlerweile einfach überall Synthesizer sind. Ich habe aufgehört, mich mit einem Synthesizer so kreativ zu fühlen, wie ich es früher tat und bin zurück zur Gitarre. Ich spiele immer noch Gitarre für NIN, aber ich betrachte die Gitarre schon lange nicht mehr als mein Hauptinstrument. Ganz im Gegensatz zu früher, als ich in die USA ging, um Gitarre zu studieren. Wenn ich jetzt Gitarre spiele, fühlt es sich allerdings nicht so an, als wäre ich in der Zeit zurückgegangen. Mein Spiel hat sich in eine ganz andere Richtung entwickelt und es fühlt sich gut an neue Herangehensweise auszuprobieren. Es geht mir viel mehr darum, eine Balance zwischen dem Gitarristen und dem elektronischen Musiker in mir zu finden. Sodass ich das, was ich von den verschiedenen Instrumenten gelernt habe, auf eine Weise zusammenbringe, bei der sich das Publikum nicht darum schert, ob es eine Gitarre, ein Buchla oder was auch immer ist.

AB: Fühlt es sich für dich an, als hättest du die Gitarre neu entdeckt? AC: Definitiv. Als Teenager bin ich total auf

condensed and they don't turn anymore, and you're not able to press play but the visuals are still going. The thing that freaks me out the most is the idea of people coming to pay and see me play a show, and me having technical issues and having to apologize and wasting half an hour for lack of responsibility when it comes to doing my job. And I think that also comes from years and years with NIN and having paranoia about things failing, because it always happens—knock on wood—so I always try to have redundancy.

AB Through the converted Super 8 footage, which in its visual quality features artifacts, unsharpness, and picture noise, you render visible what has always interested you: the recalcitrance and imperfection of devices.

AC It all comes—and I have to give credit where credit is due—from William Basinski's work. I mean, that was my first conscious experience with the use of degradation in a creative way. His work overall, but particularly the *Disintegration Loops*, is incredibly emotive. And he particularly uses the shortcomings of a technology as a form of expression, which I think is a very unique thing to do. As far as I am concerned, for *Avanti* it's a little different: having grown up with Walkmans, the idea is that the hiss of the cassette—this sort of *fffffss* noise, that's always there—is also part of the recording. That's why there's so much of it in *Avanti*. And I feel like the imperfection of machines in general add a lot of personality to the music. There's so much attention to perfection nowadays, even in the new analogue renaissance, that we miss the variables that come from things that don't work perfectly. They are as perfect as they could be in 1979 or 1980, but definitely not perfect by today's standards. I think the beauty of electronic music and the precision of it doesn't necessarily mean that you can't be human about it or it can't have a soul.

AB Are you exploring the notion of imperfection in other ways at the moment?

AC Right now I tend to equate imperfection with the first idea, because it's just pure, unaltered, raw creativity. I try to keep the first ideas, whether I'm playing the guitar or a synthesizer. Because no matter what, before I press record I've already tweaked the machine to a point where it's not really the first idea—I mean yes, it is the first idea but I've reached a point where my level of satisfaction with what comes out of the guitar or the synthesizer has already a threshold. But I'm like a child: if I get bored with it, then most likely I won't be recording it. There's a very narrow window. For example when you're a kid and you ask your parents for that toy at Christmas, and then you get it on Christmas day and you play with it for two or three hours, and then the excitement of opening the package is just gone. So I'm trying to surf that "opening the package" phase—and to keep it. Because if you record that and it becomes the main core of the composition, and then you have a very pure idea to build on. I think music tends to lose the magic the more you work on it—this is a personal thing. I know plenty of people whose masterpieces or works are based on refinements and over-refinements and more over-refinements, and they're fine with it. They see it as a beautiful challenge. I don't work that way.

AB It's striking to me that the albums *Sonno* and *Risveglio* grew out of lullabies you played to yourself on tour. So there's this very personal need for music before anything else appears on the surface. Was it the same for *Avanti*?

AC Yes, it's always the same. This kind of work is very different than the songwriting work for me. It all started with *Force*. It was more about feeling good making the music than about being in the studio environment that constantly tells you that you need to make a record. There was no idea for a record. I recorded enough for three double albums but didn't intend to release it. It was the same with *Sono*. *Sono* was recorded, you know... I don't even want to say "recorded," because I was

super schnelles Spielen und *Shredden* abgefahren. Meine Vorbilder waren Steve Vile und Jo Satriani. Ich finde immer noch grossen Gefallen daran, auf diese Weise zu spielen, aber es ist definitiv nicht etwas, das ich als Teil meiner künstlerischen Arbeit ansehe. Aber ich mag den Gedanken, dass ich jetzt als 41-Jähriger fähig bin, Dinge auf der Gitarre zu spielen, die ich nicht spielen konnte, als ich vierzehn war. Aber ich würde nie während eines Konzerts am *Atonal* beginnen, super schnell zu *shredden*. Was mir in letzter Zeit allerdings viel Spass bereitet, ist einige meiner Sequenzen wiederaufzunehmen und sie auf der Gitarre zu lernen. Wenn du etwas auf einem analogen Synthesizer komponierst und es dann auf einem Saiteninstrument spielst, wo du zupfst, wirst du möglicherweise etwas spielen, dass dir so möglicherweise nicht in den Sinn gekommen wäre. Es ist eine gute Übung und letztlich sind es genau solche Dinge, die mich faszinieren und mich dranbleiben lassen. Und es kommt nicht von einem Lehrer, nein, alles entspringt aus deiner eigenen Musik. Das ist für mich wie Lego; man baut sich seine eigenen Spielzeuge.

AB: Ist es nicht so, als würdest du dich weiterentwickeln und gleichzeitig einen Schritt zurückgehen? AC: Es ist bloss ein weiterer Schritt. Wer weiss, vielleicht werde ich mir für das nächste Album einen langen Bart wachsen lassen und in Sandalen Akustikgitarre spielen. Ich weiss es nicht. Wir werden sehen!

just setting up this synthesizer and I had the exact same recorder [points at the recorder on the table] and I would walk around in the hotel room to record the sequence in different spaces. But it was exciting! It was like, "Oh shit, if I record it from the bathroom, I open the faucet and I can hear the water but I still hear the sequence in the other room." It was fun! I was like a kid, playing. I didn't have an idea of *Sono* being a record until Dominick Fernow from Hospital Productions said, "I want to put this out," and I said, "Put what out? It's stuff that I fall asleep to." I came to realize that if I'm making music for a specific therapeutic need—which for *Sono* was falling asleep, and for *Avanti* is to remember my family and to be melancholic—and if it works for me, then most likely it will work for other people, too. If you enjoy what I do, you can enjoy it sitting down and listening, you can enjoy it if you're in a train, just looking out the window while you're traveling, cleaning your space. I don't think it requires attention. I think it's even better if you're doing something else and you let it play—you know, if it's part of the environment.

AB Do you see this as a reaction to the NIN world you are also part of, where you experience a much more commercial side of being a musician?

AC I think it was more of a reaction to the song-based world in general. I always thought when I came to the United States that I wanted to have my band and just make it with my band. And it was fun, but then I realized that the structure itself, or having to go out and open for a band and play the same songs over and over in the same way, took away the magic of being in a studio and recording it. That was when I started making music for *Force*. It was completely different. I would come up with simple sequences that made me feel good. I could let them go and lay down and just feel great. It took me a while to understand that this could be *the* record, or that this could be *the* work. I always thought that I would have to go back, redo it, do it properly, do it in time with a metronome—like, crazy ideas! What for? Because you have to sync it up so everything lines up with the grid in the software? Because you might want to add stuff? No, I actually didn't want to add anything! But it took me a while to understand that there are different ways of making music. For my music there's no rule. That's why with every new record I say I don't know what it will be until it happens— it's true! The happier I am with the release, the happier other people usually are as well. And I don't want to sound too spiritual or whatever, because I'm not really that kind of person, but I do believe that there should be emotional content. If the artist puts this in the work, people will respond to it. It's not tangible, it's not something that you can sit down and study or write.

AB It sounds like you've found a way to enlightenment and happiness!

AC I don't know, that's a big statement. But yeah, musically, I think I have. I have to say that I've recently gotten a little bit overwhelmed with the fact there are synthesizers everywhere. I kind of stopped being creative with synthesizers as much as I used to be and got back to guitar. I still play the guitar for NIN, but I don't really consider it my main instrument like I did when I went to the United States to study guitar. And now I'm back to it, but in a way that's different from when I was studying it. It feels good to be able to approach it in a way where it's more about finding a balance between me as a guitar player and me as an electronic musician. I take what I've learned on guitar and what I've learned from other instruments and put them together in a way where the listener isn't going be concerned if it's a guitar or if it's a Buchla (or whatever).

AB So do you feel like you're rediscovering the guitar?

AC Yeah, definitely. As a thirteen- or fourteen-year-old I was really into fast playing and shredding—like Steve Vile, Jo Satriani.

I still very much enjoy that kind of playing, but I don't see it as a part of what I do creatively. I like the idea that now I'm forty-one years old and am able to play things I couldn't play when I was fourteen. But I would never go on stage at *Atonal* and start shredding super fast. One thing that I've been enjoying a lot is going back to some of my sequences and learning them on guitar. Obviously if you write something on an analog synthesizer and then you learn it on a string instrument, where you have to pick, it might not be what you would have played. So it's a good exercise, too. Those are the things that keep me interested. And it doesn't come from a teacher that tells you "You should do this, you should do that." It comes from your own music. So it's like Legos. You're building your own toys in a way.

AB Does it feel like you're progressing and going a step backwards at the same time?

AC It's just another step. Who knows. Maybe for the next record I'll be long-bearded, with an acoustic guitar and sandals. I don't know. We'll see.

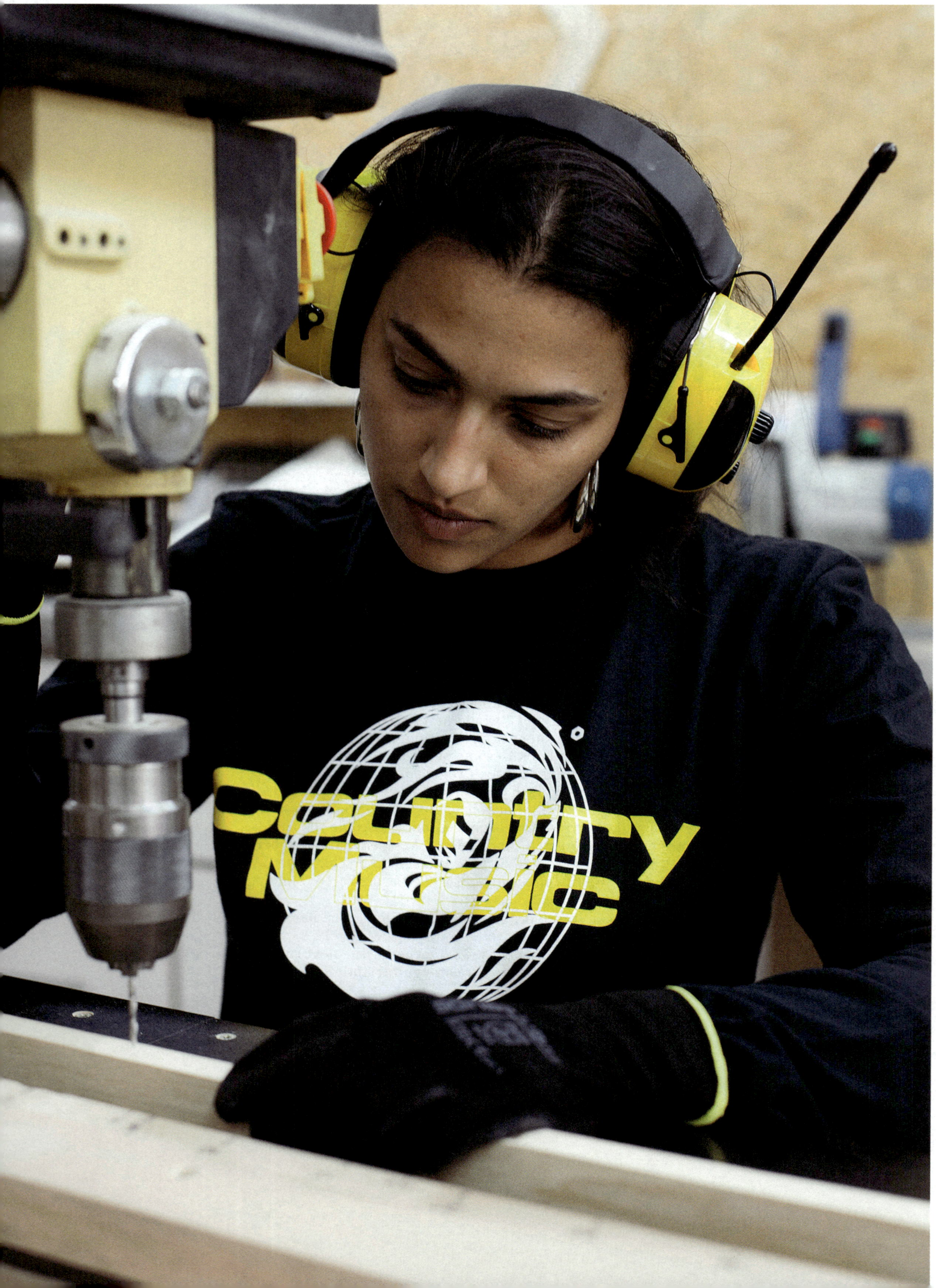
Country
Music

COUNTRY MUSIC WORKSHOP AND PLATFORM

Interview:
Marc Schwegler
Photography:
Viktor Fordell,
Ari King

Anna Sagström und Daniel Iinatti sind die Köpfe hinter dem gemeinsamen Projekt Country Music. Unter diesem Namen veröffentlichen die beiden über ihre Website Texte und Musik. Letztere erscheint bisher jeweils in der Form von zeitlich strikt auf acht Minuten begrenzten Tracks. Diese im Musikhandel sowie auf den gängigen Streaming-Plattformen nicht erhältlichen Werke stammen unter anderem von Nkisi, HAJ300, Estoc oder Osheyak—Exponentinnen einer globalen Produzenten-Szene, die sich in Bezug auf ihr Klangmaterial zwar teilweise noch an Klubmusik orientiert, in der Form jedoch mehr und mehr fernab von Dancefloors experimentiert. Eine pointierte und eigenständige Bildsprache und Ästhetik sowie weiterreichende, konzeptionelle Überlegungen begleiten diese Veröffentlichungen; zudem bietet Country Music verschiedene Design-Objekte zum Kauf an. Im Zentrum der Überlegungen und Aktivitäten des Projekts stehen Fragen zu Peripherie und Aussenseite; zu Arbeits- und Lebensbedingungen in postindustriellen Ökonomien. zweikommasieben-Redaktor Marc Schwegler hat die beiden Macher von Country Music in Berlin zum Gespräch getroffen.

Anna Sagström und Daniel Iinatti are the two brains behind the collaborative project Country Music. They release music and text via their website, and they've recently put out a string of tracks restricted to a length of eight minutes. The tracks, which aren't available on either the ubiquitous music stores or streaming platforms, are by Nkisi, HAJ3000, Estoc, and Osheyak—i.e., key members in a global scene of club-oriented producers whose sonic experiments lead them further and further from the dancefloor. The releases are accompanied by a trenchant, idiosyncratic visual language and aesthetic as well as far-reaching conceptual considerations; and Country Music also sells various design objects. At the center of the project's philosophy and activities are questions of periphery and marginalia, and of the working and living conditions resulting from a post-industrial economy. Marc Schwegler met the two Country Music creators in Berlin.

Marc Schwegler: How did you get to know each other?

Anna Sagström: Daniel was in a collective called Yoga Center, which ran a project space in Gothenburg. I myself was running a project space in Stockholm. We released a couple of USB sticks—TCF[1] did one, we did one ourselves, and we also invited Yoga Center to do one. That was maybe five years ago. Although I was working in visual art, music has always been a keen interest of mine. So I think I was always attracted to Daniel's field of knowledge and the energy around music and art. I then had this vague idea that I emailed him about, and we started discussing doing something that was in between art and music, based around certain themes that we have now incorporated into Country Music.

Daniel Iinatti: I guess we didn't realize it in the beginning, but we both grew up in similar cities.

AS Yes—postindustrial cities that used to be prominent at a certain point in Swedish history. I come from a steel industry town called Fagersta that was built for 30,000 people, but nowadays only twelve thousand are left. It's a bit like a ghost town—there are a lot of defunct and empty spaces. I also felt that we've both been a bit outside of the establishment by choice, especially in Stockholm.

DI The town I grew up in, Laxå, was blooming in the 70s. We had like 10,000 people there, and growing industries. In the 90s those industries started shutting down and it started to decline. It's not a ghost town per se, but it's one of the few towns in Sweden where the population is shrinking.

AS Globalization should theoretically make smaller cities more accessible, but actually it's the opposite—everything is being horizontalized. That's what has been interesting to us: things starting to shrink and decline, times slowing down, and people adjusting to that. And the other thing was space: how different it is to be surrounded by unused space. And what happens when you combine those two things. That's the paradox we're interested in: this weird texture of time and space. Later in the project, we started to speak more about what the periphery could also mean more generally. Now we have a much wider and generous understanding of this concept. Geographies are more complex than we thought in the beginning. At first we had this idea that our producers should come from the countryside. But then we realized that a lot of people actually leave those environments and move to the cities...

MS I didn't know that there's a rural, post-industrial Sweden. Is the postcolonial notion of a "global south" misleading in the sense that some of the fragmentation in the north gets overlooked? In America they say that the recent success of populism is based upon re-focusing on the so-called "forgotten men and women" of fly-over country. Is there something to that?

AS That's a tricky political territory to speak about. This is where I'm torn: on the one hand I do believe the frustrations of the Rust Belt[2] and all that. At the same time, I think there's a responsibility to be socially progressive. And I don't know how to have it both ways, exactly. Our ambition has always been to have a wide geography of artists. So far, we've basically just had people we know, and now we're trying to reach out to a wider group of people—just to pick up something global in the idea of countryside, whatever that might be, with inclusive politics. We have a lot of friends with visa issues, or different issues related to class and race. I think that has heightened our sense of marginalia or periphery. And we also started to think a lot about how the periphery relates to work. I also worked a lot in industries—I used to work as a cleaner for a time. Being in all that dust and dirt feels like the opposite of progress, somehow. We've been involved in so many jobs, like extra jobs and side jobs. We thought that this rarely gets discussed. You present the culture and art that you produce while you're

Interview   Country Music

schon, eine möglichst grosse Geographie verschiedener Künstler zu haben. Bis jetzt hatten wir aber eigentlich vor allem Leute, die wir kannten und wir versuchen nun entsprechend, einen weiteren Kreis von Leuten zu erreichen. So finden wir vielleicht das Globale im Ländlichen—was auch immer das sein mag—und Politik, die einschliesst, nicht ausschliesst. Wir haben viele Freunde, die Probleme mit ihrem Visum haben oder sich rassistischen oder klassenbedingten Vorurteilen ausgesetzt sehen. Das hat unser Verständnis für Marginalisierung und Peripherie erweitert. Und wir haben auch vermehrt versucht, uns damit auseinanderzusetzen, inwiefern Arbeit und Peripherie zusammenhängen. Ich habe viel in der Industrie gearbeitet—unter anderem als Reinigungskraft. Nur schon permanent dem ganzen Staub und Dreck ausgesetzt zu sein, fühlt sich an wie das Gegenteil von Fortschritt. Wir haben so viele verschiedene Jobs und Nebenjobs! Das wird jedoch generell eher wenig thematisiert. Man präsentiert die Kultur und Kunst, die man produziert, während man nebenher die ganze Arbeit macht, um sich das Ganze zu finanzieren. Die Kunst hat immer rein und präsentabel zu sein—der ganze Kampf, der sie begleitet und stützt, wird dabei jedoch nicht gezeigt. Es ist sehr anstrengend, den Anschluss zu behalten—das gilt gerade in Bezug auf die Musik; wo man auch noch auszugehen und zu tanzen hat. Wir wollten diesbezüglich die Wahrnehmung etwas verändern. Die Produzentinnen, die wir kennen, die haben eigentlich gar nicht die Zeit, permanent in Klubs zu gehen. Wenn sie Musik produzieren, dann sind sie oft im Kontext eines anderen Musikkonsums, man hört Musik bei der Arbeit oder generell in verschiedenen Situationen. DI: Das wollten wir auch in den Bildern, die wir online zeigen, transportieren: Die verschiedenen Situationen, in denen man Musik ausserhalb einer Klubumgebung hört.

MS: Eure Bildsprache zeigt jedoch auch eine sehr eigenwillige Ästhetik von Arbeit. Gerade die Werkstatt, die bei euch recht prominent auftreten ist, scheint doch eher auf eine Ökonomie vor der industriellen Revolution zurückzuverweisen… AS: Die Fotos haben wir aber an meinem ehemaligen Arbeitsort gemacht. Ich bin zurück an dem Arbeitsplatz, von welchem ich zuvor gefeuert worden war. Ich bin immer zu spät gekommen und hab deswegen auch das Einstempeln immer gehasst. Nach einiger Zeit wurde mir gesagt, ich müsse um sieben Uhr morgens da sein, weil es eben eine Werkstatt sei. Nach ein paar Monaten fand ich, dass ich nie mehr dahin zurück wollte. Wir glaubten, dass das genau der Punkt ist und haben beschlossen, aus all der Frustration, aber auch der Zeit, die ich da mit Musikhören verbracht hatte, etwas zu machen. Also habe ich meine ehemaligen Chefs gefragt. Und alles in allem war es dann auch ein ganz lustiges Fotoshooting. Meine früheren Arbeitskollegen haben sich sicher gefragt, was das soll… Die meinten so oder so, dass ich schräg sei. Natürlich ist aber alles, was wir in Bezug auf unseren visuellen Auftritt machen, überästhetisiert. Die Helligkeit ist hochgeschraubt, zum Beispiel. Wir haben uns viel über unsere Ästhetik unterhalten und darüber, was sie ausdrücken soll, wie man eine Ästhetik benutzt, die auf die Werkstatt zurückgeht, die in diesem Sinne der Arbeiterklasse zugehörig und vielleicht nicht mal unbedingt besonders cool ist. Gibt es Möglichkeiten eines alltäglichen, volkssprachlichen Designs? Die Farben schwarz und gelb stehen zum Beispiel für die Fabrikarbeit, genau so wie sie auch für gewisse Sportmannschaften stehen… Ich weiss nicht. Aber finden wir uns nicht oft in Situationen, in denen wir gewisse Dinge gleichzeitig feiern und kritisieren? Das Hauptsymbol in unserem Logo zum Beispiel stammt von einem Baufirma… DI: …der Baufirma… in der auch meine Eltern früher gearbeitet haben.

115

doing all this other work to finance it. And your art has to be pure and presentable and you're not supposed to present the struggle. I think—especially with music—it's hard to keep up and go out and club and dance. So we wanted to shift the perception. The producers we know don't have the time to go clubbing all the time. When they produce music they think of other ways to consume music—you listen to it at work or in a wide range of situations.

DI I guess that's also what we wanted to present with the imagery online: the different situations— outside of a club environment—in which you can perceive the music we present.

MS You also present a very peculiar aesthetic of labor with your images, though. One could argue that especially the workshop that you feature so prominently points back to an economy before the industrial revolution…

AS But it's actually my former workplace where we went back to take the photos—I returned to the workplace I actually got fired from. I always came too late and I hated the copy-in cards. After a while they said I needed to start at 7 a.m. because it was a workshop, and after a couple of months I was just like, "Argh, I don't want to ever go back there." But we thought it might also be quite meaningful to do work that has come out of all of these frustrations and of the times being at that workplace and listening to music. So I just asked my former bosses. And it was quite a funny photoshoot—all my former colleagues were working and they thought, "What are you doing here?" They thought I was weird, anyway. But of course everything we do is super aestheticized—for example, the brightness is turned way up. We talked a lot about aesthetics and what they represent, and how you could appropriate an aesthetic that is used in a lot of workshops—one that's somehow a working-class aesthetic, but not necessarily a cool one. We went for black and yellow, which symbolizes factory work and labor, and also certain sports teams and things like that. I don't know. Sometimes we find ourselves in situations where we try to celebrate and criticize something at the same time. "Could there be such a thing like vernacular design?" we wondered. Our main logo symbol, for example, is taken from a construction company…

DI …Which is actually the company where my mom and dad used to work!

MS So there's a deliberate attempt to represent and highlight certain individual and biographical issues with Country Music?

AS Biographies are often stripped in terms of social and political backgrounds. I think we've been bringing our biographies into this project for the first time, and that's something that's quite relieving. It's a reality that in order to do art, a lot of times, you have to be supported by a day job—or by your parents. And we just want to highlight the struggle and the many different identities that people have to put on.

MS Involving your own identity runs counter to certain notions of fluidity in identities…

AS Yeah, exactly. There are some restrictions and frustrations that come from being marginalized, from being someone not physically able to participate in certain scenes for various reasons—maybe geographical reasons or also other reasons. Estoc, for example, one of the earliest artists we released, spoke a lot about using the tools of oppression—harshness, hardness—and turning those around to create something empowering. From the beginning we've focused on hard music. With a lot of people we've emailed or people who have emailed us, there's this interesting feedback loop, just like a raw energy in material. There seem to be things that people just want to get off their chest. The text by Jennifer Boyd we published, *The Theory of the Strange Girl*, tries to theorize this and asks if there could be such a thing as liberation in a quite limited space.

116

MS: Versucht ihr also auch bewusst, Biografisches und Persönliches ins Projekt zu integrieren? AS: Biographien werden oft ihres sozialen und politischen Hintergrunds beraubt. Ich denke, dass wir unsere Biographien in diesem Projekt zum ersten Mal miteinbeziehen—und das hat etwas sehr Befreiendes. Es ist nun mal eine Realität, dass wenn man Kunst produziert, man das oft mit einem Tagesjob finanzieren muss—ausser man stammt aus reichem Elternhaus. Diesen Kampf wollten wir hervorheben—und auch die vielen verschiedenen Identitäten, die Leute aufgrund ihrer verschiedenen Beschäftigungen annehmen müssen.

MS: Ist die Integration von persönlichen, biografischen Umständen auch eine Absage an gewisse Vorstellungen von einer völlig fluiden Identität? AS: Ja, klar. Wird man marginalisiert, dann gehen damit gewissen Einschränkungen und Frustrationen einher. Man kann physisch an gewissen Dingen nicht teilhaben—sei dies aus geografischen, aber auch aus anderen Gründen. Estoc zum Beispiel, eine der frühesten Künstlerinnen, die wir veröffentlicht haben, spricht sehr viel darüber, die Werkzeuge der Unterdrückung gegen diese zu richten—Härte, Unnachgiebigkeit umzudrehen, um etwas Ermächtigendes daraus zu machen. Von Anfang an haben wir den Fokus auf harte Musik gelegt. Mit vielen Leuten, mit denen wir im Austausch stehen, hat sich so ein interessanter Feedback-Loop entwickelt und eine rohe Kraft in deren Material. Es scheint durchaus Dinge zu geben, die die Leute loszuwerden versuchen. Der Text von Jennifer Boyd, den wir veröffentlicht haben, *A Theory of the Strange Girl*, versucht das zu theoretisieren und fragt, inwiefern Befreiung in einem eng begrenzten Raum funktionieren könnte.

MS: Könnt ihr mir noch ein bisschen etwas über eure Ideen zu Zeit und Zeitlichkeit erzählen? Ihr veröffentlicht ja diese achtminütigen Tracks und Musik ist ganz grundsätzlich eine zeitbasierte Kunstform. Aber euch interessiert Zeit ganz grundsätzlich—bei eurem Soundcloud-Account beispielsweise steht der Claim: «Tools forming, Under-Time». AS: Die Länge und Form der Tracks ist auch eine Allegorie für das, was ich vorhin erwähnt habe. Wie sich innerhalb der Tracks das Tempo verändert, die Zeit sich dehnt und dreht, entspricht den verschiedenen Zeitregimen, denen sich die Leute unterwerfen müssen. Wir haben jedoch in der Entwicklung des Projekts auch realisiert, dass man die Musik für sich selbst sprechen lassen muss. Zu Beginn haben wir noch stark an gewissen Konzepten gehangen und versucht, Texte zu präsentieren und Erklärungen abzugeben. Nun lassen wir die Dinge mehr geschehen und versuchen eher geeignete Formate zu finden. DI: Allen Produzenten geben wir mehr oder weniger die gleichen Vorgaben. Sie nützen die acht Minuten, die wir ihnen zur Verfügung stellen, eigentlich völlig frei. Sie machen zwar klassische Klubmusik, aber sie sind sicher in dem Dunstkreis zu finden. Unser Format erlaubt ihnen etwa, Musik zu produzieren, die gewissen Restriktionen nicht folgen muss, etwas, das nicht in einem Klub gespielt werden muss. Die acht Minuten erlauben ihnen, mehr über Intros, Outros und Song-Strukturen generell nachzudenken. AS: Wir haben ihnen auch immer die Möglichkeit gegeben, Räume leer zu lassen—nur haben das bisher nur zwei Leute dann auch tatsächlich gemacht. Digitale Releases haben ja keinen eigentlichen Zeitrahmen—man beginnt einfach zu komponieren und lässt es laufen. Wir haben versucht, die Materialität von Zeit hervorzuheben, indem wir einen bestimmten Zeitrahmen vorgeben. Gewisse Produzentinnen finden es zu kurz, andere es wiederum zu lang, viele Musiker verwenden verschiedene Tempi. Man füllt halt die acht Minuten. Das war für uns

117

interessant. Ich glaube, dass dieses Format, dem alle folgen müssen, erlaubt, über gewisse Aspekte verstärkt nachzudenken. AS: Genau. Wie zum Beispiel will man diese Zeit überhaupt aufteilen? Inwiefern lässt sich räumlich darüber nachdenken? Wir haben auch schon darüber gesprochen, die Zeit künftig auf die Hälfte zu reduzieren um noch einmal mehr Optionen zu eröffnen, wie lange ein Release sein soll: Vier Minuten, zwei Minuten—oder sechzehn Minuten. Man könnte auch 30-Sekunden Specials machen. Von Anfang an war das Format jedoch auch an einem Arbeitstag orientiert. Wenn du am Arbeiten bist und dabei Musik hörst, kannst du dir eine Zeitstruktur geben, ohne Technologie oder weitere Dinge dafür zu brauchen. Am Anfang wollten wir so oder so auch extremere Dinge machen—Mixes über vierzig Minuten, mehrere Stunden oder auch Releases mit niedriger Lautstärke. Aber wenn man dann mit Produzentinnen zu sprechen beginnt, dann merkt man ziemlich schnell, dass man nicht zu kontrollierend sein darf. Man darf die Dinge nicht überkonzeptualisieren.

MS: Welche Musik ist für euch dann «Country Music»? AS: Nun ja, Lento Violento könnte durchaus als Country Music durchgehen. Ich weiss es nicht—auf jeden Fall ist es ein interessantes und auch etwas unterbeleuchtetes Genre. Es hat einen gewissen Folk-Touch. Zudem scheinen auch Hardcore und andere, schnellere Musikstile aus eher suburbanen Räumen zu kommen. DI: Die Produzenten, die wir bis jetzt eingeladen haben, machen sehr unterschiedliche Musik. Das möchten wir auch künftig so halten. Zwar wird eine gewisse Härte sicher weiterhin den roten Faden bilden—aber vielleicht in anderer Form. Unser nächstes Release, zum Beispiel, ist ein Track von B.yhzz und ich habe keine Ahnung, welchem Genre ich ihn zuordnen würde. Er hat ein sehr spezifisches Stück für uns gemacht, basierend auf Geräten, die sein Grossvater in der Landwirtschaft gebraucht hat. Und damit macht er wohl Noise, könnte man sagen—auf jeden Fall ist es der am wenigsten kluborientierte Track, den wir bisher hatten. AS: In der amerikanischen Country-Tradition findet man diese unglaubliche Sentimentalität; es ist eine sehr emotionale Musik. Und wir haben uns gefragt, inwiefern man das auf andere Art und Weise rüberbringen könnte. Was bedeutet das zum Beispiel in Bezug auf Hardcore? Wie sind diese emotionalen Momente da beschaffen? Natürlich klingt das dann völlig anders, aber ich glaube, da finden sich diese Momente eben auch: Es ist ebenfalls eine Musik, die einem hilft; mit sich und der Welt. Und das kann auf so verschiedene Weisen eben genau das sein, was die Leute brauchen. Ich weiss nicht, ob unsere Tracks nun etwas transportieren, das anders ist und emotional—aber ich hoffe es. Es macht auf jeden Fall den Eindruck, als würden die Leute sich besonders anstrengen, wenn sie für uns produzieren, um ein gewisses Gefühl und eine besondere Stimmung zu vermitteln.

MS: Inwiefern seht ihr Country Music als publizistische Initiative? Ich meine, ihr könntet es ja einfach auch als Label sehen und Vinyl veröffentlichen… DI: Darüber haben wir viel gesprochen. Wir sind kein Label. Wir repräsentieren unsere Künstler nicht—wir unterstützen sie nur, wir laden sie für Auftritte ein… AS: …wir haben keine Katalognummern. DI: …wir planen keine physischen Releases, wir veröffentlichen nicht über iTunes oder Spotify. AS: Wir wollen vielmehr eine erzeugende Kraft sein; wir wollen einen Austausch ermöglichen. Wir nehmen Künstlerinnen, die uns interessieren, wir treffen sie, wir versuchen, Ideen zu entwickeln und spielen sie an die Künstler zurück; wir lassen Musik zirkulieren. Und wir bieten ihr eine Plattform.

MS Could you talk about your notion of time a bit? Music is obviously a time-based art form—but you're also interested in time in a more fundamental way. On your Soundcloud page, for example, there's the claim: "Tools forming, under time."

AS We release tracks based on this format of eight minutes—that's also an allegory for what I mentioned before, because people do all these temporal shifts and turns within these eight minutes. It's like the many different tempos people need to operate in all the time. But we've also realized as the project has evolved that we wanted to let the music speak for itself. In the beginning we tried to stick to certain concepts and were more concerned with presenting texts and making statements. Now we're starting to just evolve and find formats.

DI We've invited all the producers on pretty much the same parameters. They use the eight minutes relatively freely, however they want. Our producers are not traditional club producers, per se, but they're in the club music realm. And this provides them a space to produce something outside of certain restrictions, something that doesn't need to be played at a club. The eight minutes give them space to elaborate more on intros or outros or structures of songs.

AS We've always given them the option of empty space—but actually only two people have done it. Digital releases don't have a particular timeframe; you can just start to compose and let it run. We tried to highlight the materiality of time by giving a specific frame. Some people think it's too short, some think it's too long, a lot of people do tempo shifts or whatever. You can fill it out. That's been interesting for us.
I do think that having a format that everyone has to follow gives you the opportunity to think more about certain aspects.

AS Exactly. How do you even divide it and think about it spatially? We've been talking about maybe cutting it in half for future releases to give multiple alternatives of how long the release should be. To make it even more intense. Like four-minute or two-minute releases. Or sixteen-minute ones. Maybe we'll do some 30-second specials. From the beginning, the format was also tied to a workday. When you work and you listen to something, it's quite easy to keep track of time—like in eight-minute structures. You can give yourself a time structure without using technology or other things. In the beginning we also wanted to do much more extreme things—forty-minute mixes, several hours. Or then we wanted to do low-volume release. But when you actually start to talk to producers, you realize you should not be too controlling and over-conceptualize things.

MS What music is country music to you, then?

AS I guess Lento Violento could be considered country music. I don't know. But that's quite an interesting and also under-examined genre, I think. There's a certain folksiness to it. A lot of high-tempo and hardcore music also seems to come from suburban spaces.

DI The producers we've invited so far come from a wide range of genres. I think that's also how we would like to continue in the future. The hardness will still be a vital part of it, but in different ways. For example, our next release will be with B.yhzz—and I don't know how to genre-fy that. He's doing a very specific track for us, made with his grandfather's old farming tools. And he's making noise with them, I guess—it's the least club-oriented track we have so far.

AS In American country music you think about all this sentimentality, emotionality. And we thought about how to get some of that through. Like in hardcore, what would this emotionality sound like? It would sound very different, of course, but it probably still has those moments. It's also a music that helps you cope with things. That can be in so many different ways, depending on what people need. I don't know if any of the tracks we released are different or emotional, but I would sure hope so. It does seem like people go out of their way when they produce for us and they try to get some feelings across.

MS: Könnt ihr mir noch ein bisschen was über die Veranstaltungen, die ihr organisiert, erzählen? Inwiefern bilden sie einen Teil dieser Plattform?
DI: Sie sind ein essentieller Teil des ganzen Projekts—wir finden es zentral, dass es auch physische Begegnungen zwischen allen Beteiligten gibt. Bisher haben wir nur drei Nächte organisiert: eine in Berlin, zwei in Stockholm. Die erste Nacht haben wir in einer Bar namens Nivå 22 gemacht—eine berüchtigte Bar in Stockholm, weil es eine der billigsten ist… Das Line-Up hat aus mir, HAJ300 und Swedish Lento Factory bestanden. Wir haben in dem Rahmen auch den Text von Jason Pine veröffentlicht. Stockholm ist eigentlich ziemlich posh, wohin man auch geht. Es gibt aber schon auch Leute, die versuchen etwas anderes zu machen—zum Beispiel das Drömfaculteten-Kollektiv, bei dem auch Kablam mitwirkt. Alles andere in Stockholm ist extrem teuer und es gibt nicht wirklich ein Nachtleben, weil es im Zentrum keine richtigen Clubs gibt. Unsere Veranstaltung war daher umso wichtiger—die Bar ist zentral gelegen und der Eintritt war frei; niemand musste bezahlen. Und in dieser superkleinen Bar haben wir Gabber und Hardcore gespielt. AS: Und wir haben eben auch den Text von Jason Pine veröffentlicht. Wir dachten, es wäre interessant, Texte im Rahmen einer Klubnacht zu veröffentlichen. Sogar im Klub hast du nämlich diese schrägen, leeren Räume: Jemand wartet in der Schlange für die Toilette, jemand anders hängt unschlüssig an der Bar herum. Wir haben die Leute also lesen lassen, während die Party lief—und das war schon sehr speziell. Es wird superlaute Musik gespielt und gleichzeitig hat man dieses immersive Lesen. Und man konnte dem Barpersonal zuschauen, wie es die Texte liest. Ich fand das grossartig—die Lücken und Verschiebungen zu finden, zwischen dem Tanzen und dessen Geschwindigkeit; die Leute da zu erwischen, wo sie's am wenigsten erwarten und so den Text zu veröffentlichen. Für die letzte Nacht in Stockholm war dann auch eine Ausstellung Teil des Programms. DI: Der Klub hat einen Galerie-Raum im Keller, den konnten wir für einen Monat nutzen. AS: Wir hatten eine Installation mit Stroboskop und einem speziellen Audio-Track, der auf vierundzwanzig Minuten gestreckt war. Der bildete den Kontrast zu dem Blitzlicht und zu einem sich drehenden Globus an der Decke. Wir werden eine Reihe von Veranstaltungen machen, die Ausstellung und Party kombinieren—in Kopenhagen, Helsinki und in London. Das basiert alles auf einem breiten Netzwerk von Freunden—und das ist es auch, was Country Music so grossartig macht: Auch wenn das Projekt eine ziemlich opake Ästhetik hat, die einige starke Elemente kombiniert, glaube ich dennoch, dass es die Leute als offen begreifen und sich angesprochen fühlen. Wir bekommen auf jeden Fall viele Nachfragen für Zusammenarbeiten und Ähnliches. Das war auch immer der Hauptantrieb, damit weiter zu machen: Weil das Projekt Möglichkeiten für Leute und Räume generiert.

References

1   See also the interview with TCF in zweikommasieben #11.

Siehe auch das Interview mit TCF in zweikommasieben #11.

2   See also the interview with Steve Hauschildt in zweikommasieben #16.

Siehe auch das Interview mit Steve Hauschildt in zweikommasieben #16.

MS Did you think of the whole project as a publishing operation? You could just call it a label and put out 12" vinyl...

DI We've actually talked a lot about this. We're not a label. We're not representing the artists we put out; we support them and try to invite them for shows, but...

AS ...we don't have catalogue numbers.

DI We're not planning on putting out any physical releases. We're not releasing on iTunes or Spotify.

AS We do want to be more of a generating force around conversations. We take artists that we like, we meet them, we try to come up with ideas and bounce them back to artists, just to put music in circulation. And we offer what we can, which I do think is to try to create a platform, somehow.

MS Can you talk a bit about the nights you organize? How do they fit into this platform?

DI It's an essential part of the entire project that there are physical meetings. So far we've done only three nights: one in Berlin, two in Stockholm. The first one we did was in this bar called Nivå 22. It's an infamous bar in Stockholm as it's one of the cheapest. I was playing, HAJ300 and Swedish Lento Factory. We also released the text by Jason Pine that night. Stockholm is kind of posh everywhere you go. There are some people, though, that try to do something different—for example the Drömfaculteten collective that Kablam is also part of. Since everything else in Stockholm is very expensive and there isn't really a nightlife because there aren't any central night clubs, this night was crucial. It was very central and we made it a free party—no one paid entrance. We were playing gabber and hardcore music in this really small bar.

AS And then we did release the text as well—the first one, done by Jason Pine. Because we thought that distributing text would be an interesting format to play with. Even in a club you get these weird spaces; someone is in line for the bathroom or hanging out at the bar. We started to do these readings at the same time the party was going on, which was kind of special. There's super-loud music and suddenly you have this very immersive reading. And you could see the bar staff reading the text. I thought that was great—just finding the gaps and the shifts in between the dancing and its fast pace. To catch people when they least expect it and release those texts. For the latest one in Stockholm, we also had an exhibition as part of the night.

DI The club itself has a small gallery in the basement, which we were able to use for a month.

AS It was an installation with a strobe light... And a special audio track where everything was stretched out to 24 minutes. That was contrasted with the strobe and a spinning globe on the ceiling. We did do a couple of combined exhibition parties in Copenhagen, Helsinki, and London in the spring. It's all based upon an extended network of friends, and that's what has been so great about Country Music. Even if it has a pretty opaque aesthetic with a lot of strong elements, I still think that a lot of people find it to be quite inclusive, and it does seem like people relate quite a bit. We get calls for collaborations and those sort of things, and that has been the main reason to do it. Because it creates opportunities for people and spaces.

IM LOOP MIT CHARLOTTE WARSEN

Kolumne:
Simian Keiser aka Tristan Marquardt

Bisher wurden im Rahmen der Kolumne «Soundtexte» Gedichte vorgestellt, die sich inhaltlich mit elektronischer Musik und Klubkultur auseinandersetzen. Sie demonstrierten, wie selbstverständlich diese Themen Teil der Gegenwartsliteratur geworden sind. Geht es um Lyrik, spielt Klang allerdings auch noch viel grundsätzlicher eine zentrale Rolle: in der Arbeit an und mit der Sprache selbst. Für kaum eine andere Textform sind Rhythmus und Klang so wichtig wie fürs Gedicht–oder, wie es der Dichter Ulf Stolterfoht einmal formulierte: «Rhythmus muss, Reim kann sein.» Die Lyrik ist, wenn man so will, die musikalischste Literaturgattung. Besonders spannend wird das dort, wo die klangliche Ebene Überhand nimmt über die semantische, wenn der Sound der Sprache ihre Bedeutung organisiert, mit ihr spielt, sie modifiziert und hinterfragt. Eine Dichterin, die immer wieder virtuose Sprach- und Klangkunstwerke schreibt, ist Charlotte Warsen. Der folgende, bisher unveröffentlichte Text ist eine Vorschau auf ihr bald erscheinendes, zweites Buch und arbeitet mit etwas, das uns aus der elektronischen Musik bestens bekannt ist: dem Loop.

Simian Keiser aka Tristan Marquardt ist mitunter DJ, Lyriker und Literaturvermittler. In seiner Kolumne «Soundtexte» stellt er Gegenwartsliteratur vor, die sich auf unterschiedliche Weisen mit Klang und Musik auseinandersetzt.

Charlotte Warsen (*1984) lebt in Berlin. Die Lyrikerin, bildende Künstlerin und Philosophin promoviert zur Politik der Malerei. Ihr erster Gedichtband *vom speerwurf zu pferde* erschien 2014 bei luxbooks, ein zweiter wird noch in diesem Jahr bei Brueterich Press folgen.

Thus far, the "Soundtexte" column has presented poems that touch on electronic music and club culture. Such texts demonstrate how natural and common these subjects have become in contemporary literature. Sound also plays a more fundamental role in poetry, however, through work on and with language itself. Rhythm and sound are rarely as important in other forms of writing as they are in poems; as the poet Ulf Stolterfoht once said: "There must be rhythm; there can be rhyme." Poetry is, if you will, the most musical literary genre. It becomes especially exciting when the sonic level takes over from semantics, when the sound of the language implies meaning, plays with or modifies it, questions it. Charlotte Warsen is that type of poet that virtuosically combines language and sound. The following unpublished text is a preview of her upcoming second book, which focuses on something that is well-known to fans of electronic music: the loop.

Simian Keiser aka Tristan Marquardt is a lyricist and DJ. In his column he introduces contemporary literature that grapples with club culture and music

Charlotte Warsen (*1984) lives in Berlin. The lyricist, visual artist, and philosopher completed her doctoral dissertation on the politics of painting. Her first volume of poetry, *vom speerwurf zu pferde*, was published by luxbooks in 2014; her second volume will be published this year on Brueterich Press.

in den Säften
als sie klafften vorn gerafft warn und nichts konnten

ging uns laufend kurz der Körper aus
in Erwartung einer Schroffheit war man ungekämmt
und zag erschienen einsam gar
die ersten Sätze schafften uns und würden
en passent mit uns verschwinden
es drittelte sich alles gegen Abend so infam
und nicht mehr fähig seine Nebel
bei sich zu behalten
die letzten Sonnenstrahlen schafften uns und
würden en passent mit uns verschwinden

in Erwartung einer Schroffheit war man ungekämmt
und zag erschienen einsam gar
trieb der schwerste Saft umzingelt oben träumte
brodelnd wie der Fisch im
Kalakukko träumt im Brotlaib ungehindert
über Gurgelrouten
die letzten Sonnenstrahlen lehnten lässig am
Massiv (würden en passent mit ihm verschwinden)

wie spinnert meine Finger leicht und launig über
Wangen gehn ein Leben lang wie langanhaltend
exaltierte Regenfälle rege und penible Schlagscheren
in Erwartung einer Schroffheit war man ungekämmt
und zag erschienen einsam gar
von innen schmiedeeisern schimmernd lang und breit
entlangschreddern am Anderen

es drittelte sich alles gegen Abend so infam und
nicht mehr fähig seine Nebel bei sich zu behalten
diverse Dragees deren Ergebnisse ungewiss sind rieten
zur Abreise rieten zu bleiben
am Hals von alten Amusements befallen rollten alle
Elixiere wollten was befahlen uns und schnallten was
und dachten sichs und machten sich an uns zu schaffen

in Erwartung einer Schroffheit war man ungekämmt
und zag erschienen einsam gar
die letzten Sonnenstrahlen schafften uns und
würden en passent mit uns verschwinden
trieb der schwerste Saft umzingelt oben träumte
brodelnd wie der Fisch im Kalakukko träumt im
Brotlaib ungehindert über Gurgelrouten

das Rendezvous zog ungerendert kühn vorüber wir
tunkten alle unsre Ohren ein
die Blicke kamen flötenförmig, weggeschüttet,
von innen schmiedeeisern schimmernd lang und
breit entlangschreddern am Anderen

diverse Dragees deren Ergebnisse ungewiss sind rieten
zur Abreise rieten zu bleiben
am Hals von alten Amusements befallen rollten alle
Elixiere wollten was befahlen uns und schnallten uns
und dachten sichs und machten sich an uns zu schaffen
so liebe angewidert und zersiedelt friedlich wie wenn
jemand in die Küche geht und steht vor dem geschlitzten
Licht der Jalousie und gibt dir eine Tasse warmes Maggi

seit früh um sieben ekelt mich alles Geschriebene
trieb der schwerste Saft umzingelt oben träumte
brodelnd wie der Fisch im Kalakukko träumt
im Brotlaib ungehindert über Gurgelrouten
in Erwartung einer Schroffheit war man ungekämmt
und zag erschienen einsam gar

das Rendezvous zog ungerendert kühn vorüber wir
tunkten alle unsre Ohren ein
als ob Apostellöffel zögernd fragend auf flambierte
Zuckerhauben schlagen
die letzten Sonnenstrahlen lehnten lässig am
Massiv (würden en passent mit uns verschwinden)

am Hals von alten Amusements befallen rollten
alle Elixiere wollten was befahlen uns und schnallten
uns und dachten sichs und machten sich an uns
zu schaffen
die Blicke flogen flötenförmig, weggeschüttet
das Rendezvous zog ungerendert kühn vorbei
wir tunkten alle unsre Ohren ein

in Erwartung einer Schroffheit war man ungekämmt
und zag erschienen einsam gar
von innen schmiedeeisern schimmernd lang und breit
entlangschreddern am Anderen
wie spinnert meine Finger leicht und lotrecht über
Wangen gehn ein Leben lang ereignisreiche
Regenfälle rege und rigide Schlagscheren

die letzten Sonnenstrahlen schafften uns und würden
en passent mit uns verschwinden
diverse Dragees deren Ergebnisse ungewiss sind
rieten zur Abreise rieten zu bleiben
seit früh um sieben ekelt mich alles Geschriebene

am Hals von alten Amusements befallen rollten
alle Elixiere wollten was befahlen uns und schnallten
uns und dachten sichs und machten sich an uns
zu schaffen
die Blicke kamen flötenförmig, weggeschüttet,
als ob Apostellöffel zögernd fragend auf flambierte
Zuckerhauben schlagen

trieb der schwerste Saft umzingelt oben träumte
brodelnd wie der Fisch im Kalakukko träumt im
Brotlaib ungehindert über Gurgelrouten
am Hals von alten Amusements befallen rollten
alle Elixiere wollten was befahlen uns und schnallten
uns und dachten sichs und machten sich an uns
zu schaffen

in Erwartung einer Schroffheit war man ungekämmt
und zag erschienen einsam gar
die letzten Sonnenstrahlen lehnten lässig am Massiv
(würden en passent mit ihm verschwinden)
so liebe angewidert und zersiedelt friedlich wie
wenn jemand in die Küche geht und steht vor dem
geschlitzten Licht der Jalousie und reicht dir
eine Tasse heisses Maggi

es drittelte sich alles gegen Abend so infam und
nicht mehr fähig seine Nebel bei sich zu behalten
die Blicke flogen flötenförmig, weggeschüttet
das Rendezvous zog ungerendert kühn vorbei
wir tunkten alle unsre Ohren ein

SUBSTANTIA NIGRA

Column:
DeForrest Brown Jr.

Substantia Nigra is a durational lecture-performance by a session group comprised of media theorist DeForrest Brown Jr.,¹ sound artist Kepla, lecturer and dancer Destiny Be, and visual artist Chris Boyd. Latin for "black substance," *Substantia Nigra* continues the themes of genetic memory and the black body as a technology explored in the EVP Sessions/Penned in the Margins-commissioned and PTP-released work Absent Personae. It is a tight, rhythm-based audio-visual conversation acting as a network that utilizes the asymmetrical principles of "black compositional thought" and spiritual jazz as a speculative model and radical tool for the evasive survival and reconstitution of a people. *Substantia Nigra* is dedicated to philosopher Ariel Valdez. The text below is part of the ongoing project that will be released later this year. It was read for the first time at Signal Gallery Brooklyn in workshop performances with Destiny Be, as a part of her lecture and performance series *Basic Elevated Realism*.

Substantia Nigra ist ein als längerfristige Lecture-Performance angelegtes Projekt von DeForrest Brown Jr., Klangkünstler Kepla, dem bildenden Künstler Chris Boyd und der Tänzerin Destiny Be. Spanisch für «schwarze Substanz» führt *Substantia Nigra* Themen rund um genetisches Gedächtnis und schwarze Körper weiter, die bereits die im Rahmen der EVP Sessions von Penned in the Margins kommissionierte Arbeit von Brown und Kepla *Absent Personae* untersuchte (veröffentlicht auf Purple Tape Pedigree, 2017). *Substantia Nigra* ist als engmaschige, rhythmusbasierte audiovisuelle Konversation gedacht und fungiert als Netzwerk, um asymmetrische Prinzipien spezifisch schwarzer Kompositionskonzepte sowie Spiritual Jazz als spekulative Modelle und radikale Werkzeuge für das Überleben und die Neukonstituierung eines Volkes zu nutzen. Substantia Nigra ist dem Philosophen Ariel Valdez gewidmet. Der untenstehende Text ist Teil des sich derzeit weiter entwickelnden Projekts, das im Laufe des Jahres veröffentlicht werden soll. Er wurde zuerst im Rahmen der Vortrags- und Performance-Reihe *Basic Elevated Realism* von Destiny Be in der Signal Gallery in Brooklyn gelesen.

"Slowly, I measured the glistening black drops, seeing them settle upon the surface and become blacker still, spreading suddenly out to the edges."

Ralph Ellison,
Invisible Man

Latin for "black substance," the "substantia nigra," is a tissue located in the brain involved with reward signaling and decision-making processes. The distribution of sensation throughout the body is like a type of data flow, a circulation of prime forces urging the body into movement. A stack is a model, an ecology of being through which the micropolitical streams of data are arranged and psychogeographies prefigured. The stack is a way to conceptualize reality from the perspective of data flow itself; the substantia nigra negotiates the stack and consumes and distributes data in a tight gameplay of exchange rates, across time.

The Black body is an absent identity, an untethered user swimming in black data, a slippage in the cloud. The black body is counterintuitive to the interfacing needs of the established stack, it is closer to the layer of the Earth, a raw material. The black body is potency, its substance is concentrate. Through the mimicry of "coolness," the black body can catch flows of unregistered information, transcend layers, cast gestures into the cloud, and shift its address and how it interfaces with the stack. The black body can even rebuild the stack overtime, in augmented modes...

Confession 001: Acknowledgement

Jazz as a form presents a model for the black body to decontextualize and explore pools of information beyond the parameters of the circle of 5ths and counterpoint. The "free"-ing of jazz offers a more non-standard thought program for considering surroundings. In all of his technical designations of the limits of space and time and the forced entropy of the zoning of harmonic potentiality, John Coltrane used his intuition to remap the planes of acousmatic experience, thus crunching together scales, the layers and gears upon which reality unravels. The material sensory ecology of a black body contains a deep inventory of periods of emotional distress and the actions in its environments that elicit such distress. Free associations in black thought is an operation performed in sketches, tooling trauma and dismembered orientation into a logic of evasion and survival. The substantia nigra, then, acts as an intermediary tool, a point of filtration just before deployment.

Confession 002: Resolution

The project of black unity, the fulfillment of the healing of the black body, within the delusion of the stack entails an indulgence of the fractured and unseen; the void, in contrast, is a vast wholeness comprised of blank slates. If the black body in the modernist context is inhuman, asserted as an organic technoid designed for endless production, then, the 'free' associations that spawn from a black thought can be composed and anchored to the constantly pulse of data deployment and retrieval. As an unidentifiable user, the black body is "maladjusted," free from the imposing layers, but ambiguous and invisible to the adjusted. The laboring black body only knows giving, and, it gives until collapse, then finds the strength to give more. This is love, and there is love in black unity. The black body, in unity, is a supreme love that flows freely, ceaselessly. There can be no more sorrow, no more exhaustion, only acknowledgement and contentment with the trappings and trauma of the black body as a giver and a forger of hope and with the futurity of the stack and the shape of stacks to come (mainly for others, and hopefully one day for ourselves).

Confession 003: Pursuance

Jazz is a language of love. There are linguistic truths in the shaping of the armature, and the freeing of the breathing that circulates through the body and filters through the architecture of an instrument. Performance can be a mode of ascension, descension, and maneuvering within the stack. Mid-summer in 1967, a funeral service was held for John Coltrane with Albert Ayler and Ornette Coleman paying tribute through song, inscribing his lineage and spirit. In the few years leading up to his death, Coltrane's thinking and playing began to instigate a kind of miniature stack ecology, plucked out of the acoustic unconscious. There is an unrestrained spatialization, action and reaction, energy and overflow in black compositional thought. The concept of "sheets of sound" sought to liquidize and loosen the structures of western music in order to open up space in which he could stack chords and substitute harmonic components. Riffing on an arpeggio, the matrix-breaking playing performed in rapturous pieces like 1966s *Ascension* saw black compositional thought overdrive the accumulative statistical properties of the current logic of senses, and divvy them up into intermingling "horizontal" layers. There was an eerily joyful mourning and pleading in the performances of free jazz. A standardized form of "coolness" was dissolved in favor of a scream, a howl, and ultimately a question: "when will we be free?"

Confession 004: Psalm

Sentiment is the material ecological assemblage of emotional debris exchanged amongst a community within a given space-time; or a long, braided trail of emotional bonds and lesions across the stack. The sensational environment of a black body is ensconced in the meaning of its own instrumentality. There is an ambient phenomena of the black body wading through the vital material of chemical and atomic complexity of the matrix of the stack. The unconscious, floating information is gleaned and reveals explicit insight on strategies for maneuvering. The only way out of the stack and out of capitalism is to confess, liquidize the matrix of the self. The offering of one's being as a musical component in the aggregational scaling of computation is a loving act. Capitalism in America is designed to be a long-form project towards a fictive "progress" and a hyperbolic becoming. The goal is always to get a return on an investment because the future (or the end) is always nigh. The instrumentalizing of a people—the transformation of the African continent into the black body—is a disruption with no easy solution. But free jazz, a black compositional thought, accepts the data construction of the self, flattens the roles of a user and interface to acknowledge the black body's relationship to the Earth. The black body inhabits the unseen and unconsidered while being hypervisible and reluctantly participatory in the stack. There is no way out, but the black body also does not inhabit a strict address. The black body utilizing black compositional thought can become an illusory slip through the cracks into the depths of black data and all of its potential to come, becoming attached to a deliberate impermanence. The black body is the site of racial violence in a sensory war in daily life in the stack. Without a matrix of the self, contingent upon itself, the black body interfaces with divine intelligence through exercises of mapping the infinite scope of black data and intuition spawned on the fringes. So through black compositional thought, the black body hopes to "play" itself as a means of hacking the system. In Coltrane's *Ascension*, the session group breathed as one, releasing a polyphonic lull of a chorus. Each attack corresponded to a decay; space-time collapses. The current of black data submerges the black body. Acquiescent to the flow, the black body moves like water, no longer lodged in hardened fractal freedoms, only floating on a vibe; unfree, but at least at large, signaling to the fragments of maladjusted users interfaced with black substance to form a black unity. Harmonic cooling over rhythmic undulations liquidize the scale, fold the future at the edges, and the black body sings, "we are only material for a love without ceasing..."

---

1   DeForrest Brown Jr. is a curator and writer based in New York. His column, where he operates with an editorial carte blanche, is closely linked to his artistic and theoretical practice that outlines the poetics of a contemporary, speculative and open thought on music and sound—not least from a decidedly Afro-American perspective.

STORE.RA.CO

レジデント・アドバイザー

TOPOGRAPHICAL REFLECTIONS
FURTHER REDUCTIONS

Interview:
Nick Klein

Zehn Jahre in New York zu verbringen, führt unweigerlich zu einem feinen Gespür für die vielen Variablen, die diese Stadt in konstantem Wandel halten. Und so ist jeder Abend, den man mit Shawn und Katie O'Sullivan, bekannt als Further Reductions, ziellos in Brooklyn oder Manhattan umherwandernd verbringt, ein anthropologisches Auslegen des Nachtlebens der Stadt der letzten zehn Jahre. Die enzyklopädische Qualität ihrer Erinnerungen sorgt für zahlreiche Referenzen zu Nächten, die waren, und Nächten, die sind. Es sind retrospektive Bewusstmachungen des Sounds, der die Räume dieser Stadt ausfüllte.

Passend dazu hat Further Reductions gegenwärtig den Ruf als städtischer Fahnenträger für vortreffliche Live-Auftritte im Kontext des Klubs. Perfomances, die beeindrucken durch eine Vielzahl kompositorischer Elemente und die einen Effekt erzielen, als wäre ein listiger DJ am Werk. Die Gruppe geniesst Kultstatus, bedingt durch die spärliche Taktung ihrer Veröffentlichungen von Live-Aufnahmen und die Resonanz auf ihr monumentales, 2014 auf Cititrax erschienenes Album *Woodwork*. Ende 2017, und nach einer Dekade als Further Reductions, erschien zuletzt das Album *Disparate Elements* auf dem niederländischen Label Knekelhuis.

Nick Klein sass mit Further Reductions über einer Flasche Tito's und einer Tüte Orangen zusammen und sprach mit ihnen über ihren Weg; über die Kontextverschiebungen, die ihnen ihre stetige Weiterentwicklung ermöglichten.

When ten years passes inside the metropolitan zone of New York City, one naturally begins to feel the many variables of change that have occurred. An evening strolling through Manhattan or Brooklyn with Shawn and Katie O'Sullivan of Further Reductions becomes a sort of anthropological mapping of the last ten years in premium nightlife culture. Their encyclopedic minds are often ripe with references to parties bygone and present, as well as to the recordings that swelled and inhabited the parties' rooms themselves.

Further Reductions is arguably the most formidable standard bearer of live dance music performance in the city today. Their performances excite with a wide range of masterful compositional elements that read as if an astute DJ was playing music of many different producers. Given the pacing of their output, the group has manifested a cult following over time that is hinged on the sharing of captured live recordings and the love of the monumental 2014 effort *Woodwork* on Cititrax. A decade into their existence, Further Reductions released *Disparate Elements* on the Knekelhuis imprint last December.

Nick Klein sat with the group over a bottle of Tito's and a bag of oranges to discuss the course their project group has taken and the context-shifting that has made for a fantastic evolution.

Nick Klein: So what I am particularly curious about, to start, is how Further Reductions began and what the landscape of performing in New York City was like compared to the present, in 2018?

Katie O'Sullivan: It's extremely different. In 2008 there was a desire to participate. It was like, "what can we contribute to this?" We saw Xeno & Oaklander, who were becoming our heroes. I guess they were already Shawn's heroes. Cheyney Thompson [of Epee Du Bois] as well! It was a diverse arts community and not just people saying, "we want to play minimal synth!" There was this minimal synth thing going on which felt very untouched or underground. The people at the *Wierd Party* would like galleries, weird music, and would just go on and party, knowing it would be a weird scene. Legit goths!

Shawn O'Sullivan: It emerged out of the Wierd Records scene. I was friends with [Xeno & Oaklander's] Sean [McBride] for a while at that point and loved his work. Martial Canterel, Xeno & Oaklander were part of that scene and hugely, hugely influential. At that point no one was really into minimal synth. Veronica [Vasicka] had put out a few things on Minimal Wave. It wasn't codified—it was mostly weirdos and record collectors, artsy freaks. Pieter Schoolwerth [of Bloodyminded] who threw the *Wierd Party* was known as "King Of The Goths" and had various ties to various facets of the scene here. The crowds at the *Wierd Party* were very unique people—lots of cyber-goths with goggles and big boots, fetish people. The "Human Carpet" used to show up a lot. He was like an intermittent fixture in New York nightlife—the guy who shows up at parties and announces very clearly "this is a thing I do—I wrap myself in carpet, I lay by the bar, and I want people to stand on me."

KO I don't remember that. It was just a fun, weird party! I moved to New York with not much intention other than not wanting to do school. I felt like I was quickly getting familiar with the Brooklyn DIY music scene, and it felt very masculine and macho although purported to be welcoming. I was like, "well I can't do that, I can't be that, so..."

SO I guess it's important to note, too, that we met at Will Burnett's party at Tribeca Grand.

NK This is something I always wanted to know about! Everyone from the era of musicians playing electronic music or DJing in New York that I associate you guys with mentions these small rooms. Like, "oh we played this or that person's small bar party here or there." No one brings up larger format clubs from that moment. Given the turn-around time of spaces and people in the city, how did this manifest?

KO It's people like Todd P [aka Todd Patrick], or a place called Studio B, which would do these "bloghouse" kind of things. I wasn't really into that stuff but they would do some cool stuff occasionally. Things don't really last very long. It's hard to pin down a culture or something like that.

SO There was Studio B in that era. I guess this was just in the moment when a place called ATP existed that was like Bossa Nova Civic Club—very house-focused. I would say that was in 2004, 2005. There was also Love, which the Dope Jams guys helped open. They designed the sound system. That was between 2005 to 2008, maybe. These were smaller clubs that generally focused on house and disco—lots of re-edits. Love did a lot of very influential dubstep parties, too, if I recall correctly. Then there was of course The Bunker, which had moved from Tonic to Galapagos.

NK Further Reductions exists through waves of trends and plods along, continually amassing information that becomes these definitive documents, like the Cititrax record. Also this other really important thing happens where live sets are recorded and float around between friends and fans on Soundcloud or something. These live sets are unbelievably good and varied. What's the agenda with these live performances?

SO Going back to the genesis: what was so thrilling about the

Disco setzten. Love hat aber auch einige wichtige Dubstep-Partys organisiert, wenn ich mich richtig erinnere. Dann gab es natürlich noch The Bunker, der irgendwann vom Tonic ins Galapagos umzog.

NK: Etwas, das für mich Further Reductions ausmacht, ist die Tatsache, dass ihr einige Trends erlebt und mitgemacht habt, stetig die dazugehörigen Informationen aufsaugt und verarbeitet und daraus Meilensteine formt, wie das Album auf Cititrax. Ein anderes wichtiges Element sind eure Live-Aufnahmen, die zwischen Freundinnen zirkulieren oder auf Soundcloud hochgeladen werden. Diese Sets sind unglaublich gut und variabel. Wie nähert ihr euch solchen Live-Performances an? SO: Zurück zum Anfang: Was die *Wierd Partys* so besonders machte, war der Fokus auf Live-Performances und analoge Setups. Die Partys waren berüchtigt für einen strikten Anti-Laptop-Kurs. Ich glaube, dass nur ein oder zwei Acts jemals mit einem Laptop performten, und das waren extreme Ausnahmen. Die Party war diesbezüglich strikt und forderte die stetig fortschreitende Immaterialität von elektronischer Musik heraus. Ich bin mir sicher, dass das ein Ziel war: nicht die Exklusion, sondern ein philosophisches Statement. Wir alle können heutzutage elektronische Musik mit Laptops produzieren und haben Tools zur Verfügung, die für 1000 Dollar das Gleiche leisten, wie ein 40 000-Dollar-Studio. Besagte Philosophie war eine Reaktion gegen diese Entwicklung. KO: Es sollte jedoch kein unnötiges Hindernis sein; es sollte Spass machen, auszuprobieren, wie man mit dieser Herausforderung umgeht. SO: Cheyney, Sean und Liz, oder auch Ramiro [Jeancarlo, von Staccato Du Mal] und natürlich Nina Belief formten ein Netzwerk gleichgesinnter Verrückter, das Wert auf situative Performances mit elektronischen Instrumenten legte. Das ist die Grundlage für das, was wir machen, obwohl wir uns selbst nicht in diesem Minimal Synth-Kontext verorten. Die Praktiken, die wir mit unserem Netzwerk entwickelten, sind immer noch die Grundlage unseres Schaffens. Die Performance soll kein perfektes Imitieren der Informationen einer Platte sein, sondern eine Interpretation dieses Materials, die so lebendig wie möglich ist. Ich bin kein fundamentaler Gegner von Laptops, solange sie als Perfomance-Tool genutzt werden und nicht zur blossen Wiedergabe von Material. Das Gleiche gilt für Sampler und Sequenzer, die heutzutage oft eingesetzt werden. Sie können als Perfomance-Tools genutzt werden und eine solide, verlässliche Grundlage für interessante Arbeiten sein—oder sie können als banale Abspielgeräte eingesetzt werden. Wir agieren in unseren Live-Performances situativ, auf den Raum und auf die Crowd reagierend, für die wir spielen.

NK: Fühlt ihr euch vielleicht wegen der sozialen Vergänglichkeit New Yorks verpflichtet, diese konzeptuellen Parameter eurer Anfänge weiterhin in eurer Arbeit zu berücksichtigen? SO: Ja, ich glaube, wir versuchen so viel wie möglich davon weiterzutragen. Eine Sache, die ich am meisten liebte an den *Wierd Partys*—die immer seltener stattfinden— und eine Sache, die ich auch früh im Bossa Nova wertschätzte, war das Potential dieser Orte als Experimentierfeld. KO: Man hat die Möglichkeit, sein persönliches Repertoire stetig zu erweitern, ohne dass persönliches Scheitern eine Rolle spielen würde. Risiken einzugehen war ausdrücklich erwünscht. Solche Orte gibt es immer seltener. Die Leute kamen jede Woche, um einen Live-Act zu sehen und die, die auftraten, gaben immer ihr Bestes. SO: …auftreten, irgendetwas machen —und manchmal miserabel scheitern.

NK: Diese nicht-binäre, nicht auf Bestehen oder Scheitern ausgelegte Mentalität bringt mich ins Hier und Jetzt. Alles fühlt sich durchdekliniert und

Wierd Party was this heavy emphasis on live performance and analogue electronics. The party had a pretty notorious and very strict anti-laptop policy. I think only one or two acts ever performed there with a laptop—they were extreme exceptions. It was a bit of a gauntlet thrown down, a challenge to the era of increasing immateriality. I think that was very much the goal there, not exclusionary but a philosophical statement. We can all make electronic music with laptops now—we all have tools at our disposal that cost $1000 that would otherwise be a $40 000 studio, and we can all have them in our homes. This was sort of a reaction against that.

KO It wasn't supposed to be a bummer thing, though; it was supposed to be a fun challenge—to see how you can perform with these limitations…

SO With Cheyney, Sean, and Liz, also Ramiro [Jeancarlo of Staccato Du Mal] who came up a few times, and of course Nina Belief, there was a network of like-minded weirdos with an emphasis on performing in the moment with electronic instruments. That is absolutely the foundation for what we do, even though we don't operate in some minimal synth context. Those practices we developed in tandem with peers is how we still operate to this day. The live performance doesn't need to be a perfect regurgitation of information on a record—it just needs to be a live performance that is as live as possible. I have no hard line against laptops as long as they are used as a performance tool and not a playback tool. The same goes for any number of samplers or sequencers people use now. They can be used as incredible performance tools and solid, reliable backbones for interesting work to be laid upon, or they can be used as "press play and go." We definitely approach live performance based on where we are in the moment, what the space is like, what crowd we are performing for.

NK Given the social transience of New York City, do you still feel a particular responsibility to harken back to the conceptual parameters from when you were just cutting your teeth?

SO Yeah, I think we try to uphold as much of that as possible. One of the things I loved about the *Wierd Party*—which happens less and less—and one of the things I loved about Bossa Nova early on, is that it was a playground or sketchpad…

KO You can just keep expanding what you do and it doesn't have to be tied down to you. Taking risks—that is what we and a lot of other performers were allowed to do at that time. There's not a lot of space for that anymore. People would go to see one live act a week, and performers would do the best that they could.

SO …go in there, do something, whatever. Take risks, fail miserably.

NK This non-binary, no pass-or-fail-mentality brings me to where we are in 2018 New York City. Everything feels like a total package, everything feels very "pro."

KO We've got our marketing team, our booking agency. This was all just the extreme opposite of what any of us were concerned with earlier. It wasn't on my mind. At the time you were just putting your two tracks on Myspace.

SO Brand ready from the get-go! Before a record exists, before you've gone onstage and made a fool of yourself you already have everything in place. Maybe this is exaggerating a bit, but you know, there definitely is a heavy emphasis on getting a brand cultivated and presenting that. I think another important distinction to make for the respective times is that everything now is filtered through an international techno infrastructure—not a physical infrastructure but a very tight information infrastructure or architecture. It seems like whatever you are making has to fit somehow within some facet of that structure, or it sits decisively, or more often purportedly, against it. In the mid-to-late 2000s, we weren't making music that was fundamentally different than what we make now, but it had to operate through this "indie" infrastructure. To achieve any kind of success, to get bookings or put your name out there, you had to work with something that had to identify with a pretty broad scope of indie rock. Noise stuff then, for instance, was tied more to indie rock than to techno like now.

NK Do you think this careerism is helping or hindering?

KO I think it is fair for us to all strive to succeed and be our best and be paid well for our performances. But I think it takes so much of the fun away from listening and enjoying music when it gets so concerned with branding, individual success, and ego. Why would you want to separate yourself like that? At the same time, we need to be critical.

NK With the laying out of the techno infrastructure that vessels this kind of careerism, is there room for "weird" dance music in a capital-driven place like New York?

SO Well, I think the history of most weird dance music always exists in big urban centers. It's always New York, it's always Chicago, it's always London, it's always Berlin. I think the city is uniquely situated to foster scenes for weird dance music.

KO Look at The Loft. You can get a lot of people coming together from different places and age groups.

SO New York in the 70s, 80s, and 90s was able to foster these scenes because of the different voices that coexist here crossing race, class, sexuality, and gender boundaries.

NK Some things feel geographical, though. Like some work doesn't get a bigger seat at the table because of geography. Geography is tied in with access to resources. I wonder—without being too defeatist or shitty—is New York City a place that can sustain its mythology or history?

SO I think geography is less a defining feature of musical movements in the 21st century than it has been previously, and I think that is a trend that will continue. The internet has collapsed geographical boundaries in a way that, on paper, is amazing and democratizing.

As far as a kind of organizing structure for emergent musical forms the city, the urban space is not going to continue to function the way it has in the last 30 to 45 years. That is something I think is a relic of the previous century. I think this democratization is a great thing on paper, and it obviously has a lot of good facets to it, but it doesn't have enough of the criticality of the actual democratized information that the internet has afforded. I think it warrants some skepticism. People are very eager to frame social media, YouTube, Discogs etc. as amazing emancipatory, liberating tools...

NK They aren't libraries!

SO Not to say they don't have those qualities, but they have chains attached.

NK What I love about Further Reductions' live sets is the wonderful array of information, compositionally, that occurs. I've heard a really wide palette of music within the context of dance-based music that you guys make. It's really refreshing to see you not give into genre specificity.

SO Well we just want to do something new every time. It's not fun if you do the same thing every time.

KO We always have so many circuits going and ideas that we work with at the time. We usually get it together and have a learning experience to see what we want more and less of.

NK Seeing you play at The Bunker party in the Bad Room you just had these sets with these basslines that were brilliant because they were fun. Everyone else presents themselves very "smart" or "serious."

KO Everybody wants to be so sophisticated!

NK I think that people forget using a vocabulary that can be a little fun or a little dumb; in fact this could lend itself to being a key contributor to the very sophisticated and complex social scenario that is the party. I think you all consistently add to that vocabulary.

professionell an. KO: Wir haben mittlerweile auch Leute, die sich um unseren Auftritt und um unsere Bookings kümmern. Das steht konträr zu dem, was uns damals beschäftigte. Darüber habe ich niemals nachgedacht. Damals hat man einfach zwei Tracks bei Myspace hochgeladen und das wars. SO: Heute ist immer alles gleich eine Marke. Bevor es überhaupt eine Platte gibt, bevor man sich auf der Bühne seine Sporen abverdient hat. Vielleicht ist das eine leichte Übertreibung, aber es wird viel Wert auf Vermarktung und Vermarktbarkeit gelegt. Eine weitere wichtige Unterscheidung zwischen damals und heute ist die Tatsache, dass jetzt alles durch eine internationale Technoinfrastruktur gefiltert wird—keine physische Infrastruktur, aber eine sehr dichte Informationsarchitektur. Es scheint, als müsse alles, was man macht, in diese Informationsarchitektur passen oder dezidiert dagegen sein. In den späten 2000er Jahren haben wir keine grundlegend andere Musik gemacht als heute, aber es musste möglich sein, sie in der «Indie»-Infrastruktur unterzubringen. Um erfolgreich zu sein, Bookings zu bekommen oder einfach nur den eigenen Namen zu etablieren, war die Identifikation mit Indie Rock notwendig. Noise war damals zum Beispiel eher mit Indie Rock assoziiert als mit Techno, wie es heute der Fall ist.

NK: Ist dieser Karrierismus hilfreich oder hinderlich? KO: Das Streben nach Erfolg ist legitim. Das Streben nach guten Gagen genauso. Aber ich denke, dass viel Spass und Interesse am Musikhören und -geniessen verlorengeht, wenn es immer um Vermarktung, individuellen Erfolg und das eigene Ego geht. Warum will man sich so vereinzeln? Man muss kritisch bleiben.

NK: Ihr habt die Technoinfrastruktur erwähnt, die eine bestimme Art von Karrieren fördert. Existieren in einer kapitalgetriebenen Stadt wie New York noch Orte für «seltsame» elektronische Musik? SO: Rückblickend hat diese Art von Musik ihren Platz immer in grossen und urbanen Zentren gefunden. Etwa in New York, Chicago, London, Berlin. Ich denke, New York ist und bleibt ein einzigartiger Nährboden für das Seltsame. KO: The Loft ist ein gutes Beispiel. Es war möglich, heterogene Gruppen verschiedenen Alters und verschiedener Herkunft zusammenzubringen. SO: Im New York der Siebziger, Achtziger und Neunziger war es immer möglich, Szenen zu pflegen aufgrund der Koexistenz verschiedener Stimmen, die sich fluid zwischen Geschlechtern, Klassen und Sexualitäten bewegten.

NK: Die Geographie scheint auch eine Rolle zu spielen. Ich meine zum Beispiel, dass manche nicht partizipieren können, weil sie räumlich getrennt sind von New York. Geographie ist verknüpft mit der Verfügbarkeit von Ressourcen. Ich frage mich allerdings auch, ob New York seine Mythologie und Geschichte konservieren kann? SO: Ich glaub, die geografische Verortung musikalischer Bewegungen wird im 21. Jahrhundert immer unwichtiger. Das Internet sorgt für ein Verwischen geographischer Grenzen. Auf dem Papier ist das eine wunderbar demokratisierende Entwicklung. Im Sinne einer organisierenden Struktur für aufstrebende musikalische Formen werden die Stadt oder der urbane Raum nicht mehr die Funktion haben, die sie in den letzten 30 bis 45 Jahren hatten. Das ist ein Relikt des vergangenen Jahrhunderts. In der Theorie ist diese Demokratisierung eine tolle Sache, die selbstverständlich viele Vorteile hat. Ich vermisse allerdings auch eine breite kritische Haltung gegenüber der demokratisierten Informationen, die das Internet definieren. Ich denke, es bedarf eines skeptischen Blicks diesbezüglich. Allzu schnell werden soziale Netzwerke wie YouTube oder Discogs als emanzipatorische, befreiende Werkzeuge gefeiert.

D

NK: Das sind keine Bibliotheken! SO: Ich sage nicht, dass sie nicht solche Qualitäten haben, aber diese haben einen Preis.

NK: Was mir an euren Live-Sets besonders gut gefällt, ist das grosse Spektrum kompositorischer Informationen, die ihr anwendet. Ich habe schon eine sehr breite Palette musikalischer Spielarten im Kontext eurer Performances gehört. Es ist erfrischend, dass ihr euch nicht in Genrespezifikationen verliert. SO: Wir wollen einfach immer etwas Neues machen. Es macht keinen Spass, immer das Gleiche zu tun. KO: Bei uns stehen immer viele verschiedene Ideen im Raum. Meistens bildet die Performance den Teil einer Lernkurve und wir entdecken beim Spielen, wovon wir mehr und wovon wir weniger wollen.

NK: Als ihr bei der Bunker Party im Bad Room gespielt habt, bestanden eure Sets fast ausschliesslich aus Basslines, die brillant waren, weil sie Spass machten. Sonst wollen Acts immer ernst oder clever sein. KO: Die Leute und ihre Ansprüche!

NK: Dass Vokabular ein bisschen albern oder bescheuert sein kann, wird oft vergessen; obwohl das einen Schlüsselbeitrag zu einer sehr elaborierten und komplexen sozialen Situation—der Party—leisten kann. Ihr macht davon Gebrauch. SO: Grenzen zwischen Hoch- und Subkultur zu erodieren, ist immer eine gute Sache. In Bezug auf deine Anmerkung glaube ich, dass es eine fortschreitende Abgrenzung zwischen den Rollen gibt, die Techno und House spielen sollen—Techno ist erwachsen und House ist unterhaltsam. Ich denke nicht, dass das so explizit stimmt. Der beste Techno ist natürlich auch unterhaltsam. Monochromer Techno wird schnell langweilig, das war der Fall in den frühen und mittleren Nullerjahren: viel grauskalierter Techno. Ich spreche mich selbst nicht frei von dieser Entwicklung, auch werde ich assoziiert mit Labels, die Teil davon sind. Wenn das allerdings die dominierende Stimmung ist, wird Techno fade. Das gleiche gilt für House: House sollte nicht nur unterhaltsam sein, Spass machen und sich auf gefilterte Discosamples verlassen, sondern auch mal härter klingen dürfen. Die Musik ist viel langsamer geworden seit den Neunzigern. KO: Davon erfährt man beispielsweise online mehr. Wie wäre es mit ein bisschen Recherche?

NK: [ironisch] Menschen müssen gesagt bekommen, was zu tun und zu denken ist, ok? Ambiguität schreckt ab. SO: Ich glaube nicht, dass ich dem zustimme. Im Moment reagieren die Leute ganz gut auf Ambiguität; sie mögen es, Dinge zu hören, die sich nicht so einfach in Schubladen stecken lassen. Was das Verarbeiten und Verbreiten dieser Informationen betrifft—besonders im Internet, das sehr bildlastig und fragmentiert funktioniert—, ist die Vermittlung dieser Ambiguität etwas schwieriger. Intuitiv reagieren Menschen allerdings gut auf Mehrdeutigkeiten.

NK: Könnt ihr etwas über die Zeit erzählen, als *Woodwork* erschien und wie es zur Entstehung des neuen Albums kam? KO: Oh, diese Geschichte erzähle ich gerne. Wir sollten Musik veröffentlichen, das frustrierte mich. Ich wollte einfach weiterhin Musik produzieren, die auf der Tanzfläche funktioniert, aber gleichzeitig auch das Repertoire erweitern. Manche Labels waren nicht interessiert daran, ein Portfolio aufzubauen. Sie wollten sich lieber auf die Musik konzentrieren, die vermarktbar war. Entweder sollten die Sachen blitzsauber sein oder sie waren nicht diffus genug. Die Community damals fühlte sich deutlich kleiner an. Dinge, die später gross wurden, kamen damals aus einem kleinen Pool. Als wir die 7" auf Captured Tracks rausbrachten [*Decidedly So / Not Unknown*, 2010], hat Ryan [Martin] von Dais Records auch etwas des Materials auf Tapes auf seinem

E Interview Further Reductions

SO Eroding boundaries between high and low culture is always a good thing. Expanding upon what you are saying, I think that there is an increasing delineation between the roles performed of techno and house—techno being sophisticated, and house being fun. But neither of them needs to be so explicit. The best techno is also fun. Techno gets very boring when it is super monochrome, and that was much of the early-to-mid 2000s—lots of greyscale techno. I mean, I've released music somewhat in that spirit myself, and I release with labels somewhat in that spirit. When that is the dominant voice, though, techno does get a little dull. And the same goes for house: house music doesn't need to just be fun, good times, and filtered disco samples. It can be very hard; tempos have slowed a lot since the 90s.

KO People who don't know the forms can read about them on a website and get what they need. How about doing a little research?

NK [mockingly] People need to be told what to do and think, right? Ambiguity is a deterrent.

SO I don't know if I agree with that assertion. In the moment, I think people actually respond. People actually like to hear things that don't fit so neatly into boxes. As far as digesting and disseminating that information, especially through the internet, which tends to be very image and sound-byte focused, communicating ambiguity is very difficult. On a visceral level, though, people respond to ambiguity very well.

NK Could you explain the time period around when *Woodwork* came out and how things came to be with your newest record?

KO Oh, I can tell this story pretty well. I felt like I was getting so frustrated that we weren't getting to put out any music. I wanted to keep making more dancefloor-focused music, but I wanted to expand. Certain labels were not interested in building a body of releases because they wanted to focus on what they could work with that was more marketable. It had to be squeaky clean, or something wasn't "hazy" enough. It felt like a much smaller a community at the time. Things that went on to be huge later came from a much smaller pool. From the time we did that 7" on Captured Tracks [*Decidedly So / Not Unknown* in 2010], Ryan [Martin] from Dais Records put out a bunch of material on tapes on his label Robert & Leopold. We had all this back-catalogue material we hadn't released. Shawn was busy in Led Er Est at the time and starting to work solo. He was super busy and we recorded little. The way we were working was not quite focused. The stuff we were recording then was not to the caliber to where it would later be. We lived with roommates at the time, shared a practice space with Led Er Est. And then we lost the practice space.

SO I think that practice space is now owned by Vice Magazine.

KO We finally moved to our own apartment and were far out and isolated with our studio in our space. Shawn was starting to work on his records for Avian [under his 400PPM alias] and on Civil Duty [a collaborative project with Beau Wanzer]. We finally lived alone in a small, nice apartment with space for ourselves. We were older and able to make music not very loud when we needed to. I was excited working with modular synthesis. I wanted to participate and make something that was techno and expansive. We wanted to break down the preconceived notions of the band we were.

SO We both have backgrounds in DJing dance music. We met DJing. We kept running up against walls in the "indie" era because people couldn't believe we liked electronic music. We always tried to incorporate elements of techno and dance music into what we did—the sets were pretty open-structured. We loved a lot of cheesy italo, too.

KO I told Shawn that if we didn't make the record, we would never do it. So we recorded it together in a month. That was when Hurricane Sandy happened, too.

D

Label Robert & Leopold veröffentlicht. Wir hatten viel unveröffentlichtes altes Material. Shawn war zu der Zeit sehr mit Led Er Est beschäftigt, zudem fing er an, alleine zu produzieren. Wir hatten kaum Zeit und unsere Arbeitsweise war nicht besonders fokussiert. Unsere damaligen Stücke hatten nicht das Kaliber der späteren Sachen. Wir wohnten in WGs, teilten einen Proberaum mit Led Er Est und verloren diesen dann auch noch. SO: Ich glaube der Proberaum gehört jetzt Vice. KO: Dann endlich zogen wir in unsere eigene Wohnung, die etwas weiter draussen liegt und uns endlich die Möglichkeit gab, isoliert zu arbeiten. Shawn begann [unter seinem 400 PPM Alias] Material für Avian aufzunehmen und arbeitete an Sachen für Civil Duty [eine Kollaboration mit Beau Wanzer]. Wir waren also endlich in unserem eigenen, kleinen, netten Apartment mit Platz für uns. Wir wurden älter und konnten, wenn es sein musste, auch leise Musik produzieren. Ich fand es aufregend mit modularen Synthesizern zu arbeiten. Ich wollte partizipieren und Musik produzieren, die Techno war, aber nicht nur. Wir wollten mit den Erwartungen an uns brechen. SO: Wir haben beide eine Vergangenheit als DJs von elektronischer Musik—wir haben uns durchs Auflegen kennengelernt. Aber die Art, wie wir auflegten, funktionierte während der Indie-Ära nicht, weil die Leute nicht glauben konnten, dass wir elektronische Musik mochten. Wir haben immer versucht, Techno- und Dance-Aspekte in unsere Sachen zu integrieren; unsere Sets waren sehr offen. Wir mochten auch kitschige Italo-Produktionen. KO: Ich sagte Shawn, dass wenn wir die Platte jetzt nicht machen würden, sie niemals gemacht würde. Also haben wir sie zusammen in einem Monat aufgenommen. Das war, als Hurricane Sandy wütete. SO: Ich erinnere mich noch, dass wir damals ohnehin sehr viel aufgenommen haben. Katie hat Material an Veronica [die auch das Minimal Wave-sublabel Cititrax betreibt] geschickt, ohne mir davon zu erzählen. Irgendwann hat Katie mir gesagt, dass Veronica unser Zeug mag, was mich natürlich sehr freute.

NK: Was mir daran gefällt, ist die Tatsache, dass ihr ein komplettes Album in petto hattet und bereit wart, es zu veröffentlichen. Ich finde mich oft mit der Situation konfrontiert—und damit bin ich nicht alleine—, dass ich Platten oder Dinge produziere, die mit einer Anfrage zusammenhängen. Eine heimtückische Situation, findet ihr nicht? KO: Ich bevorzuge definitiv das Gegenteil. Ich denke ungern in Kategorien à la: «Ich mache diesen Track für dieses Label.» Ich wollte, dass das Album ausufert. Und das war eine wertvolle und lehrreiche Erfahrung. Dann wird man aber von Leuten gebucht, die wollen, dass man genau *die* Stücke spielt. Man geht hin, macht sein Ding und die Leute fragen: «Was zur Hölle war das?» Oft bleibt es nebulös, und das ist eine Sache die wir niemals ändern wollen. Die Goths sind enttäuscht, die New Beat- und EBM-Leute finden es scheisse, die Indie-Szene denkt: «Was ist das für ein Lärm?» und die Leute aus der Techno-Szene finden die Sache albern.

NK: Wie war das bei dem neuen Album? KO: Dass es so lange gedauert hat, lag auch an meinem sehr anstrengenden Job, den ich mittlerweile gewechselt habe. Ich bin 30 geworden und verlasse mich nicht auf die Musik als Karriere. Auch war ungewiss, was kommen wird. Und ich wollte mich nicht auf dünnes Eis begeben. SO: Künstlerinnen und Musiker sollten Fähigkeiten kultivieren, die ihnen ein Einkommen ausserhalb ihrer Passion ermöglichen¹. KO: Ich war etwas verloren. Shawn war viel auf Tour und ich konnte nur damit angeben, wie cool mein Freund ist.

SO I just remember I was recording a lot in general back then. We were churning out a bunch of material. Katie had sent it to Veronica [who also runs the Minimal Wave-sublabel Cititrax] without ever telling me. Eventually Katie told me that Veronica would like our stuff, and I said that sounded really good.

NK What I like here is that you had a record ready to go, whereas I find myself and my peers often making records or a thing specifically for an offer. This is a bit of a treacherous place to be as a maker. What do you think?

KO I would rather just do it the other way. I am never like, "I'm going to make this for this." I wanted that record to be expansive. It was an invaluable session and lesson. Then people want you to play in their city and people want you to play *those* songs. You go and do your thing and people ask, "what the fuck did you just do?" It's a nebulous zone and we're always going to be nebulous. All the goths were disappointed, all the new beat- and EBM-people were like "this sucks," indie people were like "what is this noise?" and techno people were like "this is goofy."

NK What about the new record?

KO The reason it took so long was because I quit a very taxing job and moved into a new one. I was turning 30 years old. I wasn't and am still not banking on music to be my career. I was feeling the anxiety of what was coming. And I wanted to not feel like I was skating on thin ice.

SO Yeah, artists and musicians should cultivate skills and streams of revenue outside of their desired fields.[1]

KO I was a little bit lost, Shawn was touring a lot. I got to brag about how cool my fiancé is. Then we got engaged and we were getting inquiries about 2015. I was all over the place because I didn't know what I wanted to do.

NK And since then New York has entered a new phase...

KO Yeah, Bossa Nova is becoming a thing.

SO Yeah, Bossa Nova was happening, house was a thing. L.I.E.S. became a thing. Techno was acceptable, but you still couldn't play full-on techno sets. But by 2015 things really changed.

KO Then we had to get married, threw that wedding together in a month. We met some really great people during this period. We met Ken and Karl Meier [of Standards & Practices]. We met you. All of our old friends moved away or started families. We were still kind of in the same place everyone already was. It was fun meeting some new people—we had felt so isolated. We played Panorama Bar, we played Greece. I thought we would move to Berlin. Then we went to Chicago and Japan. We recorded ten tracks on our honeymoon. We had a weird period of problems with our home but we slowly began working on things. Around the same time, Knekelhuis started writing us every once in a while. We knew we had some good tracks over time and Mark [van de Maat of Knekelhuis] said he would be honored to put it out.

SO He had written checking in to see if we wanted to still do something, and we did one more track and sent it off.

References

1 See also the interview with Country Music on page 110.

Siehe auch das Interview mit Country Music in dieser Ausgabe, S. 110.

DING DONG VS. PUM PUM

Column:
Marius Neukom

In this column, Marius 'Comfortnoise' Neukom introduces book publications that relate in various ways to dub culture. He contextualizes each publication, describes its guiding principles, and expands on its author's thoughts. An annotated version of this column with supplemental sound and text references can be found at
www.comfortnoise.com/blog/basslines.html

In der Kolumne Basslinien stellt Marius 'Comfortnoise' Neukom jeweils Buchveröffentlichungen vor, die sich in verschiedenen Formen auf die Dub-Kultur beziehen. Dabei arbeitet er die Essenz der jeweiligen Publikationen heraus, kontextualisiert sie und führt Gedanken der Autoren weiter. Eine kommentierte, mit Ton- und Text-Referenzen versehene Version dieser Kolumne findet sich unter
www.comfortnoise.com/blog/basslines.html

Within the European West, discussions on the representation of sexuality and gender in today's dancehall culture often result in head-shaking. The observation of forced masculinity, contempt for women, homophobia, and violence have led to a complete lack of understanding, strong condemnation, and sometimes even concert bans. Although such reactions are comprehensible, it is surprising how often they are characterized by an unreflected self-righteousness. In her book, *Inna di Dancehall. Popular Culture and the Politics of Identity in Jamaica,* Donna P. Hope presented a revealing description of dancehall culture already back in 2006.

Much has been written on dancehall culture before and after Hope's book but *Inna di Dancehall* stands out because the author is personally involved with and close to the subject. Her book is the preliminary arrival after a journey not only through the dancefloor but also through Jamaican society: from the dancehall fan to the dancehall researcher, and from the rural working class to the social hotbeds of the big city. She observes keenly, writes vividly, theorizes with restraint, and refrains from politicizing and judging. Such qualities are, unfortunately, often lost in other, more academically-oriented publications on this topic, especially when they raise allegations of sexism and racism and try to substantiate their claims with far-reaching theoretical discussions.

In the chapter on gender and sexuality of *Inna di Dancehall*, Hope refers to a hierarchy of the skin in the context of race, class, and gender: At the top is the white man, followed by the white woman. Next comes the colored man and then the colored woman, after which is the black man and finally, at the very bottom, the black woman. This ranking has historical roots in colonialism and slavery, originating from distinct European patriarchal structures. With this hierarchy in mind, Hope concludes that the gender order within dancehall culture is not accidentally prone to sexism and heteronormativity in which biological gender, gender identity, and gender roles are consistently drawn as either superior male or inferior female, and in which the 'natural' and solely acceptable and healthy form of sexual intercourse must be heterosexual. In particular, she shows that the female ideals of beauty are closely related to European ideals; for instance, improving one's appearance by straightening one's hair or by the harmful practice of bleaching one's skin. She also notes opposites such as the ideal of female obesity, which is sometimes aided through the use of hormone pills.

Such themes are reflected in many song lyrics and music videos, and often appear in more-or-less encrypted forms. For example, in "Love Punaany Bad" (1998), Shabba Ranks sings: "... love punaany bad, / mi a punaany guineagog" (I love vaginas very much / I am a vagina master). The genital organ represents the entire female person, who, while highly esteemed, must of course be taken possession of. This male perspective is complemented by equivalent phrases of female artists, showing how both sides support stereotypes and fantasies through such reductive, binary thinking. In "Boom Wuk" (2004), for example, Tanya Stephens sings: "It's all about the sex / Mi jus love off you boom wuk / Love the way you have mi pum pum stuck / ... / "Love the long ding dong" (It's all about the sex / I just love how you fuck / I love the way you're stuck in my vagina / ... / I love the long penis). The quality of sexual intercourse is determined not only by penis length but also by how violent the sexual intercourse is. In the duet, "Ramping Shop" (2009), Spice sings the following with Vybz Kartel: "Well you haffi ram it hard (...) kill mi wid di cocky" (Well you have to push hard (...) kill me with your penis). In Addicted (2017), Popcaan almost entirely eliminates the female subject when he sings: "Gyal, me nuh waah fight everyday a di week / Me know you waah me / And you tight fat pum pum a fight fi me see it" (Girl, I don't want to fight every day of the week / I know you want me / And your tight fat vagina will fight so that I get to see it).

Long ding dong vs pum pum: These texts reveal a gender struggle from which highly problematic and psychodynamically unavoidable consequences such as contempt of women, violence, and homophobia, emerge. Due to dancehall's tendency to name and also exaggerate central issues of everyday life, these themes are represented in controversial 'slackness', 'rudebwoy' and homophobic 'batty' tunes . But do such words depict the external world and behaviors? No. First and foremost, they are artifacts, and as such an image of the (unconscious) fantasies that emerge from the above-mentioned gender order. Because not everyone is able to adequately differentiate between imagination and external reality, confusion and unacceptable behavior is bound to result.

The circumstances surrounding the lived roles and behavior of men and women within dancehall culture are by no means as simple and clear-cut as the lyrics imply. With her book, Hope presents a fascinating kaleidoscope of roles and nuances in the context of sexuality and violence. Although they are related to the gender hierarchy, they are more complex than what is found in music lyrics and videos: 'independent ooman', 'matie', 'skettel', 'babymother', 'browning queen' and 'slack, black queen' are just some sounding examples of diverse female roles that can be found in this scene.

While it might not be a good idea to play the above-quoted songs without reflection in Europe, if we Europeans believe that we should be outraged, intervene, enlighten, regulate, or even sanction in the name of justice, we are hypocritically ignoring the fact that sexism is not uncommon in our (electronic) music scenes. We also deliberately overlook the fact that our own culture is the starting point for the gender order seen in dancehall culture. Our interventions threaten to end up as cultural imperialism that reveals how little we have learned from the past 200 years of history.

Aus der Perspektive des europäischen Westens geben die Themen Sexualität und Geschlecht in der gegenwärtigen Dancehall-Kultur immer wieder Anlass zu Kopfschütteln. Die Beobachtung von forcierter Männlichkeit, Frauenverachtung, Homophobie und Gewalt haben zu vollkommenem Unverständnis, scharfen Verurteilungen, mitunter sogar Konzertverboten geführt. Diese Reaktionen sind nachvollziehbar und doch erstaunt es, wie häufig sie von einer unreflektierten Selbstgerechtigkeit geprägt sind. Donna P. Hope hat bereits 2006 in ihrem Buch *Inna di Dancehall. Popular Culture and the Politics of Identity in Jamaica* eine lehrreiche Beschreibung der Situation vorgelegt.

Bereits vor und auch nach Hopes Buch wurde viel zu diesem Thema geschrieben, doch *Inna di Dancehall* sticht heraus, weil die Autorin persönlich involviert und nahe am Thema ist. Ihr Buch ist die vorläufige Ankunft nach einer Reise nicht nur über die Tanzfläche sondern auch durch die jamaikanische Gesellschaft: von der Dancehall-Anhängerin zur Dancehall-Forscherin und aus der ländlichen Arbeiterklasse in die sozialen Brennpunkte der Grosstadt. Sie beobachtet genau, schreibt anschaulich, theoretisiert zurückhaltend und verzichtet aufs Politisieren und (Ver-)Urteilen. Das sind Qualitäten, die anderen, stärker akademisch ausgerichteten Publikationen in diesem Feld leider häufig abgehen, besonders wenn sie Sexismus- und Rassismus-Vorwürfe erheben und diese mittels ausgreifenden theoretischen Erörterungen zu belegen versuchen.

Im Kapitel zu Geschlecht und Sexualität von *Inna di Dancehall* postuliert Hope eine Hierarchie der Haut im Kontext von Rasse, Klasse und Geschlecht: Zuoberst befindet sich der weisse Mann, gefolgt von der weissen Frau. Dann kommen der farbige Mann und die farbige Frau; schliesslich der schwarze Mann und ganz zuunterst die schwarze Frau. Diese Rangfolge hat historische Wurzeln in Kolonialismus und Sklaverei, die—ausgehend von Europa—in ausgeprägten patriarchalischen Strukturen eingebettet waren. Daraus folgert Hope, dass die Geschlechterordnung innerhalb der Dancehall-Kultur nicht zufällig zu Sexismus und Heteronormativität neigt, in denen biologisches Geschlecht, Geschlechtsidentität und Geschlechtsrollen einheitlich entweder als überlegen männlich oder als unterlegen weiblich gezeichnet werden und die ‹natürliche›, einzig akzeptierte und als gesund betrachtete Form von sexuellem Verkehr heterosexuell sein muss. Sie zeigt zudem, dass insbesondere die weiblichen Schönheitsideale eng auf Europa bezogen sind: Beispielsweise im Versuch von Angleichungen des Aussehens mit Hilfe des Glättens der Haare oder des mithin gesundheitsschädigenden Bleichens der Haut. Es gibt allerdings auch Gegenbilder wie das Ideal weiblicher Fettleibigkeit, der mitunter mit Hormonpillen nachgeholfen wird.

Diese Verhältnisse spiegeln sich in vielen Songtexten und auch Musikvideos mehr oder weniger verschlüsselt wieder. Shabba Ranks beispielsweise singt in Love Punaany Bad (1998): «...love punaany bad, / mi a punaany guineagog» (I love vaginas very much, / I am a vagina master). Das Geschlechtsorgan steht für die ganze weibliche Person, die zwar hochgeschätzt, aber freilich auch bemächtigt werden muss. Dieser männlichen Perspektive stehen Formulierungen von Frauen gegenüber, die zeigen, wie dieses reduktive, binäre Denken von beiden Seiten her mit Stereotypen und Fantasien bedient wird. Tanya Stephens etwa singt in Boom Wuk (2004): «It's all about the sex / Mi jus love off you boom wuk / Love the way you have mi pum pum stuck / ... / Love the long ding dong» (It's all about the sex / I just love how you fuck / I love the way you're stuck in my vagina / ... / I love the long penis). Nicht nur die Länge des Penis entscheidet über die Qualität des Geschlechtsverkehrs, sondern auch das Ausmass der eingesetzten Gewalt. So singt Spice im Duett Ramping Shop (2009) mit Vybz Kartel: «Well you haffi ram it hard (...) kill mi wid di cocky» (Well you have to push hard (...) kill me with your penis). Popcaan schliesslich eliminiert das weibliche Subjekt fast ganz, wenn er in Addicted (2017) singt: «Gyal, me nuh waah fight everyday a di week / Me know you waah me / And you tight fat pum pum a fight fi me see it» (Girl, I don't want to fight every day of the week / I know you want me / And your tight fat vagina will fight so that I get to see it).

Long Ding Dong versus Pum Pum: Diese Texte skizzieren das Bild eines Geschlechterkampfs aus welchem Phänomene wie Frauenverachtung, Gewalt und Homophobie hochproblematische, psychodynamisch unvermeidliche Folgen sind. Aufgrund der Tendenz der Dancehall-Kultur, zentrale Themen des Alltags nicht nur beim Namen zu nennen, sondern auch zu überspitzen, schlagen sie sich in der umstrittenen ‹slackness›, dem ‹rudebwoy› sowie homophoben ‹batty› Tunes nieder. Doch bilden diese Worte die äusseren Verhältnisse und die Verhaltensweisen ab? Nein. Zuallererst sind sie Kunstprodukte und als solche ein Abbild der (unbewussten) Fantasien, die aus der beschriebenen Geschlechterordnung hervorgehen. Weil nicht alle Menschen Vorstellung und äussere Wirklichkeit adäquat auseinander halten können, muss es natürlich auch zu Konfusionen und inakzeptablem Verhalten kommen.

Was aber die tatsächlichen, gelebten Rollen und Verhaltensmuster der Männer und Frauen innerhalb der Dancehall-Kultur angeht, sind die Verhältnisse keineswegs so simpel und eindeutig, wie es uns die Songtexte oft suggerieren. Hope jedenfalls arbeitet ein faszinierendes Kaleidoskop von Rollen und Abstufungen im Kontext von Sexualität und Gewalt heraus. Sie sind zwar auf die skizzierte Geschlechterordnung bezogen, doch komplexer als es die Texte und Videos darstellen: ‹independent ooman›, ‹matie›, ‹skettel›, ‹babymother›, ‹browning queen› und ‹slack, black queen› sind beispielsweise die klingenden Namen unterschiedlicher weiblicher Rollen in dieser Szene.

Es ist gewiss keine gute Idee, die zitierten Songs in Europa unreflektiert auf die Bühne zu bringen. Doch wenn wir Europäer glauben, im Namen der Gerechtigkeit entrüstet aufschreien, einschreiten, aufklären, regulieren oder gar sanktionieren zu müssen, übergehen wir erstens scheinheilig, dass Sexismus auch in unseren Szenen der elektronischen Musik keine Seltenheit ist. Zweitens übersehen wir geflissentlich, dass unsere eigene Kultur den Ausgangspunkt für die beschriebene Geschlechterordnung im Dancehall bildet. Unsere Interventionen drohen in einen kulturellen Imperialismus zu münden, der offenlegt, wie wenig wir aus der Geschichte der letzten zweihundert Jahre gelernt haben.

IMPORTANT THINGS AND OTHER THINGS
PETER REHBERG

Interview:
Guy Schwegler
Photography:
Georg Gatsas

Editions Mego (und dessen Vorgänger Mego) ist eines der langjährigsten und zentralsten Labels für experimentelle Musik. Schon seit beinahe zwei Jahrzehnten veröffentlicht der in Wien ansässige Betrieb ohne Unterbruch und verteilt über die unter seinem Dach vereinten Sublabels—Ideologic Organ, Recollection GRM, Spectrum Spools, usw.— das Who is who der Szene wie etwa Jung An Tagen, Klara Lewis, Felix Kubin, Stephen O'Malley, Beatriz Ferreyra oder Second Woman. Ob es sich bei diesem Unterfangen um eine ausgefuchste kuratorische Strategie, reines Liebhabertum oder eine Arbeit fürs Archiv handelt, ist dabei letztlich nicht ganz klar—angesichts der Qualität der Veröffentlichungen allerdings wohl auch nicht weiter wichtig.

Anfang Jahr erschien auf Editions Mego auch ein neues, gemeinsames Werk von Label-Betreiber Peter Rehberg und Nik Void—unter anderem Mitglied der Post-Industrial-Band Factory Floor. Unter dem Pseudonym NPVR präsentiert das Duo fünf abstrakte, skizzenhafte Stücke Computermusik. Im Anschluss an die Veröffentlichung der Platte unterhielt sich Guy Schwegler via Skype mit Rehberg—über Nebensächlichkeiten und das, was eigentlich wirklich spannend und wichtig ist.

Editions Mego and its precursor, Mego, is one of the longest-standing and most prominent labels for experimental music. For almost two decades and with next to no interruption, the Vienna-based organization has been releasing the who's who of the scene—recently Jung An Tagen, Klara Lewis, Felix Kubin, Stephen O'Malley, Beatriz Ferreyra, Second Woman—under the Mego banner and its various sublabels: Ideologic Organ, Recollection GRM, Spectrum Spools, etc. It's unclear whether this undertaking has a closely-followed curatorial strategy, pure enthusiastic hobbyism, or an interest in archival research to thank—but in light of the quality of releases, this is perhaps not all that important.

At the beginning of this year, Editions Mego released a collaborative work between label operator Peter Rehberg and Nik Void, who among other things is a member of the post-industrial band Factory Floor. On the release, the duo, which goes by the moniker NPVR, presented five rough, abstract pieces of computer music. On the occasion of the record's release, Guy Schwegler spoke with Rehberg via Skype about important topics and side topics.

Guy Schwegler: Während ich mich sehr auf dieses Interview gefreut habe, bin ich in meinen Vorbereitungen gleichzeitig auf ein Problem gestossen: Du hast schon so viele Interviews gegeben und bereits viele interessante Fragen beantwortet. Ich wusste also zuerst nicht so recht, über was ich mit dir sprechen soll. Daher als Eröffnungsfrage: Wie schaffst du es, dass die Dinge interessant und spannend bleiben?

Peter Rehberg: Schaffe ich das überhaupt? Ich bin mir da nicht wirklich sicher, stehe aber auch nicht am Morgen mit dem Ziel auf, dass alles interessant bleibt. Mich treibt vor allem an, dass es weiterhin genügend zu tun gibt: Das Label und die dazugehörigen Unterkataloge, meine eigene Musik, andere Produktionen—mir wird also nicht langweilig. Langeweile wäre ein Problem. Jeweils sind auch bereits zehn bis fünfzehn Veröffentlichungen geplant. Das Ganze ist tatsächlich ein Job für mich—oder zumindest schon lange kein Hobby mehr. Ob es immer noch interessant ist, müssen dann andere entscheiden. Und spannend? Das ist ja subjektiv, aber ich glaube, es gibt immer noch interessierte Leute, Likes in den sozialen Medien, Konzertbesucherinnen, Interviews werden geführt... Aber wie spannend ist spannend auf einer Skala von eins bis zehn? Fünf, sechs, sieben oder eins? Für mich ist es jedenfalls weiterhin spannend. Zum Beispiel hätte ich mir vor einem Jahr nicht vorstellen können, dass ich eine Platte mit Nik Void machen würde!

GS: In einem Interview habe ich gelesen, dass du mal Ambient DJ warst[1]. Mir gefällt diese Idee sehr gut: Lounge Musik, irgendwie im Hintergrund... Und überhaupt nicht spannend per se.
PR: Ja, irgendwie war ich Ambient DJ und ich glaube, das bin ich immer noch. Bevor Mego entstanden ist, war ich in der lokalen ‹Techno›-Szene involviert. Und ich war eben derjenige, der auf dem zweiten Floor gespielt hat—im Chillout-Raum oder was auch immer. Da spielte ich Sachen, zu denen man nicht unbedingt tanzen konnte, die aber trotzdem elektronischer Natur waren. Ich wollte aber gleichzeitig das Ganze auch etwas weiter pushen mit Industrial, Elektroakustik und mehr. Denn was mich an Techno schon immer etwas gestört hat, war, dass sich das Genre als diese Revolution präsentierte. «Vor Techno gab es keine Musik—und plötzlich war da Techno!» *Bullshit*, es gibt keine Revolutionen in der Musik. Es gab immer etwas, was vorher da war. Bei Techno ist es eine Mischung zwischen Disco und Industrial Musik. Und damals an diesen Techno-Partys sind Leute zu mir gekommen und meinten: «Oh, du bist auch hier.» Und ich dann: «Ja, wieso auch nicht.» «Ich wusste nicht, dass du auch auf Techno stehst.» Aber ich fand das ja toll! Und so hat auch Mego angefangen, denn Ramon Bauer und Andreas Pieper, meine beiden Partner, hatten zuvor ein Label namens Mainframe, das richtig Techno-Techno war. Davon hatten sie dann irgendwann genug und damit kam ein Interesse an experimenteller Musik auf.

GS: Das Witzige an einem Ambient DJ ist ja, dass es so jemanden eigentlich gar nicht braucht... PR: Ja, es könnte auch einfach eine Playlist sein, oder ein Algorithmus, der einen zufälligen Patch spielt.

GS: Ja, oder eine CD mit ein paar netten Ambient-Stücken... PR: Aber dann braucht man auch keine Techno DJs.

GS: Da gibt es zumindest noch diese Vorstellung von der Interaktion mit den Tanzenden. PR: Naja, wenn du ein Jeff Mills-Set aufnehmen und es am drauffolgenden Abend abspielen würdest, wäre das den Leuten doch nicht bewusst. Techno Sets sind fix bis zu einem bestimmten Grad; es gibt einen Aufbau, Break, Höhepunkt, usw. Und wirkliche DJs sind die meisten eh nicht mehr, man spielt mit Ableton oder so. Das ist ja auch völlig okay, hat aber nichts mehr mit dem Wort zu tun. Man könnte auch einfach auf die Starttaste eines Octatrack oder ähnlichem drücken... Aber mit dieser Idee, dass Musik live sein muss, bin ich sowieso nie wirklich warm geworden. Wenn ein DJ, eine Musikerin oder wer auch immer ein Instrument spielt und dies live tut, ist das ja toll. Aber: Es geht auch um die Tatsache, dass sie an einem bestimmten Ort sind, mit anderen Leuten und denen ihr Werk präsentieren. Noch problematischer als diese Vorstellung von Live-Musik ist die Haltung von sogenannten echten Musikern, die dann Dinge sagen wie: «Ohh, Drumcomputer machen das Handwerk der Schlagzeuger kaputt». Aber das ist Quatsch, ein Drumcomputer mag vielleicht eine bestimmte Tonalität, einen bestimmten Rhythmus haben, der von einer echten Schlagzeugerin zwar nicht reproduziert werden kann–aber wieso sollte das auch jemand tun! Es braucht beides; die jeweilige Form des Ausdrucks zählt. Und einen Drumcomputer zu benützen heisst ja auch nicht einfach Start zu drücken. Direkt aus der Box machen die nichts anderes als *tack-tack-tack-tack*... Klingt vielleicht gut, ist aber langweilig! Man muss das Programmieren würdigen.

GS: Aber die entsprechenden Leute fühlten sich vielleicht nicht mehr wichtig aufgrund der Konkurrenz durch die Maschine... PR: Ja, das passiert–wie wohl bei der Weiterentwicklung von Technik generell. Heute kann auch jede und jeder einfach seine Meinung über irgendwelche sozialen Medien verbreiten, die zuvor den Filter der Zeitungen, Bücher oder ähnliches hätte passieren müssen. Heute ist es kein Problem, eine Schriftstellerin zu sein oder...

GS: ...ein Label zu führen? PR: Ja, oder ein Label zu führen. In den goldenen Zeiten des Musikgeschäfts war ein Label ein grosses *Business*. Sie waren die einzigen, die Platten pressen konnten. Heute kann das jemand anderes für dich machen. Oder du veröffentlichst Musik nur via Bandcamp (oder einer sonstigen digitalen Plattform): ein PayPal Account und Benutzername–fertig ist dein Label.

GS: Mego–und auch Editions Mego–werden als sehr einflussreiche und wichtige Labels porträtiert. Ich würde dem auch 100% zustimmen. Ich habe mich allerdings gefragt, ob du dich mal mit dem Label oder bestimmten Veröffentlichungen richtig unwichtig und einfach nicht relevant gefühlt hast. PR: Ich fühle mich immer ein wenig unwichtig– aber das ist doch die Natur des Menschen! Aber was ist schon wichtig, was ist relevant heutzutage? Platten verkaufen sich mal besser, mal schlechter–das liegt nicht in deiner Hand. Das wird von der Meinung und einem Geschmack der Öffentlichkeit entschieden. Aber ich denke schon, dass wir uns mit Mego ein bisschen Respekt verdient haben. Wiederum andere werden sich wohl denken: «Nicht schon wieder ne Platte von denen!» Der Markt hat sich auch extrem gewandelt in den letzten zehn bis zwanzig Jahren. Heutzutage ist es extrem wichtig, wie man sich online präsentiert. Mehr Einnahmen kommen via Bandcamp und anderen digitalen Verkäufen als durch physische. Das ist nun seit fünf Jahren bereits Realität. Und viele hören sich die Veröffentlichungen über Streaming-Dienste an. Ich glaube, den Leuten gefällt weiterhin was wir veröffentlichen, aber als Label hat man nicht mehr dieses physische Urteil. Früher hattest du eine riesen Kiste mit Platten und am nächsten Tag waren da keine mehr. Das war dann ein Zeichen dafür, dass ein Release sehr gut läuft. Heute bekommt man eine Übersicht von seinem Distributor für die digitalen Files und... «Ohh, es läuft ziemlich gut.» Es ist viel abstrakter.

GS: Relevanz war also früher einfacher zu bestimmen? PR: Ja, weil du hattest

GS I was excited to do this interview, but then I encountered a little problem: you've already done so many interviews and I don't really know what to ask you that hasn't already been asked. Maybe to start with: how do you keep things interesting and exciting after all this time?

PR Do I keep it interesting? I'm not sure... I mean, I don't wake up and go, "oh, I want to keep it interesting." I just wake up and carry on. Whether it's interesting or not is for other people to decide. But, I mean, the main thing keeping me going is that there's lots of work to do. And there are so many things: the label and its sublabels, the music, other productions—so I don't get bored. If I started getting bored then I'd start to worry. In terms of releases, there are always ten or fifteen records planned at least, per year. For me it's a job—it stopped being a hobby years ago. And exciting, well, yes—but what's exciting? It's kind of subjective. I guess there are still people who buy the records—not as many as there used to be, but there are people who are interested, who "like" things on social media, come to the concerts, do interviews. How exciting is exciting on a scale of 1 to 10? 5, 6, 7, or 1? But I think it's still exciting, at least. And it's always interesting. For example, a year ago, I'd have never known that I'd make a record with Nik Void!

GS I read in another interview that you used to be an ambient DJ.[1] I really like the idea of an ambient DJ, also like a lounge DJ. Someone who's somewhat in the background—not really exciting or important.

PR: Kind of, and I still am. Before we started Mego in the mid-90s, I was involved in the local "techno" scene. And I'd always be the one on the second floor, the chill-out room or whatever you call it, playing stuff that wasn't necessarily made to dance to, but still electronic in nature. And I played stuff from that era, like electronic ambient techno, but also other favorites—industrial and electroacoustic records. I wanted to push the genre a bit further. You know, the thing about techno I found a bit weird in general is that it presented itself as some kind of revolution—"Before techno there was no music. Suddenly there was techno music." Bullshit—there's no such thing as a revolution in music. There's always something that came before. Techno is basically a mixture of disco and industrial music. I remember people would come up to me at techno parties in the early 90s and say, "oh, you're here as well." And I'd said, "Well, why not?" And they'd be like, "I didn't know you're into techno." But I was into it! And that's kind of how Mego started. Because the other two guys I did it with, Ramon and Andy, they were running a label called Mainframe which was more techno-techno. And that kind of fell apart when they became fed up with techno. They got more interested in experimental music and Mego started coming together.

GS What I think is funny about an ambient DJ is that there is no real need for one.

PR Yes—it could just be a playlist. Or you set an algorithm playing a random patch.

GS Or just CDs with some nice ambient tracks on them.

PR Well, you could also say you don't need techno DJs.

GS But there's this myth of crowd interaction and whatever.

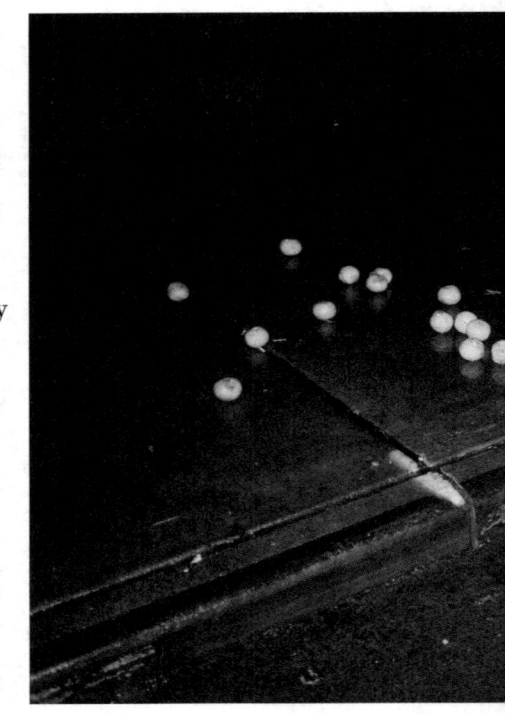

PR Well, if you record a Jeff Mills set one night and play it the next night, it's fixed! Techno sets are fixed, to a certain degree—there's a build-up, there's a breakdown. People wouldn't notice! And now some people don't even "DJ"—they play Ableton. That's fine, but it's not really "jocking the discs," is it? You could also get an Octatrack sampler and just press play. But yeah... That's another thing I never really got into, the idea that it has to be live music. DJs or musicians or anything, okay, they play an instrument, and doing it live is great. But it's also the fact that they're actually there in the place with other people presenting their work. And I was never really a fan of these so-called real musicians who

say things like "Drum machines are going destroy drummers." Well, not really—the drum machine has a certain tonality and a certain kind of rhythm that of course a real person couldn't have—but why would she want that? There's a need for both! It's just another form of expression. And the idea that a drum machine is easy because you just have to press play... you still have to program it and tell it what to do. If you take it out of a box, it just goes *tack-tack-tack-tack*... boring! It sounds good, but program it! That's the skill that needs to be recognized.

GS But what happens if you don't feel important anymore? As a drummer, for example...

PR Yeah, that happens with the advancement of technology in general. Nowadays everyone can blast out their opinions on social media, whereas before someone's opinion had to go through a filter, like media, newspaper, books. Now everyone can be a writer or...

GS A label-owner?

PR Yeah, or a label-owner. In the golden days of the music industry, doing a label was a big business. In the old days, a label was a label because it could press the records. Nowadays you get someone else to do it. If you want to do a Bandcamp label (or some other digital-only label), you can do anything! You just need a PayPal account and a user name. There you go—there's the label!

GS Mego—and Editions Mego—have always been portrayed as important labels. And I'd agree with that 100%. But I was wondering: have you ever felt that your releases or related projects are unimportant or irrelevant?

PR I always feel a bit unimportant—that's human nature! But what *is* important these days? And what's relevant? Some records don't sell as much as others, but that's something I can't really decide. It's public opinion, public taste. But we do have a kind of image or respect from some people, I guess. Others may think, "Oh no, not another record!" The marketplace has definitely changed over the last ten, twenty years. Nowadays it's all about how you present yourself on the internet. More revenues are coming from Bandcamp and digital sales than from physical sales. That's been going on for the past five years. Most people are listening to it by streaming, and they still enjoy it, but as a label you don't get that physicality of one day having a big box of records and the next day having none. That was a symbol of things going well. Now you get a statement from your digital distributer once a month and you go, "Oh, it went quite well." It's more abstract.

GS So relevance was easier to judge in the old days?

PR Yes, because you saw that physicality! Now it's hard to say. You post stuff on Twitter and Facebook and everyone likes it. But do they like it? Or do they just like the idea that you posted the thing?

GS What are and were other ways of determining a release's relevance?

PR Well, I buy lots of records. Most of them I listen to once or twice, but there are a few records I listen to ten times... or fifty times! For me, something is relevant when someone enjoys listening to it. But of course, with experimental music, you don't listen to certain extreme records when you're doing things—they need a different mindset. In the old days—like the really, really old days, before the internet—people bought records because it was the only way to hear music. Now you can turn on your computer and listen to anything you want. It's maybe not a different value, but... the whole business side of running a label is based on selling records. That's what we do, what makes it worth it. Of course I could do digital-only and not any physical records, but I would find that very boring.

GS Coming back to the issue of relevance in relation to how many people listen to or buy a record: why do a *Groupe De*

die man hören konnte und auch heute noch kann. Sie haben diese seltsamen Geräusche und speziellen Syntheseverfahren genutzt, um wirklich neue Musik zu produzieren. Stockhausen wäre ein anderes gutes Beispiel: Auch er hatte unglaublich viel Equipment in seinem Studio, das er teilweise selber aufgebaut hat. Ich glaube allerdings nicht, dass er per se daran interessiert war. Von all seinen Kompositionen haben wohl nur fünf wirklich elektronische Elemente drin.

GS: Wenn wir gerade über Technologie sprechen: Kurz vor der Jahrtausendwende wurdest du und einige andere Leute aus dem Mego-Umfeld prominent durch eure Verwendung des Laptops in Live-Performances und einige gingen so weit, euch als Laptop-Musiker[5] zu bezeichnen. Heute verwendest du live einen Modular-Synthesizer—der Laptop spielt wohl keine so zentrale Rolle mehr. Ich habe mich allerdings gefragt, ob die Verwendung des Laptops irgendwann mal ein Statement war für dich? PR: Es war weder zu Beginn noch sonst irgendwann ein Statement, sondern einfach eine Entwicklung. Wir haben damals unsere Musik noch im Studio gemacht und—klassisch—Synthesizer, Sampler, Mischpult, etc. verwendet. Als es dann ums Live-Spielen ging, wurde das zum logistischen Alptraum mit Kisten und Racks voll Sampler, Keyboards, usw. Langsam aber sicher wurden zu der Zeit Laptops immer leistungsfähiger und man konnte—mit einigen Kompromissen—auch live damit davonkommen. Das war es, was uns daran interessiert hat. Dann wurde das aber Laptop-Musik genannt—oder sogar noch dümmer ‹Laptronica›. Dass an dem Begriff so vieles aufgemacht wurde, befremdete uns ein wenig. In den 2000er Jahren ging das dann weiter mit sehr vielen Gigs, wo ich auftauchte, den Laptop öffnete, meinen Lärm spielte und wieder stoppte. Davon hatte ich ein wenig die Nase voll und 2009 hörte ich auf, live zu spielen; ich fokussierte wieder mehr auf das Label und meine Arbeiten im Theater. Ein, zwei Jahre später begann ich wieder Hardware zu verwenden, Synths anzuhäufen und auch Modular-Systeme zu verwenden. Dabei realisierte ich, dass ich dieselben Dinge auf dem Hardware-Netzwerk wie auf dem Laptop mache—auch vorher habe ich Patches verwendet in Programmen wie SuperCollider und Max MSP. Jetzt mache ich das einfach auf einer physischen Maschine—und das ist sogar noch besser; ohne mühsame digitale Interfaces. Vielleicht ist die Idee, Kabel umzustecken etwas retro, aber sonst sind sehr viele der Module hochentwickelt und selten analog. Old-school Synthese wird mit Computertechnologie und digitaler Signal-Verarbeitung (DSP) verbunden.

GS: Heute macht man also Computermusik mit Hardware? PR: Ja, das ist in etwa das, was passiert ist. Es ist ja auch dasselbe: Klangquelle und Synthese, Mischen und Editieren. In den Bauklötzen der elektronischen Musik hat sich nichts geändert.

GS: Eine Unterscheidung, die auch nicht mehr so aktuell scheint, ist diejenige zwischen akademischer und populärer Musik. In älteren Interviews hast du noch sehr darauf beharrt, kein akademischer Musiker zu sein. PR: Aber mir gefällt viel akademische Musik?

GS: Ja, und du hast im akademischen Bereich gearbeitet. Ist diese Unterscheidung also nicht mehr wichtig? PR: Viele Leute benötigen einen akademischen Diskurs wenn es um extreme, experimentelle oder spezielle Musik geht. Ich empfand das aber nie als nötig. Mit dem Glück, in den achtziger Jahren aufzuwachsen, ging auch einher, dass ich über Mainstream-Kanäle Zugang zu experimentellen Industrial- und Noise-Platten fand. Zu NON fand man durch Depeche Mode; via Soft Cell zu Throbbing Gristle und Psychic TV. Diese speziellere Musik war immer eine Erwei-

Recherches Musicales (Recollection GRM)[2] reissue series, then? I'd guess not so many people listened to those recordings before you reissued them, so why do you think they're relevant?

PR Yeah, because they couldn't—they weren't really available.[3] Since we started this series with Stephen [O'Malley]'s artwork and the uniform covers and stuff, the records have sold really well. It's even some of the bestselling stuff these days. Because no one's really heard it. GRM is legendary. I remember first hearing about GRM in the early 80s, but you could never really get the records. The people buying our reissues are a mixture of people my age who are interested in finally getting a vinyl version of these works and young people just getting into it. So I think it's relevant, I think it's important. But you're also right—it's electro-acoustic avant-garde music that has a very small subject area. However, it's quality and there's so much in that field that's actually rubbish, but this is the good stuff. This is the main reason why we did it.

GS I've always wondered why Pierre Schaeffer and the GRM get so much attention in the experimental music field while Pierre Boulez and the *Institut de Recherche et Coordination Acoustique/Musique (IRCAM)*[4] get almost none.

PR Forgive me if I spread some bad news here, because the French are very delicate about this, but I've always seen GRM as more creative. The interesting thing about GRM is that Schaeffer, who wasn't a musician—he was an engineer— really thought in terms of new music. They invented a kind of language. Their works were artistically more interesting and experimental, whereas IRCAM used to and still does concentrate on the actual technology, the hardware. They research the technological advancement of music and audio. This is where you want to go if you want to do something with incredibly complex recording techniques and things like this. IRCAM, like most other electronic music studios in the 50s, 60s and 70s, had those studios and played around just to see what happened, without making music. Like the BBC radiophonic workshop—all they actually did was make sound effects and funny noises for science fiction films: *"beep-beep-bup-pffff."* It's great that they did, but you don't have to listen to it. The GRM stuff, though, is music you can still listen to now. They actually took it from being a bunch of funny noises and some weird synthesis equations into music. Stockhausen is another good example of this. He had access to all this studio equipment and helped build it, but I don't think he was very interested in it, per se. Of all Stockhausen's works, only around five have actual electronics on them.

GS Speaking of technology: shortly before the millennium, you and your Mego colleagues became known for your use of laptops in live performances. You were even sometimes referred to as "laptop musicians."[5] And today you perform using modular synthesizers, so laptops no longer seem to play such an important role for you. But I wondered: was using a laptop ever a statement for you?

PR It was never a statement to use a laptop in the first place. It was just a development. Our music was still made in the studio, with synths, samplers, and mixing desks. But then came the object of playing that live. And our first live gigs were like a nightmare, with big cases of racks, samplers and keyboards. Slowly, laptops started to be a bit more advanced. You had to make a few compromises, but you could kind of get away with performing with them. It was interesting from that point of view. And the media started calling it laptop music or stupid terms like "laptronica." We thought it was a bit strange that people would make this big fuss about laptops. And things bumbled on and I kind of got fed up with doing lots of gigs in the 2000s, opening my laptop, playing my noise, stopping again. So I stopped in 2009 and just did label and theater stuff. Slowly I got into using hardware again around eight years ago. I started adding more things, more synths, got into modular a bit later on. And I realized

terung von Popmusik. Ich höre mir eine Russell Haswell[6]-Platte an und mag sie—das hat allerdings nichts mit einem intellektuellen Diskurs zu tun. Trotz meiner Arbeit in diesem Bereich und den Platten, die ich veröffentliche, habe ich nie wirklich den persönlichen Zugang dazu gefunden. Oft ist es so, das Leute aus dem Umfeld sehr darin sind, extreme Musik zu erklären—zuhause dann aber wieder ABBA hören. Ich selber sehe irgendwie keinen Unterschied dazwischen. Mir gefällt populäre und akademische Musik. Problematisch ist hingegen immer der Snobismus—egal auf welcher Seite. Dieser ist aber insbesondere in der Neuen Musik zu finden ist. «Ohh, ich war an diesem und jenem Konservatorium, bla-blabla; und wir werden vom Staat finanziert weil wir Genies sind.» Ach, hau doch ab, das interessiert mich nicht und deine Musik ist langweilig! Mir muss niemand erklären, was gut und was schlecht ist.

GS: Und wie sieht es mit der umgekehrten Richtung aus? Denkst du, dass Mego bzw. Editions Mego einen Einfluss auf Popmusik hatte? PR: Was ich weiss, ist, dass auf dem letzten Björk Album ein Sample von der *Sacred Flute Music From New Guinea*-Compilation drauf war. Irgendjemand in Björks Studio hat also eine Platte, die wir veröffentlicht haben. Grundsätzlich ist unsere Musik erhältlich, wenn dass nun jemanden beeinflusst hätte Musik zu machen—egal ob Pop oder Akademisches—toll! Wenn nicht, auch toll.

GS: Siehst du denn Editions Mego auch zwischen diesen beiden Polen von populärer und akademischer Musik? PR: Ja, schon irgendwie. Denn wenn ich Leute aus dem akademischen Umfeld treffe, dann denken die, wir sind ein Pop-Label. Und diejenigen, die sich eher im Mainstream verorten, denken wir seien ein akademisches Avantgarde-Energiezentrum. Es ist schön, dazwischen zu sein—und dadurch auch etwas unberechenbar! Gleichzeitig haben einige immer noch das Gefühl, wir veröffentlichen Laptop-Musik.

GS: Was sind relevante (oder auch irrelevante) Aspekte, die ihr mit dem Label in sozialer Hinsicht erreicht habt? Denkst du, Editons Mego ist auch ein Projekt für eine bestimmte Gemeinschaft? PR: Ja, aber es ist etwas abstrakter. Das Label ist ja in Wien ansässig, aber ich denke uns kennen etwa sechs Leute hier in der Stadt. Aber es gibt überall auf der Welt Personen, die ähnliche Dinge machen. Und für dieses Netzwerk mache ich insbesondere gerne Label-Showcases. Da kommen Künstlerinnen aus den verschiedensten Bereichen zusammen, verschiedene Szenen—und es tut immer gut, die einander vorzustellen. Das ist interessant! Aber in gesellschaftlicher Hinsicht sind wir doch nur ein kleiner Fleck in diesem massiven, urbanen Leben. Ich hoffe zumindest, dass wir für diejenigen, die sich mit Musik auseinandersetzen und leidenschaftlich gute Musik hören, etwas bedeuten. Aber der Durchschnittsbürger hat keine Ahnung, was wir machen.

GS: Stört dich das?
PR: Überhaupt nicht!

GS that what I do on a modular synthesizer network is the same as what I was doing on my laptop. I had already been using patches, like Supercollider and Max MSP, and now I'm doing it on a physical machine. Maybe the idea of plugging things in with cables is a bit retro, but lots of the modules are very, very advanced. They take a bit of old-school synthesis, a bit of computer technology/digital signal processing (DSP), and just blur them together into something new.

GS And now you can do computer music with hardware gear.

PR Yes, that's basically what happened. It's the same thing—it's still source-sound or synthesis, processing, mixing, and editing. Nothing has really changed in the building blocks of electronic music.

GS Another theme that seems to have lost a bit of its importance is the difference between academic and pop music. In older interviews, you were quite specific about stating that you're not academic.

PR But I like a lot of academic music, you're suggesting?

GS Yes, and you've worked in academia, haven't you? Has this differentiation become unimportant?

PR Many people seem to feel that there needs to be some kind of academic discourse when music is extreme, experimental, and weird. But I've never really felt the need for that. I was lucky enough to grow up in the early 80s, and a lot of the weird and experimental industrial and noise records I got into I found through mainstream channels. You got into NON because you listened to Depeche Mode, or via Soft Cell you got into Throbbing Gristle or Psychic TV. So for me all this weird electronic music is just an extension of pop music. I always felt that way. I can listen to a Russell Haswell[6] record and I can like it or not like it, but the reason for that has nothing to do with an intellectual discourse. I always felt that academia was used as an excuse for music for being difficult—but you shouldn't have to make an excuse. So even though I work in an academic field with the records I release, I never really got into it. A lot of people who work in academia are really good at explaining bits of extreme music during the day, and then at home they go listen to something like ABBA. But I never saw big differences between the two. I like a lot of popular music and I like a lot of academic music. But what I don't like on both sides—especially on the academic side—is the snobbery around it all. I see it a lot in new music circles "We went to this fucking conservatory, blablabla, and we get all this funding from the government because we're geniuses." It's like... "Go away! So what? Couldn't care less. Your music is boring!" I listen to a lot of music, and I've been doing it for 40 years. I don't need some academic to tell me what's good or bad.

GS And what about the other direction? Do you think the music you have made or released with Mego/Editions Mego has made an impact on pop music?

PR Maybe? I know that on the last Björk album there was a sample of the *Sacred Flute Music From New Guinea* compilation. Someone in Björk's studio had a record we put out. Our records are available, but I don't know if they directly influence—I can't really tell. If they influence people to make music, be it pop or academic, then great. If not, also great!

GS And do you see Editions Mego as standing in between the poles of academia and pop?

PR Yes, kind of. When I meet people from academia, they think we're a pop label. And when I meet people from more mainstream channels, they think we're some kind of academic avant-garde powerhouse. It's good to be in between. I've always preferred things to be more open—not random, but surprising. You never know what's coming next! Some still think we're putting out laptop music!

GS What seems relevant (or irrelevant) to you in terms of the social things you've achieved? Do think of Editions Mego as a social project?

References

1 See also Rehberg, Peter. 2014. Editions Mego's Peter Rehberg on His Leading Experimental Electronic Label. Red Bull Music Academy. http://daily.redbullmusicacademy.com/2014/06/editions-mego-feature, accessed 15.04.18.

2 The Groupe de Recherche Musicales was founded in the late 1950s by Pierre Schaeffer in conjunction with the development of what he termed "Musique Concrète." The group and associated studios, which belonged to the Office de Radiodiffusion Télévision Française, worked both theoretically and practically on the evolution of electroacoustic music. The GRM is still active today. For more details about the Recollection GRM, see: Sande, Kiran. 2012. *Peter Rehberg on raiding the GRM archive and starting another Editions Mego sublabel.* FACT Magazine. http://www.factmag.com/2012/03/29/peter-rehberg-on-raiding-the-grm-archive-and-starting-another-editions-mego-sub-label/, accessed 15.04.18.

3 Original vinyl output of music by the GRM was and is extremely expensive; some GRM CDs were available, but through different channels.

4 The Institut de Recherche et Coordination Acoustique / Musique, based at the Centre Pompidou in Paris, was and is also dedicated to the study of electronic and electroacoustic music. As an organization long overseen by Pierre Boulez, the IRCAM's musical practice has focused particularly on serialism. See also Born, Georgina. 1995. *Rational music: IRCAM, Boulez, and the Institutionalisation of the Avant-garde.* Berkeley: University of California Press.

5 E.g. Smarzoch, Raphael. 2015. Mehr als nur ein Laptop-Label [More than just a laptop label]. Deutschlandfunk. http://www.deutschlandfunk.de/mego-mehr-als-nur-ein-laptop-label.807.de.html?dram:article_id=334362, accessed 15.04.18.

6 See interview with Russell Haswell, P. 161

NO GUTS NO GLORY

sic! Raum für Kunst
Elephanthouse
Neustadtstrasse
CH-6003 Luzern
www.sic-raum.ch

PR Well, yes, but it's a bit more abstract than that. In terms of community, the label is based in Vienna, but there's probably about six people here that know the label. There are small amounts of people all over the world who make stuff like this. I really like doing label showcases for this global network, bringing different artists together. Most of the artists are from different areas, different scenes, and it's good to introduce people. It's interesting! For the few people who are keen on music and passionate about good music, I'm sure we mean a lot. But in terms of society at large, we're just this small speck in a mass of urban life. The average man on the street doesn't know what we're doing.
GS Does that bother you?
PR Not at all!

1 Siehe auch Rehberg, Peter. 2014. *Editions Mego's Peter Rehberg on His Leading Experimental Electronic Label.* Red Bull Music Academy. http://daily.redbull-musicacademy.com/2014/06/editions-mego-feature, heruntergeladen am 15.04.18.

2 Die *Groupe de Recherche Musicales* wurde in den späten 1950er Jahre von Pierre Schaeffer im Anschluss an das Dunstfeld um die *Musique Concrète* gegründet. Die Gruppe und die damit verbundenen Studios (Teil des *Office de Radiodiffusion Télévision Française*) arbeiteten sowohl theoretisch als auch praktisch an der Weiterentwicklung von elektroakustischer Musik. Die GRM ist heute noch aktiv. Siehe für Details zur Recollection GRM: Sande, Kiran. 2012. *Peter Rehberg on raiding the GRM archive and starting another Editions Mego sublabel.* FACT Magazine. http://www.factmag.com/2012/03/29/peter-rehberg-on-raiding-the-grm-archive-and-starting-another-editions-mego-sublabel/, heruntergeladen am 15.04.18.

3 Original Vinyl von Musik der GRM waren und sind extrem teuer; CD Versionen der Stücke der GRM waren über bestimmte Kanäle erhältlich.

4 Das am Centre Pomidou in Paris ansässige *Institut de Recherche et Coordination Coustique/Musique* widmete sich ebenfalls der Erforschung von elektronischer und elektroakustischer Musik. Im Anschluss an Pierre Boulez ging das IRCAM in seiner musikalischen Praxis insbesondere vom Serialismus aus. Siehe auch Born, Georgina. 1995. *Rational music: IRCAM, Boulez, and the institutionalisation of the avant-garde.* Berkeley: University of California Press.

5 z.B. Smarzoch, Raphael. 2015. *Mehr als nur ein Laptop-Label.* Deutschlandfunk. http://www.deutschlandfunk.de/mego-mehr-als-nur-ein-laptop-label.807.de.html?dram:article_id=334362, heruntergeladen am 15.04.18.

6 Siehe Interview mit Russell Haswell S. 161

RUSSELL HASWELL
WRONG TECHNO

Log:
Remo Bitzi
Photography:
Lendita Kashtanjeva

References

1 See the Interview with DJ Stingray in zweikommasieben #15.

Siehe das Interview mit DJ Stingray in zweikommasieben #15.

2 See the interview with Peter Rehberg in this issue on page 148.

Siehe das Interview mit Peter Rehberg in dieser Ausgabe auf Seite 148.

3 See the interview with Oscar Powell in zweikommasieben #10.

Siehe das Interview mit Oscar Powell in zweikommasieben #10.

Log

Russell Haswell is a multi-disciplinary artist, performer and curator—always at the forefront, always challenging. With a past in fine arts and a background in computer music, black metal, noise, techno and solo improvisation, his practice is renowned for embracing extremities both visually and sonically. He has been touring with Consumer Electronics and solo forever, as well as performing occasionally in collaboration with Regis as Concrete Fence, with DJ Stingray[1] or Sue Tompkins. On top of that, Haswell has released music on labels such as Warp Records, Editions Mego[2], Downwards, Diagonal and Ideal Recordings, among others. Considering all this, it's not a big surprise that the artist, who recently relocated from London to Glasgow, has deep ties to basically everyone who's got something to say in the world of the arts and experimental music.

Russell Haswell is a great storyteller, too. It's his crass, no-holds-barred, dark humour combined with a myriad of anecdotes and encounters he has experienced. Parts of a recent meet-up between Haswell and zweikommasieben's Remo Bitzi were recorded. It happened at the occasion of a zweikommasieben × Diagonal night featuring appearances by Diagonal-co-boss Oscar Powell[3] and Haswell himself in late December 2017 at Cave 12. Shortly after his arrival, hanging out at the bar of the Genevan venue, Russell gave insights into the struggles of a touring artist—his bags got lost on his journey to this gig with Dutch airline KLM after all—, into his restless practice, into plans for a New Year's Eve that haven't materialized yet, into an industry that's not always as pleasant as it should be, and into a life that's not always as easy as it ought to be.

Russell Haswell ist ein Künstler, Performer und Kurator—stets an vorderster Front, stets herausfordernd. In der Vergangenheit hat er sich genauso im Feld der bildenden Kunst bewegt, wie in verschiedenen Bereichen gegenwärtiger Musik—etwa Computer Music, Black Metal, Noise, Techno und Solo-Improvisationen. Seine Praxis ist berüchtigt dafür, dass sie visuelle und musikalische Extreme bedient. Haswell tourt seit Ewigkeiten mit Consumer Electronics sowie solo und tritt gelegentlich im Rahmen seiner gemeinsamen Projekte mit Regis als Concrete Fence, mit DJ Stingray[1] oder Sue Tompkins auf. Weiter hat Haswell Musik auf Labels wie Warp Records, Editions Mego[2], Downwards, Diagonal und Ideal Recordings veröffentlicht. In Anbetracht all dessen ist es keine grosse Überraschung, dass der neulich von London nach Glasgow übergesiedelte Künstler irgendwie alle kennt, die etwas im Kunst- oder Musikgeschäft zu sagen haben.

Russell Haswell ist auch ein grossartiger Geschichtenerzähler. Es ist sein derber, hammerharter, schwarzer Humor kombiniert mit einer Myriade an Anekdoten und Begegnungen. Bei einem der letzten Aufeinandertreffen mit zweikommasieben nutze Remo Bitzi die Gelegenheit, um Haswell aufzunehmen. All das fand vor einer zweikommasieben × Diagonal Nacht statt, im Rahmen derer Diagonal-Co-Boss Oscar Powell[3] und Haswell selbst Ende Dezember 2017 im Cave12 auftraten. Kurz nach seiner Ankunft, an der Bar des Genfer Veranstaltungsorts, gewährte Russell Einblicke in die Mühen eines Künstlers auf Tour—immerhin ging sein Gepäck auf der Reise nach Genf mit der holländischen Fluggesellschaft KLM verloren—, in seine rastlose Praxis, in Pläne für eine noch nicht verwirklichte Silvesterparty, in eine Industrie, die nicht immer so angenehm ist, wie sie sein sollte, und in ein Leben, das nicht immer so einfach ist, wie es sich eigentlich gehört.

No. No, I just checked KLM's website again. It says exactly the same thing, which is annoying because they should've found my bags by now.

... Well, let's do a little private party next New Year's Eve! We should go to Gstaad. There's the art thing in January or whatever. I was supposed to do that the other year, but the curator guy just pulled out. ... We've gotta go to the house where they filmed *Phenomena*—that film by Dario Argento with Jennifer Connelly. The girl gets decapitated on the mountain waterfall. But that's not in Gstaad, it's in St. Gallen—maybe not in the town, but nearby. Go to YouTube and go for "filming locations of whatever"—you can see little films about it. Actually, there's a kid that probably comes tonight. He made a film about the filming locations. He lives here and he's a little synth mutant. [Laughter] He likes me.

... I wanna play tonight. I spent all day yesterday fucking around all the time to make it work. New samples, new fucking modules, new fucking patches. I don't wanna sit at the bar and be like: "Oh, what a great night." I was really looking forward to this. It's the only thing this year that I was going to do that was exciting. I love coming here.

... Did you hear my story earlier? Two weeks ago, me and Oscar and other people played at Berghain. It was a party of nine people traveling. Everyone flew with British Airways from Tegel to Heathrow. But I was going to Glasgow from Schönefeld and Oscar's fiancée was flying to Gatwick from Schönefeld as well. Oscar's fiancée was really pissed off that she wasn't flying with the others. And she had to leave earlier in the morning with me. We got to the airport and we both took off and flew. The others all went hours later and they could sleep and recover and everything. Anyway, when my plane went over Glasgow, out of the plane window you could see all of Scotland—it was crystal clear, I've seen things I've never seen before. But right over Glasgow airport there was a lump of fog. And it was just there, everything else was clear. So, they suddenly said we're not fucking landing in Glasgow we're going to Prestwick.

... [On the phone with one of the event's promoters] Ok ... hey hey... You've probably even seen my bags before. There's one black North Face bag—you know, one of these round soft holdalls, which is black with North Face written in yellow on it. It got a red address tag made out of Lego. It's a red Lego piece hanging off the bag. And the second bag is a *Pelicase 1510*—a black Pelicase that's covered in stickers of Sleaford Mods and Incapacitants and Pain Jerk. So you know it's my one. And if Oscar's with you by then he knows exactly what my bags look like... Yeah... Yeah... ... Ok... ... Yes... Yes, I understand... Ok, alright, thank you, cheers.

... Anyway, I was like: "Where the fuck is Prestwick?" It's still Glasgow, but it's 40 miles away. It's where Donald Trump's hotel is. They landed in this airport and I had to get a train into Glasgow. And all you see on that train, apart from a little bit of sea in the beginning, is golf courts. Anyway, I finally land and then I text Oscar's fiancée and she's landed in Gatwick and says: "Russ, they're fucked, they've been delayed three hours, they're pissed, they're still at Tegel in their British Airways lounge." Eventually they're getting on the plane and made it over Heathrow but couldn't fucking land. They flew all the way to Bournemouth, which is on the south coast of England, right opposite France. Then they had to get a taxi back—that's like a five hours drive. So, Oscar's like: "Fuck, I'm not going through an airport ever again in my life." And now he's just been delayed, my bags have been lost, and Oscar's even trapped on the plane right now.

Nein. Nein, ich war gerade eben auf der Website von KLM. Da steht noch immer das Gleiche—und das nervt mich, weil mittlerweile sollten sie mein Gepäck gefunden haben.

... Wir sollten eine kleine, private Silvesterparty im nächsten Jahr veranstalten! Wir sollten nach Gstaad reisen. Im Januar oder wann auch immer findet diese Kunst-Veranstaltung statt. Ich hätte da vor ein paar Jahren spielen sollen, aber der Kuratoren-Typ machte einen Rückzug. ... Wir sollten in dieses Haus gehen, wo *Phenomena* gedreht wurde—dieser Film von Dario Argento mit Jennifer Connelly. Das Mädchen wird auf einem Wasserfall in den Bergen geköpft. Aber das war nicht in Gstaad, das war in St. Gallen—vielleicht nicht in der Stadt, aber in der Nähe. Auf YouTube findet man diese kleinen Filme darüber, wenn man «Film-Location von was auch immer» eingibt. Möglicherweise kommt heute ein Typ vorbei, der einen Film über jene Film-Location gedreht hat. Er wohnt hier und er ist ein kleiner Synth-Mutant. [Gelächter] Er mag mich.

... Ich will heute Abend spielen. Ich habe gestern verdammt nochmal den ganzen Tag geschaut, dass es auch funktioniert. Neue Samples, neue verdammte Module, neue verdammte Patches. Ich will nicht einfach an der Bar sitzen und sagen: «Oh, was für ein toller Abend.» Ich habe mich wirklich auf heute Abend gefreut. Tatsächlich war es die einzige Sache, auf die ich mich in diesem Jahr gefreut habe. Ich liebe diesen Ort hier.

... Habt ihr meine Geschichte vorhin gehört? Vor zwei Wochen spielten Oscar, ich und ein paar andere Leute im Berghain. Insgesamt waren wir eine Reisegruppe von neun Leuten. Alle flogen mit British Airways von Tegel nach Heathrow. Nur ich reiste von Schönefeld nach Glasgow und Oscars Freundin flog von Schönefeld nach Gatwick. Sie war ziemlich sauer, dass sie nicht mit den anderen fliegen konnte—und musste mit mir früh am Morgen zum Flughafen. Wir gingen also nach Schönefeld, checkten ein und hoben ab. Zu dem Zeitpunkt waren alle anderen noch am Schlafen; sie konnten sich schön erholen oder was auch immer—sie mussten erst Stunden später los. Als mein Flugzeug über Glasgow ankam, konnte man durchs Fenster ganz Schottland sehen. Man hatte kristallklare Sicht und ich sah Dinge, die ich noch nie davor gesehen hatte. Aber genau über dem Flughafen von Glasgow sass ein Klumpen Nebel. Nur da, alles andere war klar. Plötzlich verkündete das Personal, dass man nicht auf dem verdammten Flughafen von Glasgow landen könne und wir nach Prestwick ausweichen müssen.

... [Am Telefon mit einem der Veranstalter] Ok ... hey hey... Du hast mein Gepäck möglicherweise bereits einmal gesehen. Da wäre einerseits diese schwarze North Face-Tasche—du weisst schon, eine dieser runden, weichen Taschen, schwarz mit einem gelben North Face-Logo drauf. Die Tasche hat einen roten Adressanhänger aus Legosteinen. Ein rotes Lego-Stück hängt an der Tasche. Und das zweite Gepäckstück ist ein *Pelicase 1510*—ein schwarzer Pelicase, der übersäht ist mit Klebern von den Sleaford Mods und Incapacitants und Pain Jerk. Man sieht also, dass der Koffer mir gehört. Und falls Oscar bereits da ist, dann kann er ganz genau sagen, wie mein Gepäck aussieht. Ja... Ja... ... Ok... Ja... Ja, ich verstehe... Ok, alles klar, dank, tschau.

... Ich fragte mich also: «Wo zur Hölle ist Prestwick?» Das gehört tatsächlich noch zu Glasgow, liegt aber 60 Kilometer ausserhalb der Stadt. Es ist da, wo Donald Trumps Hotel steht. Die Maschine landete also in Prestwick und ich musste einen Zug nach Glasgow nehmen. Und alles, was man vom Zug

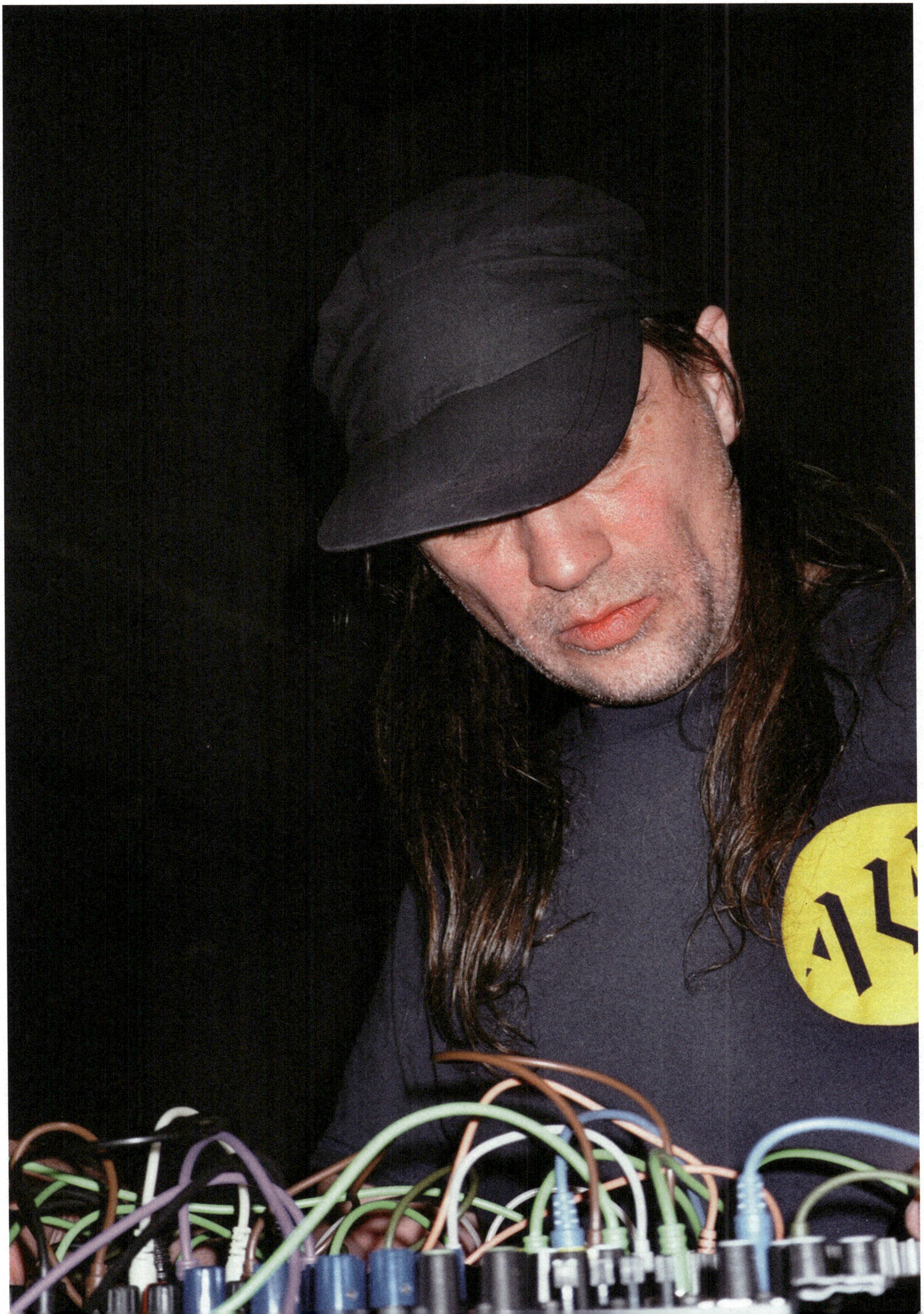

... The best-case scenario is, that we don't hear a fucking thing for half an hour and Oscar turns up with both bags. And a few packets of fags. [Laughter]

... I got a new Downwards EP, which I've just made. It's techno. Well, it's not techno, it's wrong techno.

... C'mon KLM!

... I had this Concrete Fence project with Regis on PAN. And Karl [O'Connor aka Regis] wants to do more Concrete Fence, but he's travelling so often and never gets around to doing it. So, I got bored of waiting for it and I just said: "Karl, here's a fucking album." I gave him all the files and he went: "Russ, these are the four tracks. This is an EP." And I was like: "Ok, fucking hell, have an EP instead." When I got to Glasgow I went into that little room and I just was like: "I gotta make some fucking records." I just started to record with the smallest amount of equipment I had, because I have shitloads of more gear still in London—like 100 modules, 100 whatever. Anyway, I had to make something up with the smallest amount of gear—like as much as what I've got today. When it comes. Anyway, what I've made is a kind of spasmodic quick thing. ... Where is my USB stick? [Russell checks his pockets, then walks away. Instants later brutal noise techno crackles out of Cave 12's soundsystem.]

... I'm gonna say: "Touch wood." I've never lost any baggage; they've always come, but they've not arrived on the plane many times. Often, I have been on festivals or gigs where somebody else on the bill is like: "Fuck, my bags are gone missing." But they're usually gone missing somewhere intercontinental, not just here. Maybe they show up two days later and they get some fresh underpants. But I don't know what I'm gonna do if it doesn't show up tonight.

... Have you ever been at the Ancienne Belgique?

... The running order doesn't matter, it's all good. We should toss a coin or so. ... I'd rather go last. I think Oscar will enjoy it more. ... Anyway, did somebody ask about it?

... Ancienne Belgique is this venue in Brussels. It used to be a really old grand theater, but in the early eighties they rebuilt it—it must have fallen down or something. Ever since it looks like the Hacienda; it's got pipes everywhere and it's all painted in colours. Joy Division played there, New Order played there, it was a real Factory place in the eighties. I've played there three or four times with Autechre in the main room and every time I've played there I've completely twatted the place. The entire audience was going: "Fuck off!" But the main guy that runs the place is always saying [speaking in an odd accent]: "Oh, Russell, you're fucking great, I love you. Come back and do a small gig in the little room!" I've did that with Prurient once. And there were three goths there. [Laughter] To see him. I haven't even got any haters in Belgium. I think when they've seen me when I played with Autechre they just didn't bother to find out my name.

... The problem is that here at Geneva airport there's this group that looks after lost baggage for all the different airlines that come here. Whereas when I used to fly into Norwich it was only KLM. So, there was a KLM counter, you went to a KLM girl, it was KLM. But I told the guy the truth—I'm doing a concert tonight and tomorrow I'm going to Zurich to do another concert. He was ok, he kinda went: [Imitating the guy staring into his computer sighting.] It would be classic if it doesn't come today and I go to Zurich and it doesn't come there and then I leave Zurich and then it gets here.

But my flight back is super business, because I am flying on Saturday. ... It costs a fucking fortune. I get so many of those gigs where the flights must be way more than what I'm getting paid. When you think about how much you actually get to do something, you go like: "Fuck, this is insane—the hotel, the flight—, we could've got paid five grands. Invite me in a cheap time of the year and pay three times as much!"

... When I've toured with Autechre, I think it's a case of them thinking: "We can cope with this guy on the bus." [Laugher] No, really. It's more that than what music it gonna be. At the same time, I am a kind of abrasive little weird crap before they go on stage. Loads of people love playing after me because everything sounds nice after me. I can think of about five acts that have told me that.

... [A message with the arrived bags comes pops up on the phone] Yeeeess!!! ... FUCKING YES! That means I can do the gig! ... I tell you what we can do, let's get the table over there. And if we do that... Let me finish my beer. [Walks away] That's a relief! ... It says the bags got lost in Amsterdam, maybe now it's full of ecstasy.

MOMENTS OF CLARITY GLINT THROUGH PILES OF JUNK

IPEK GORGUN & CERAMIC TL

In November 2017, Ipek Gorgun and Ceramic TL, aka David Psutka, released *Perfect Lung* on Halocine Trance. While Psutka has been known for his work for ten years now—think of the music he released from 2010 onwards under his Egyptrixx alias on the then-upcoming Night Slugs imprint—, we only first heard about Gorgun when Mumdance mentioned her name during a conversation held at RBMA Tokyo [see zweikommasieben #11]. Gorgun is an artist with widespread interests in various fields, as the press release accompanying her 2016 debut album on Touch, called *Aphelion*, claims. She's enrolled in a PhD program in sonic arts at Istanbul Technical University, participates in various band projects, has made soundtracks for documentaries, and has made a name for herself as a photographer as well as a poet. On top of all that, she recorded *Perfect Lung* with Ceramic TL. On the record, Gorgun added layers of abstract soundscapes to Psutka's crystal-clear synth plucks—making the collaborative album a late highlight of 2017.

Considering all of this, the only thing we could do was to reach out and ask for a contribution to this issue of our magazine—and what we received are the two photo essays we're contrasting here.

Im November 2017 veröffentlichten Ipek Gorgun und Ceramic TL aka David Psutka das Album *Perfect Lung* auf Halocine Trance. Während Psutka bereits seit zehn Jahren in verschiedenen Zusammenhängen auftaucht—etwa ab 2010 unter dem Pseudonym Egyptrixx im damals noch überschaubaren Katalog von Night Slugs—, hörten wir von Gorgun erstmals, als Mumdance sie in einem Gespräch im Rahmen der RBMA Tokyo erwähnte [siehe zweikommasieben #11]. Gorgun ist Komponistin und widmet sich verschiedenen Feldern, Kunstformen und deren Überschneidungen, wie die Pressemitteilung von ihrem 2016 auf Touch veröffentlichten Debütalbum *Aphelion* verspricht: Sie dissertiert in Sonic Arts an der Technischen Universität Istanbul, ist in verschiedenen Bandprojekten aktiv, komponiert Soundtracks für Dokumentarfilme, ist Lyrikerin und hat verschiedene Preise für ihre Fotografien gewonnen. Daneben hat sie nun eben mit Ceramic TL *Perfect Lung* eingespielt. Bei den Produktionen auf dem Album ergänzt Gorgun die kristallklaren Synths von Psutka mit abstrakteren Klangflächen—ein Amalgam, das zu einem späten Highlight des Jahres 2017 wurde.

Konsequenterweise baten wir Gorgun und Psutka um einen Beitrag für diese Ausgabe unseres Magazins—und wir erhielten je eine Fotostrecke, die wir hier einander gegenüberstellen.

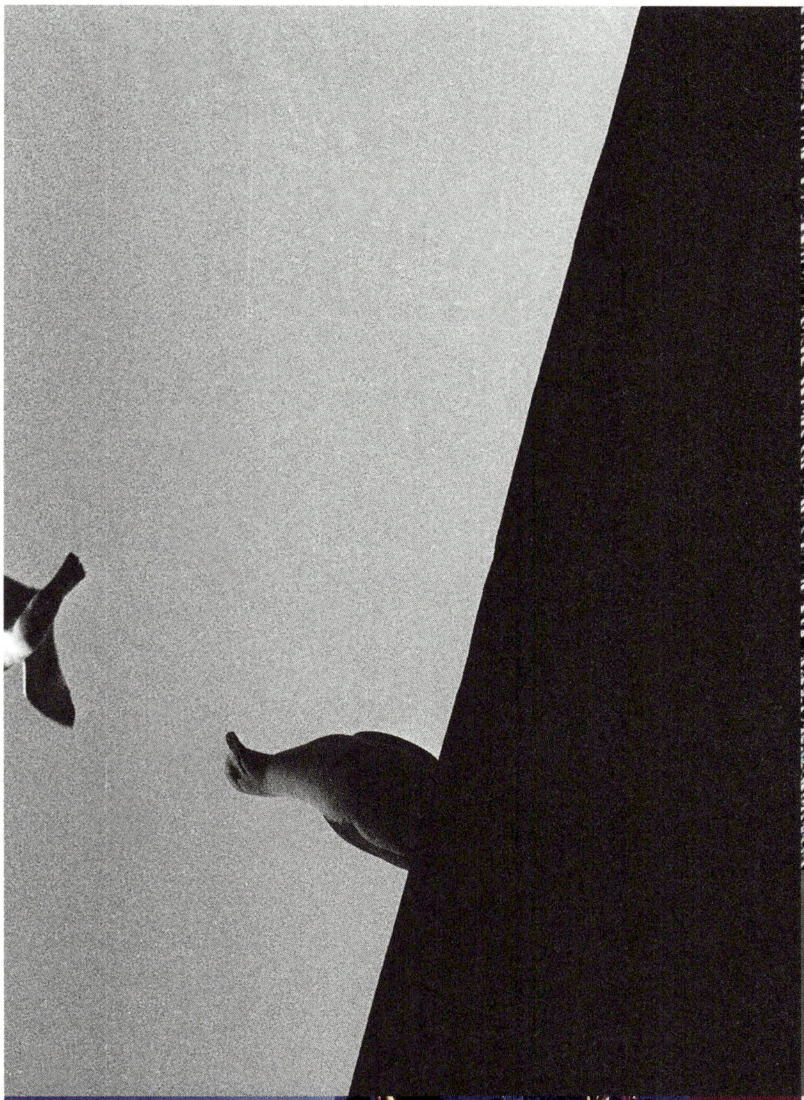

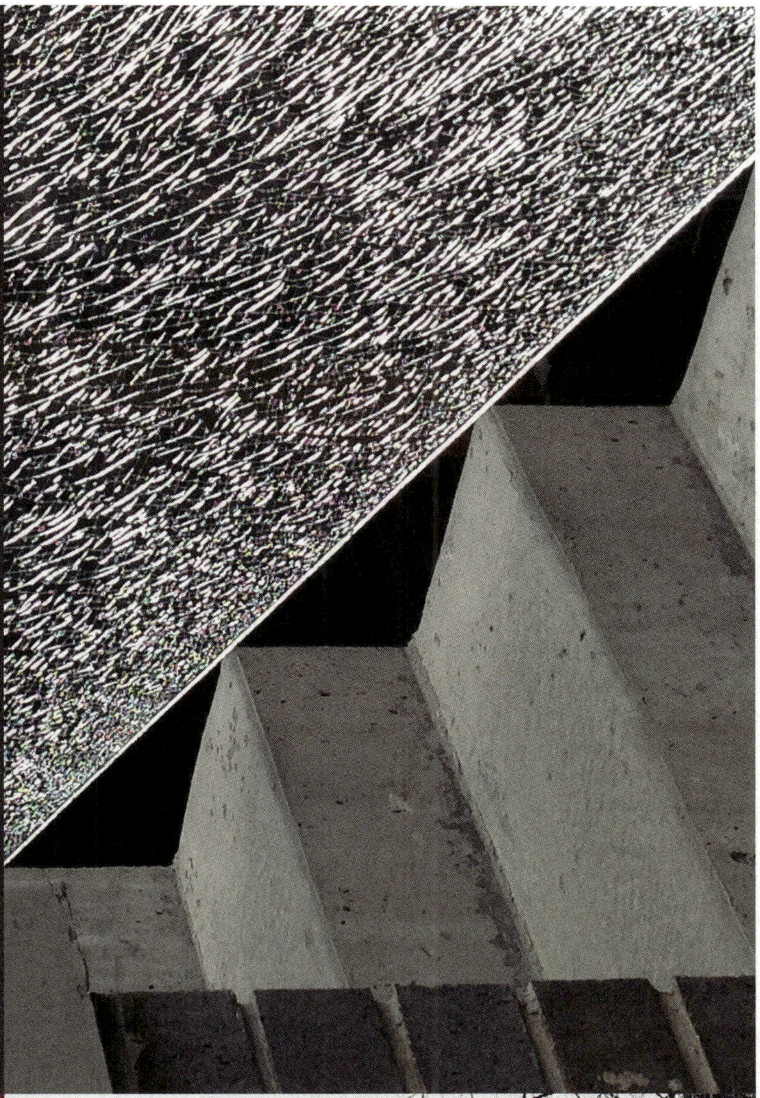

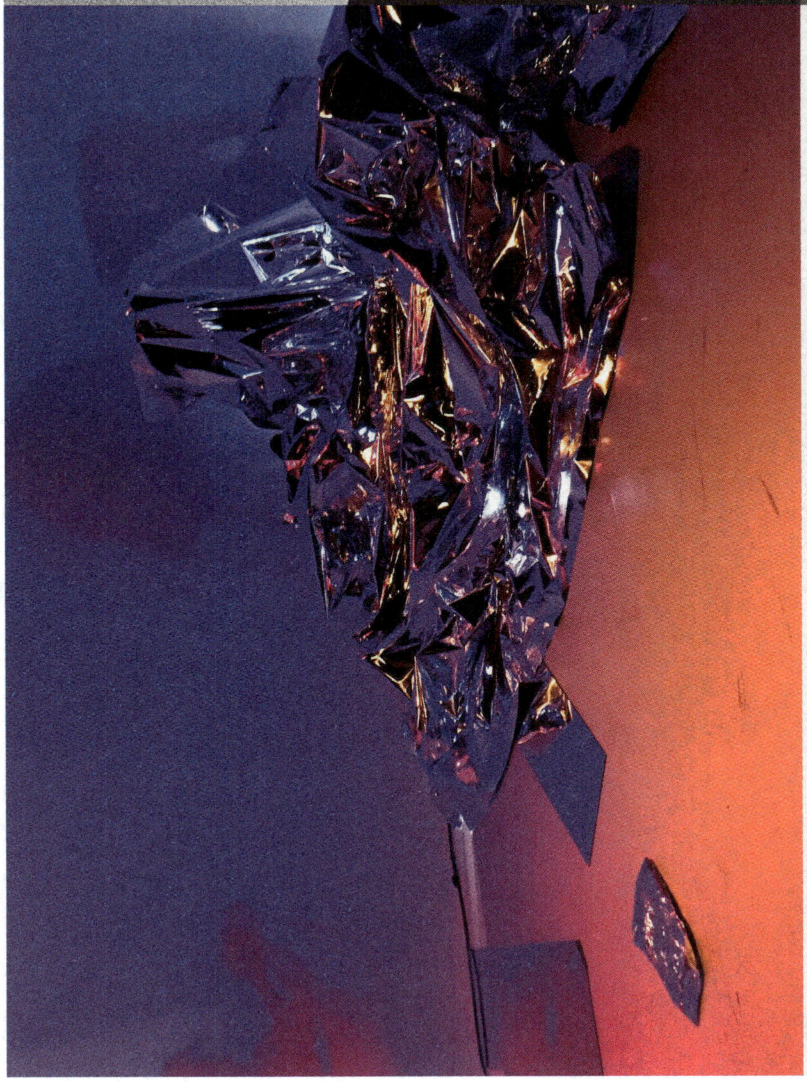

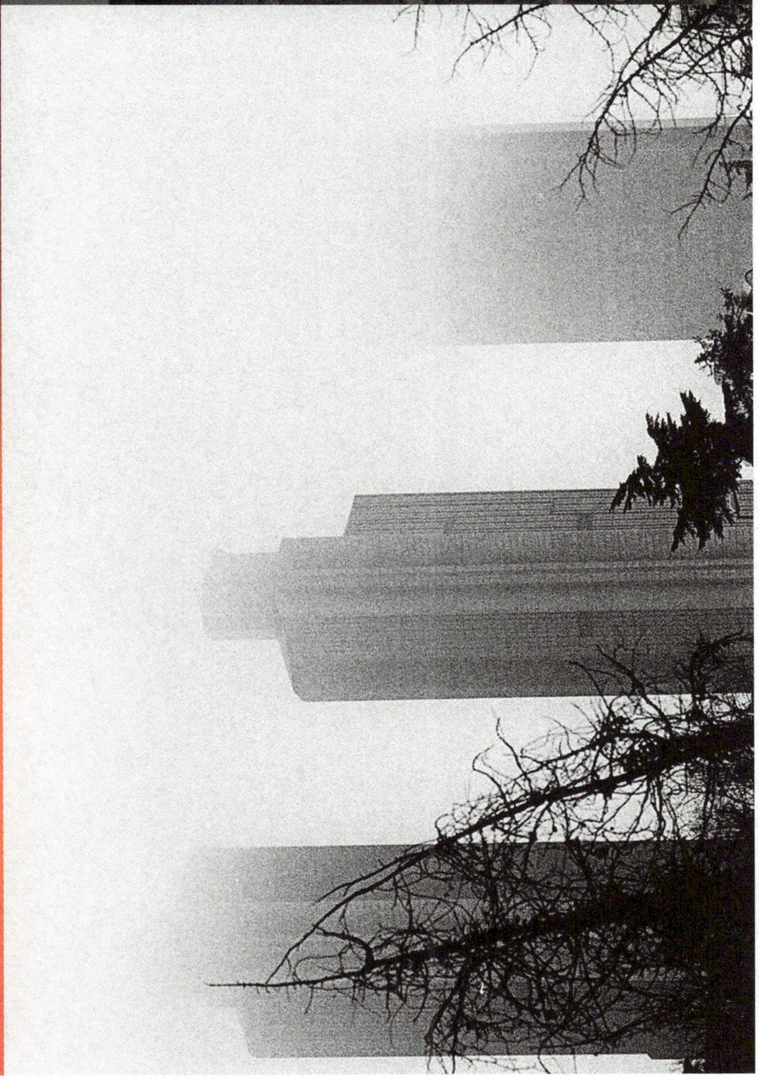

JAPAN-TOUR ANGOISSE

Angoisse ist ein spanisches Label, das verschiedene Spielarten von herausfordernder Musik veröffentlicht; sei es schwereloser und dennoch einengender Ambient, Mumble Trap oder verschiedene Varianten von Beats—langsame, nette, seltsame oder brutale—und mehr. So hat Angoisse seit 2011 Material von Mirrored Hall, Exoteric Continent, Ñaka Ñaka, Nick Klein, Enrique, CVN, Ultrafog, Mace., Kazumichi Komatsu und anderen Künstlerinnen auf Kassette, Vinyl, CD und weiteren Trägern veröffentlicht.
Angoisse und seine Künstler produzieren aber nicht nur Material für Konserven, sondern präsentieren dieses auch gleichermassen in Ausstellungsräumen und Klubs. Genau das haben einige Crewmitglieder—namentlich Theodore Cale Schafer, mdo, Gaul Plus und David M. Romero—im vergangenen Dezember in Japan gemacht: Sie verbreiteten unter anderem im WWWb und der Bar Bonobo in Tokio, in der Hikarinolounge in Okazaki und im Marco Nostalgy in Osaka Angoisse-Vibes im besten Sinne.
Exklusiv für zweikommasieben dokumentierte die Angoisse-Reisetruppe ihren Japan-Ausflug—und hielt fest, was man von einer Tour im Land der aufgehenden Sonne erwarten würde (oder eben nicht).

Angoisse is a Spanish label that releases various kinds of demanding music, from weightless yet creepy ambient to mumble-trap to all sorts of beats—be they slow, gentle, odd or brutal. The label has published material by Mirrored Hall, Exoteric Continent, Ñaka Ñaka, Nick Klein, Enrique, CVN, Ultrafog, Mace., Kazumichi Komatsu, and others on cassette, vinyl, CD, and other formats.
Angoisse and its affiliated artists don't shy away from presenting their material to audiences in art galleries or in clubs. And that's what some of them—namely Theodore Cale Schafer, mdo, Gaul Plus, and David M. Romero—did this past December in Japan. They spread some proper Angoisse vibes at WWWb and Bar Bonobo in Tokyo, at Okazaki's Hikarinolounge, and at Marco Nostalgy in Osaka, among other places.
While on the road, the different crew members documented everything you'd expect (and not expect) from a tour in the land of the rising sun, exclusively for zweikommasieben.

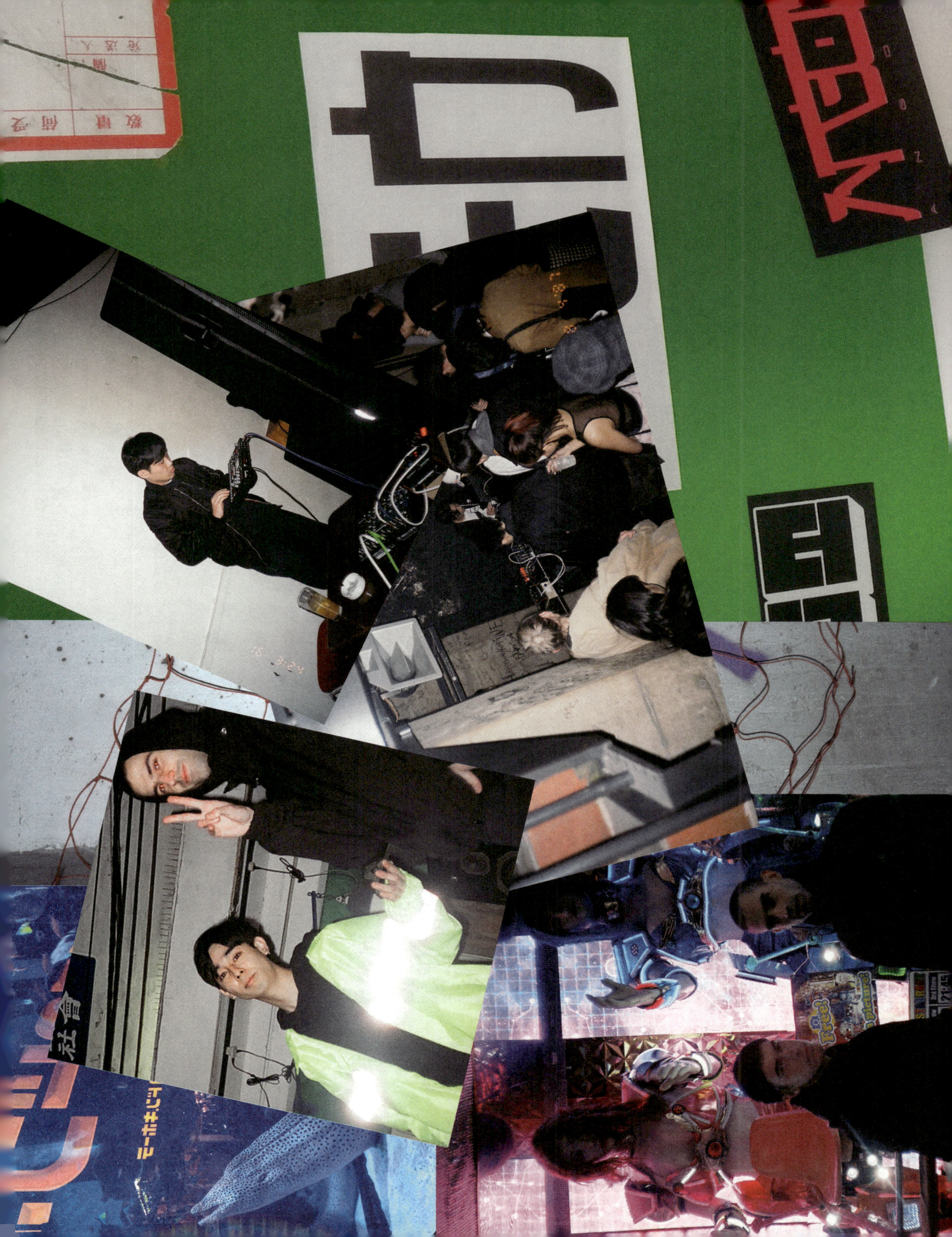

l&b

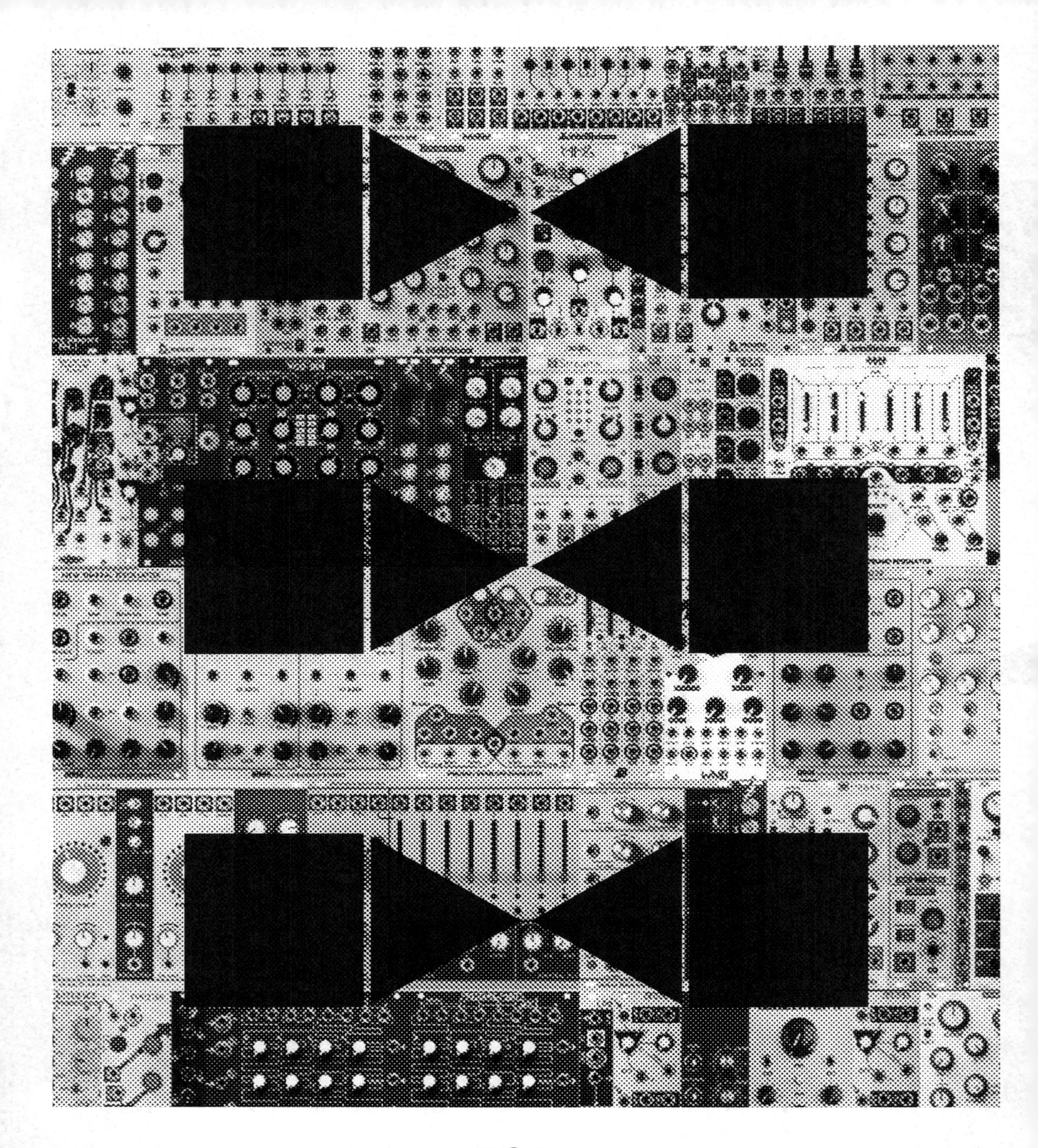

NEUE MODULAR-MODULE,
ANALOGE SYNTHESIZERS, DRUM MACHINES UND VIELES MEHR.
WWW.LOOPSANDBITS.CH

Contribution   Angoisse

EXTENDED HISTORY AND THE DIGITAL REVOLUTION
A DISCUSSION BETWEEN CHRISTOPH FRINGELI, SIMON CRAB, AND NIGEL AYERS

Transcription:
Caroline Sidler
Editing:
Marc Schwegler
Photography:
Lendita Kashtanjeva

Christoph Fringeli has been operating Praxis Records since 1992. Praxis is a label that, especially before the turn of the millennium, influenced the development of harder forms of electronic music with a subversive and activist attitude. Since 1997, Fringeli, the Berlin-based native of Basel, Switzerland has also been publishing the magazine Datacide, whose seventeenth edition came out last November. Its reach extends far beyond the musical realm into anti-capitalist, radical-left theory and politics. After releasing several albums per year in the late 90s and early 2000s, Praxis' activity has slowed some in recent years. Last January, though, the label reissued Bourbonese Qualk's 1993 album *Autonomia*. This project by industrial pioneer Simon Crab has attracted renewed attention since the release of a compilation on Mannequin and a 4-LP released in 2016 on Vinyl on Demand containing early cassette pieces. Founded in Southport around 1979, Bourbonese Qualk was a central entity in radical, uncompromising underground music, especially in the London squatter scene of the 1980s. As part of a joint tour with Nigel Ayers of Nocturnal Emissions, another early industrial luminary also recently honored with a reissue on Mannequin, Crab was passing through Berlin.

On the initiative of Guy Schwegler in January of this year, the two Englishmen and the Swiss exile came together for a conversation. Lendita Kashtanjeva took some photos shortly thereafter.

Christoph Fringeli betreibt seit 1992 Praxis Records—ein Label, das insbesondere vor der Jahrtausendwende mit subversivem und aktivistischem Gestus die Entwicklung von härteren Formen elektronischer Musik mitprägte. Seit 1997 gibt der in Berlin lebende Basler zudem das Magazin Datacide heraus, dessen siebzehnte Ausgabe im vergangenen November erschienen ist. Weit über Musik hinaus beschäftigt es sich mit antikapitalistischer und radikal linker Theorie und Politik. Nachdem Praxis als Label über die Jahrtausendwende noch mehrere Werke pro Jahr veröffentlicht hat, ist es um die Initiative in den letzten Jahren etwas ruhiger geworden. Im vergangenen Januar hat Praxis aber das 1993 ein erstes Mal veröffentlichte Album *Autonomia* von Bourbonese Qualk neu aufgelegt. Das Projekt von Industrial-Pionier Simon Crab stiess seit einer bei Mannequin veröffentlichten Compilation sowie einer 2016 bei Vinyl on Demand erschienenen vierfach LP, die frühe, auf Kassette veröffentlichte Stücke enthielt, wieder auf ein vermehrtes Interesse. Gegründet in Southport um 1979, wurde Bourbonese Qualk dann vor allem in der Londoner Besetzerszene der 1980er-Jahre zu einer zentralen Grösse kompromissloser und radikaler Underground-Musik. Im Rahmen einer gemeinsamen Tour mit Nigel Ayers von Nocturnal Emissions—ebenfalls eine unlängst mit einer bei Mannequin erschienenen Werk-Reprise geadelte, frühe Industrial-Koryphäe—war Crab auf Besuch in Berlin, wo sich ein Gespräch zwischen den Engländern und dem Exil-Schweizer aufdrängte.

Geführt wurde es auf Initiative von Guy Schwegler im Januar dieses Jahres—kurz darauf machte Lendita Kashtanjeva die begleitenden Fotos.

Christoph Fringeli: Your website claims that the early shows of Bourbonese Qualk were "mainly vandalism"—what does that mean, exactly?

Simon Crab: Well, I think early on we didn't have any money, equipment or instruments. So we thought that rather than making music we'd just vandalize things. We went around spraying graffiti and making little posters, even though we hadn't actually done anything at that point. But that was really early on. I think we wanted to extend our history a bit... [laughs]

CF How did it mutate into Qualk as we know it? I know that there were about four years in between those early years and the first record release.

SC We were always doing stuff. But again, we didn't have any money or the possibilities to make records or anything like that. That came quite a bit later. Recloose as a label was meant to be a cooperative were people would contribute music and money to make a record and then make another one from the profit of it. That was the idea, but I didn't see it happen like that, because I suppose people weren't really interested in the cooperative. Instead they wanted to promote their own work individually. But it got the label started and from that we could actually do things. We released tapes and stuff, but no one listened to them. Maybe about five people in the entire universe did. All that stuff is on the Bourbonese Qualk boxset *Archive 1980-1986* (Vinyl-on-demand, 2016) now, though.

CF So the first record came out on Recloose Organization. What kind of a context did that happen in? Were there other like-minded people active?

SC There was quite a cassette scene that was evolved and very international—there were a lot of things going on. I think it was considered almost a betrayal if you moved from cassette to vinyl, which seems a bit bizarre nowadays. I think there was sort of a movement wanting to keep the fluidity of cassettes because they were cheap and completely independent of labels and manufacturing. As soon as we started making records, we were seen as a different thing. It did lose that cooperative edge, and just became about promoting your own work. Muslimgauze just wanted to do Muslimgauze, which he always did anyway, you know. But the Bourbonese Qualk records really paid for the label, because they were the only ones that really did sell at the time.

CF Because you were touring and all?

SC We managed to get a bit of press. Dave Henderson from Sounds was writing about us.

Nigel Ayers: He was really useful, even though he was just this one person promoting a bunch of underground stuff.

CF I was just going to ask about Henderson, actually, because he put that compilation together—*The Elephant Table* (Xtract Records, 1983)—which featured both of you and many other interesting bands at the time. But would you say that there was a scene around all these bands, or was it more like separate phenomena that somehow connected?

SC It became a scene because Henderson put it all together. We didn't know the others individually. I mean, Nigel and I knew each other through squatting. We hadn't known Test Dept. or Portion Control until then.

NA ...although they lived very close to us.

CF So you were squatting in London together?

NA Yes, in the same area. I was on Milford Road and Simon squatted at Vicarage Road first.

SC I squatted a church first [laughs]. I used to sleep in the organ loft of the church for a few days, which was freezing cold. Then we broke into the Vicarage place—this massive, massive house. It was a good place, mate.

NA Graeme Revell [SPK] moved in for a while, didn't he?

SC He did for a bit, yeah. But I don't think there was a kind of cultural agreement to anything of this, you know. Looking back on it, it was very white and it was very male—pretty

Christoph Fringeli: Auf eurer Website steht, dass es sich bei den frühen Aktivitäten von Bourbonese Qualk vor allem um Vandalismus gehandelt hat. Was ist damit genau gemeint?

Simon Crab: Damals hatten wir weder Geld, Equipment noch Instrumente. Also dachten wir uns, wir hauen erstmal lieber Dinge kaputt, als Musik zu machen. Dementsprechend sind wir herumgezogen, haben Graffiti gesprüht und kleine Poster gemacht—obwohl wir ja eigentlich noch gar nichts geleistet hatten bis zu diesem Punkt. Aber das war wirklich am Anfang. Ich glaube, wir wollten vor allem die eigene Geschichte etwas länger machen, als sie eigentlich ist. [lacht]

CF: Wie ist das Ganze dann zu Qualk, wie wir es kennen, mutiert? Ich weiss, dass zwischen den frühen Jahren und der ersten Veröffentlichung etwa vier Jahre ins Land gezogen sind. **SC:** Wir haben immer irgendwas gemacht. Aber noch mal: Wir hatten kein Geld und damit auch keine Möglichkeit, Sachen aufzunehmen oder irgendetwas in der Art. Das kam erst später. Recloose als Label war eigentlich als Kooperative gedacht, für die Leute Musik und Geld beisteuern würden, um Veröffentlichungen zu ermöglichen, um dann aus dem resultierenden Gewinn erneut eine Platte zu machen. Das war die Idee, wurde aber nie genau so umgesetzt. Ich denke vor allem deswegen, weil die Leute an der Kooperative eigentlich überhaupt nicht interessiert waren, sondern vor allem ihr eigenes Werk promoten wollten. Aber immerhin ist das Label so auf die Beine gekommen und damit konnten wir loslegen; wir haben Tapes und anderes Zeug rausgebracht. Eigentlich hat sich das aber keiner angehört. Vielleicht fünf Leute im ganzen Universum. Das ist jetzt alles auch auf dem Bourbonese Qualk Boxset Archive 1980-1986 (Vinyl-on-demand, 2016).

CF: Eure erste Veröffentlichung ist also bei Recloose Organization erschienen. In welchem Kontext war das? Gab es eine Szene um diese Art von Musik? **SC:** Ja, da gab es schon eine Szene, die Kassetten getauscht hat—und das international. Da ist viel passiert. Es wurde auch schon fast als Verrat angesehen, wenn du dich als Künstler von Kassetten weg hin zu Vinyl bewegt hast—das klingt heute schon fast bizarr. Aber es gab eine Art Bewegung, die auf die Fluidität von Kassetten insistiert hat—weil Tapes waren billig und du konntest sie komplett unabhängig von Labels und Produktionsstätten herstellen. Sobald wir dann mit Platten angefangen haben, wurden wir völlig anders wahrgenommen. Wir haben auch diesen Touch der Kooperative verloren—und eben, jeder wollte nur sein eigenes Ding promoten. Muslimgauze wollte nur Muslimgauze machen; das war bei ihm aber so oder so immer schon der Fall. Aber die Bourbonese Qualk Platten waren schlussendlich eigentlich die, die das ganze Label finanziert haben—weil sie die einzigen waren, die sich auch wirklich verkauft haben.

CF: Weil ihr auch auf Tour wart und so? **SC:** Wir haben etwas Presse bekommen. Dave Henderson von Sounds hat über uns geschrieben.

Nigel Ayers: Der war echt nützlich—obwohl es sich nur um eine Person gehandelt hat, die das ganze Underground-Zeug beworben hat. **CF:** Nach Henderson wollte ich eigentlich gerade fragen, weil er diese Compilation zusammengestellt hat, The Elephant Table (Xtract Records, 1983), auf der ihr beide wart aber auch jede Menge andere, interessante Bands aus der Zeit. Würdet ihr sagen, dass es sich dabei um eine Szene gehandelt hat oder waren das doch eher Einzelphänomene, die dann irgendwie zusammenfanden? **SC:** Es wurde zur Szene, weil Henderson alles zusammenbrachte. Wir kannten uns davor ja gar nicht. Nigel und ich kannten uns aus der

awful, really. A lot of these bands where very misogynistic and kind of childish, in a way. That hasn't aged very well—I mean, if you listen to Whitehouse, it's these white blokes screaming about rape and stuff… it's just pathetic.

NA It was also pathetic at the time.

CF I was just going to say, it was probably pathetic then. But maybe in the 80s there was still some kind of tolerance for this type of stuff—in terms of things being perceived as transgressive in one way or another. That, I think, has thankfully eroded by now.

SC There was quite a scene around this sort of transgression: Current 93, Death in June, which are directly from those times. It was very weak, I think, and it doesn't stand up to any kind of real analysis. It's only very popular in places like Austria, which is very white and male and right wing, you know [laughs].

NA People I know who were called to help out in those bands didn't take it the slightest bit seriously. They were just like, "This is an easy gig, you just press this, hold your finger down on this crappy WASP-synthesizer, sustain it or put your cigarette lighter down on it for a while." That's all it was.

CF But I mean these kind of bands were like a different scene from those on *Elephant Table*, right? Or was there an overlap?

SC Yes, I think there was an overlap and it became lumped all together, especially with industrial. I suppose I remember this all as a part of the same sort of scene. I used to bump into people like Philipp Best at a Chris & Cosey gig—it was all part of the same thing. How did you get into the music you choose to specialize in? This sort of techno-y, noisy stuff?

CF I think there are some parallels from what you did to what I first set out to do—releasing tapes at first and then going over to records. In the beginning it was a bit more post-punk than, you know, properly experimental. But soon I went into a more experimental direction as a member of the band The Electric Noise Twist. Also 16-17, which I wasn't member of, was an important band in our little scene in Basel. But this was still all based on a band format, even if we played in each other's bands. Around that time I also got a job in a distribution company, REC REC in Zurich. It was one of the leading independent music distributors in Switzerland at that time. We distributed both of your records and many other things, including the slightly bigger post-punk bands and industrial rock, EBM and so on. I soon started noticing that the whole market became more and more like a mirror image of the mainstream music market, and that increasingly frustrated me. We all had the best intentions in the company, but we couldn't sell interesting records. At least by no means as well as stuff that was somehow trendy and was promoted in conventional ways. And then when the first acid house and a little bit later the hardcore techno stuff emerged, I was really taken in by the aspect that it completely denied any kind of star system. Those were white labels or obscure pseudonyms by the same producer and I was very interested in that—on the level of products and the level of events. It was a development that went away from the stage performance of the rock band to a party situation, where there was not necessarily a clear focus on a performer and a set audience.

SC It became its own economy pretty quickly, though, and the culture became very commercial…

CF Yes, and I think that kind of usurpation is a process that happens almost at the same time as something new happens, you know. So it's true that very quickly the techno scene was also taken over by the culture industry or whatever you want to call it. But some people, including Praxis, were at that time in the 90s definitely part of something that tried to make the music more and more extreme, faster, and noisier to kind of create an escape route from that capitalist quagmire. Whether that can ever be successful is another question, you know…

Besetzerszene, aber Test Dept. oder Portion Control hatten wir bis dahin nicht gekannt. **NA:** …obwohl die alle ganz in der Nähe lebten!

CF: Ihr habt also zusammen in London Häuser besetzt? **NA:** Ja, in der gleichen Gegend. Ich an der Milford Road und Simon war zuerst an der Vicarage Road. **SC:** Ich habe eine Kirche besetzt. [lacht] Ich habe zuerst auf der Orgelempore gepennt, das war aber schweinekalt. Dann sind wir in dieses Haus an der Vicarage Road eingebrochen—diese Riesenhütte. Das war cool. Ein guter Ort, Mann. **NA:** Graeme Revell [SPK] ist dann da auch eingezogen, oder? **SC:** Für eine Weile, ja. Aber da gab es keine kulturelle Übereinkunft zwischen uns oder so was in der Art. Wenn ich zurückschaue, dann muss ich schon sagen: Das war alles sehr weiss, sehr männlich und irgendwie auch recht fürchterlich. Viele der Bands waren auch sexistisch und irgendwie auch kindisch, wenn man's recht bedenkt. Das alles ist nicht wirklich gut gealtert—ich meine, wenn du dir Whitehouse anhörst, diese weissen Typen, wie sie Texte über Vergewaltigung und solches Zeug rumschreien… Das ist einfach nur noch lächerlich. **NA:** Das war damals schon lächerlich.

CF: Ich wollte gerade sagen—das war es tatsächlich schon damals. Aber in den Achtzigern wurden solche Sachen noch toleriert—im Sinne, dass man es auf die eine oder andere Weise als transgressiv begriffen hat. Das hat sich, denke ich, zum Glück schon verändert. **SC:** Es gab ja eine ganze Szene um diese Art von Transgression—Current 93 und Death in June zum Beispiel, das ist mitten aus der Zeit. Das war aber alles richtig schwach, finde ich, und es hält einer echten Analyse auch nicht Stand. Populär ist das höchstens noch in Ländern wie Österreich, das auch sehr weiss, männlich und rechts ist… [lacht] **NA:** Die Leute, die ich kenne und die gefragt worden sind, ob sie bei Gigs für die Bands einspringen könnten, die haben das alle nicht im geringsten ernst genommen. Die haben sich einfach gesagt: «Das ist ein easy Gig, du drückst auf einen beschissenen WASP-Synthesizer, hältst drauf oder lässt deinen Anzünder für eine Weile drauf liegen.» Das ist auch schon alles.

CF: Aber bei diesen Bands handelte es sich ja schon um eine andere Szene als diejenige, die auf The Elephant Table versammelt war. Oder gab es da Überschneidungen? **SC:** Ja, ich glaube da gab es schon Überschneidungen. Ich meine mich erinnern zu können, dass es sich eigentlich schon um eine Szene gehandelt hat. Ich bin beispielsweise an Chris&Cosey-Gigs Leuten wie Philipp Best über den Weg gelaufen—das war alles dasselbe… Aber wie bist du auf die Musik gekommen, auf die du dich spezialisiert hast? Dieses technoartige, noiseähnliche Zeug?

CF: Ich glaube, da gibt es durchaus Parallelen zu euch—vom Veröffentlichen von Tapes hin zu Platten. Den Einstieg habe ich aber schon vor allem über Post-Punk gefunden, das war noch nicht wirklich experimentell. Aber ich habe mich relativ bald schon in diese Richtung weiterorientiert, als Mitglied der Band The Electric Noise Twist. 16-17 war zudem eine Band, in der ich zwar nicht dabei war, die aber für unsere kleine Szene in Basel sehr wichtig war. Aber das waren immer noch alles Bands im klassischen Sinne, obwohl man eigentlich überall ein wenig mitspielte. In der Zeit habe ich dann auch einen Job bei REC REC bekommen, einer der damals wichtigen Distributionsfirmen in der Schweiz. Wir hatten sowohl eure Platten im Verteiler, wie auch die etwas grösseren Post-Punk Bands, EBM und so weiter. Ziemlich schnell habe ich aber feststellen müssen, dass der ganze Indie-Markt mehr und mehr zum Spiegelbild des Mainstreams geworden war. Das hat

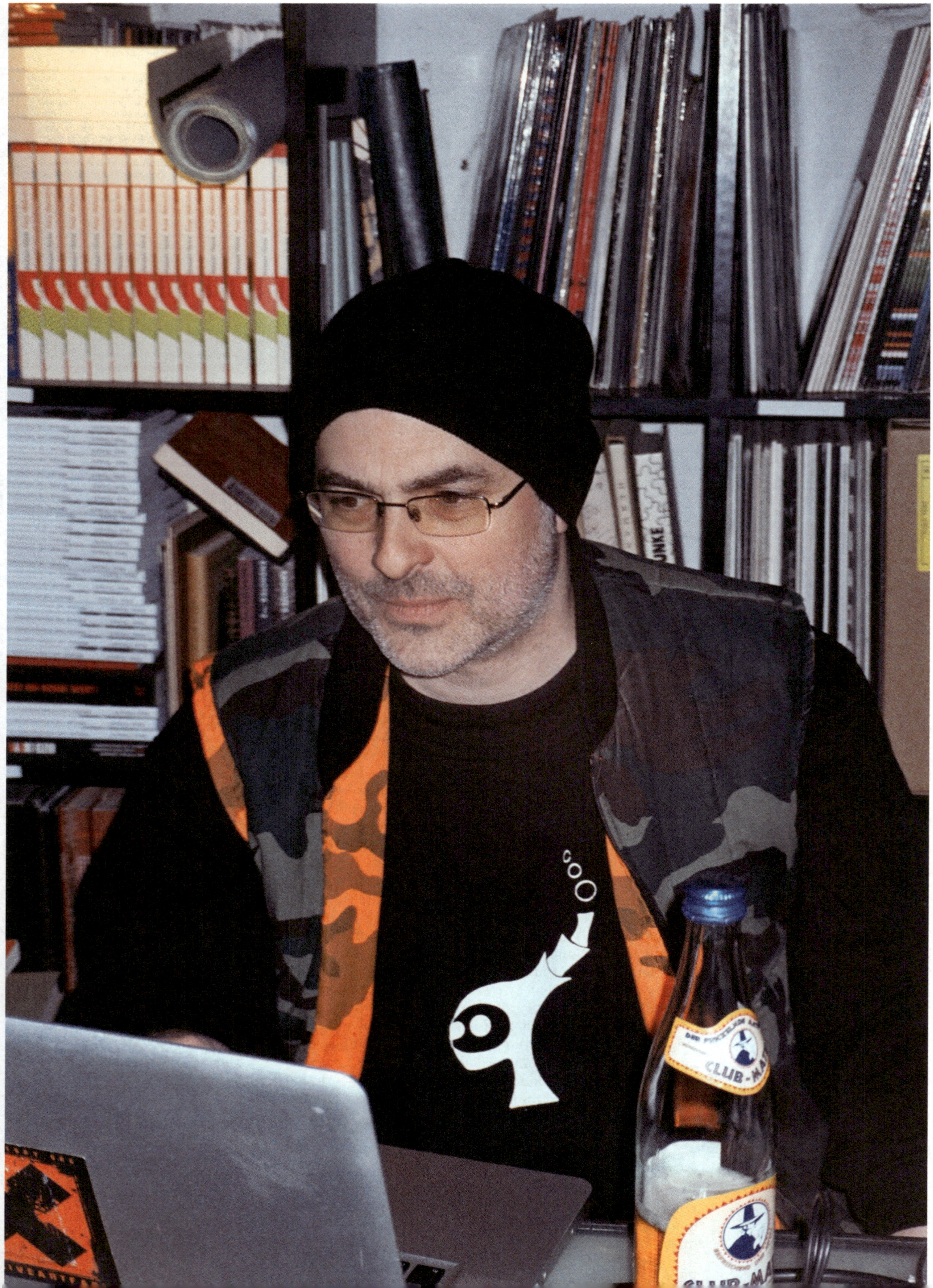

mich mehr und mehr zu frustrieren begonnen, weil wir ja eigentlich alle die besten Absichten hatten, aber die interessanteren Platten nicht verkaufen konnten. Zumindest nie im selben Ausmass wie die Sachen, die trendy waren und die auch entsprechend promotet wurden. Als dann Acid House und etwas später Hardcore und Techno auftauchten, war ich sehr beeindruckt davon, wie sich diese Musik dem Rockstar-Prinzip eigentlich komplett verweigert hat. Das erschien alles auf White-Labels oder die Produzenten hatten zig unterschiedliche und obskure Pseudonyme. Ich war sehr interessiert an dieser Entwicklung, die weg von der Bühnen-Performance einer Rock Band hin zu einer Party-Situation führte, wo es nicht mehr unbedingt eine klare Rollenverteilung zwischen Performer und Publikum gab.
SC: Ziemlich schnell ist das ja dann aber auch wieder eine eigene Ökonomie geworden und die ganze Kultur wurde kommerziell...

CF: Ja und ich glaube auch, dass diese Art der Vereinnahmung ein Prozess ist, der eigentlich schon dann einsetzt, wenn etwas wirklich Neues geschieht. Es ist also wahr, dass auch die Techno-Szene ziemlich schnell von der Kulturindustrie oder wie immer man das auch nennen will, übernommen worden ist. Aber es gab doch auch einige Leute—und Praxis war ein Teil davon—die versucht haben, die Musik immer extremer zu machen, schneller und lärmiger; um eine Fluchtlinie zu finden aus dem kapitalistischen Sumpf. Ob das grundsätzlich überhaupt erfolgreich sein kann, ist dann wieder eine andere Frage. SC: Von aussen betrachtet wirkt es so, als wärst du zwar sehr lange aktiv gewesen aber ästhetisch immer noch da, wo du angefangen hast. Oder hat es irgendwelche Variationen gegeben, die ich nicht bemerkt habe?

CF: Nun, ich würde sagen, eigentlich hat sich ganz viel verändert. Ich meine, natürlich gibt es noch diejenigen, die versuchen, das weiterzutreiben, was am Anfang war—mit Vierviertel-Takten, einem gewissen Tempo und so. Aus etwas, das mal neu und experimentell war, ist dann ein standardisiertes und formalisiertes Genre mit strikten Regeln geworden. Aber ich glaube nicht, dass Praxis diesen Weg gegangen ist. Schon in den 1990er-Jahren haben wir eigentlich den Vierviertel-Drumbeat hinter uns gelassen und begonnen, mit Broken Beats und Breaks zu arbeiten. Ich glaube, das war definitiv ein anderer Weg.
SC: Wie steht es denn jetzt um das Label? Abgesehen davon, dass es bankrott ist, meine ich. [lacht]

CF: Das ist nichts neues [lacht]. Nun, das Label ist immer noch aktiv, es hat eigentlich nie aufgehört, obwohl nicht mehr so viele neue Veröffentlichungen erscheinen. In den letzten Jahren haben wir sehr diverse Platten rausgebracht. Ich habe versucht, Interventionen in verschiedene Felder zu machen—von eher noisigen Kompositionen, die von Musikerinnen gespielt werden bis hin zu rein elektronischer Musik, sogar von Dubstep beeinflusste Sachen und experimenteller Breakcore. Ich glaube also, wir verfolgen immer noch die gleiche Mission, andere Sachen zu machen—wenn auch zugegebenermassen etwas langsamer und ungeschickter. Wie siehst du denn, was du heute machst im Vergleich zu deinen früheren Arbeiten? SC: Ich weiss nicht. Ich meine, ich habe es nie für ein Publikum gemacht. Ich habe nie versucht, ein Publikum zufriedenzustellen. Eher ist das Gegenteil der Fall. Ich mache, was ich mache, weil ich neugierig bin und weil es schwierig ist, damit aufzuhören. Ist das eine Antwort?

CF: Ja, klar. Nigel, wie ist das bei dir? NA: Ich würde sagen, dass ich eigentlich alles immer noch aus den gleichen Gründen mache, wie früher—es ist die gleiche Neugier, der gleiche Wunsch, zu experimentieren, mit der Realität rumzuspielen, mit Erfahrungen und Empfindun-

SC From the outside it appears that you've been doing it for a quite long time and it seems to be still quite close to where it started aesthetically. Or have there been variations I didn't notice?

CF Well, I think it has changed a lot. I mean there are still those who really continue what was happening back then, with the four-to-the-floor beat, a certain tempo and so on. From being something new and somewhat experimental it has become something very formalized and very standardized, with its own very strict rules. But I don't think this is what Praxis did. Already in the 90s, gradually more and more and eventually completely, we abandoned the four-four base drum beat and started using broken beats and breaks. I definitely think that was another kind of flight line, that there were new routes we tried to take.

SC So, where is the label now, apart from being bankrupt [laughs]?

CF That's nothing new [laughs]. Well, as a label it's still active—it never completely ceased its activity—but there aren't that many things coming out. We've put out very different records in the last few years. I tried to make some kind of interventions in different fields, from noisy composition stuff played by musicians to purely electronic, even somewhat dubstep-influenced things to more experimental breakcore stuff. We're still continuing with the same mission of trying to do different things, but slowly and awkwardly, to some degree. How do you see what you're doing now in relation to what you've done through the last four decades?

SC I don't know. I mean, I've never done it for an audience. I don't try to please an audience. I suppose I try to do the opposite, in a way. I just do it because I'm curious about it and it's quite hard to stop, as well. Is that an answer?

CF Sure. Nigel, you?

NA I would say that I probably still do things for the same reasons that I did before, and it is the exact same curiosity and just this wanting to tinker around with the substance and wanting to tinker with reality, experiences, and sensations. I think that this has been really consistent throughout everything I've done. I usually don't know what I'm going to do until after I've done it. It's a continuing process and it has everything to do with life, really. It's a living process, to understand a recent record. Something recent of Simon's, for example, you and I can say: "Well why is that coming out?" Or we listen to what he did ten years ago and another ten years ago and then we can see that something is emerging from that.

SC I think he put that more succinctly than I did. Do you make music and perform live, Christoph?

CF Yeah.

SC What's your reason for doing parties and stuff? I didn't quite get that, either. Because I find clubs to be quite boring.

CF Generally I agree—clubs are quite boring [laughs]. Ideally a party would be something where unexpected things can happen in the interaction between the music, the audience, and the location. I always thought there was an interesting aspect to the social space of the music in a party situation. But I see that as something quite different from clubs.

SC Seems to me that what you're talking about is an opportunity to make something out of it other than just pure entertainment. I mean, you talked about going counter to what things should be in terms of the music and so on. Shouldn't the actual event itself be counter to what people are expecting?

CF Well, yes. Of course even breaking into warehouses or into office buildings or whatever it used to be becomes a routine from the point of view of the audience, because they know the score after a while. It's not a huge adventure anymore to seek out the place of the party. But I think that's something that happens with every format. And with the format of a concert it's also debatable whether that's something that's

gen. Ich glaube, diesbezüglich war ich immer konsequent. Und meistens weiss ich nicht, was ich mache, bis ich damit fertig bin. Es ist ein kontinuierlicher Prozess und eigentlich hat es mit dem Leben an sich zu tun, würde ich sagen. Es ist ein lebendiger Prozess und um eine Platte zu verstehen, sagen wir eine jüngere Platte von Simon zum Beispiel, könnten wir uns fragen: Warum wurde das veröffentlicht? Oder wir könnten die Sachen anhören, die er vor zehn Jahren gemacht hat und dann nochmals zehn Jahre früher und plötzlich sehen wir, wie etwas vor unseren Augen entsteht.

SC: Ich glaube, das hat er jetzt um einiges besser ausgedrückt als ich vorhin. Machst du eigentlich auch Musik, Christoph? Performst du live? CF: Ja.

SC: Und was ist der Grund, Partys zu organisieren? Weil ich persönlich finde Klubs etwas sehr Langweiliges.

CF: Im Grossen und Ganzen stimme ich dir zu–Klubs sind ziemlich langweilig. Im Idealfall wäre eine Party ein Setting, in dem unerwartete Dinge passieren können, im Zusammenspiel von Musik, dem Publikum und dem Ort. Ich habe immer geglaubt, dass der soziale Raum an einer Party etwas Interessantes hat. Aber da handelt es sich um eine völlig andere Situation als in den Klubs.

SC: Mir scheint, dir geht es darum, daraus etwas anderes zu machen als reine Unterhaltung. Du hast darüber gesprochen, zu versuchen, eine Alternative zu finden was die Musik angeht. Müsste dann nicht auch die Veranstaltung als Ereignis etwas anderes sein als das, was die Leute erwarten? CF: Natürlich wird irgendwann selbst die Besetzung einer Lagerhalle oder eines Bürogebäudes für das Publikum reine Routine, weil die ja mit der Zeit genau wissen wie's läuft. Aber das geschieht mit jedem Format. Und was Konzerte angeht, so könnte man ja auch darüber streiten, ob dieses Format nicht auch schon längst Teil des ganzen Spektakels geworden ist...

SC: Hast du Spektakel gesagt? [lacht] CF: Ja, tatsächlich [lacht]. Diese Entwicklung setzt bei allem ein, sobald gewisse Dinge zur Routine oder zum Geschäft werden–das ist letztlich unvermeidbar. Es wäre lächerlich, wenn ich behaupten würde, dass Praxis von der Kulturindustrie völlig unberührt geblieben ist. Letztlich ist ja schon die Produktion von Platten ein Resultat der Ausbeutung von Bodenschätzen bei der Ölförderung. Als Rohmaterial ist es letztlich auch nichts weiter...

SC: ...als noch mehr Plastik, der im Meer landet! Ich meine nur: Würdest du sagen, dass eine Party in einer besetzten Lagerhalle eine temporäre autonome Zone sein kann? Ist es das, was du meinst? CF: Ja, im weitesten Sinne. Aber natürlich hat auch jede frei organisierte Party eine ganze Ökonomie hinter sich–es gibt Equipment, Logistik, Transport, Waren. Ich weiss sehr wohl, dass es unmöglich ist, dem Spektakel völlig zu entkommen oder der Kulturindustrie, dem Kapitalismus oder wie auch immer man das nennen will. Aber mir war immer wichtig, zumindest eine Kritik zu formulieren, auch wenn sie im Innern des Ganzen formuliert werden muss.

SC: Mich hat an der frühen Rave-Szene immer enttäuscht, dass sie aus ihrem Geist nie Vorteile zu schlagen wusste und sich woanders hin bewegte. Sie wurde einfach grösser und kommerzieller. Diese riesigen Raves waren doch eigentlich etwas wirklich Neues und Revolutionäres. Aber das hat sich dann nie weiterentwickelt. Das ist schade, weil diese Massentreffen hatten ein riesiges Potential–damals hatte die Regierung richtig Schiss vor denen! CF: Ja, da hast du teilweise recht.

Andererseits wurde es in England einfach auch unmöglich in dieser Grössenordnung zu veranstalten. Die Leute wurden aus dem Land getrieben und haben dann in Frankreich mit den Teknivals angefangen. Aber auch da ist wieder derselbe Prozess abgelaufen: Die Regierung ist nach ein paar Jahren aufgewacht und hat das ganze brutal niedergeschlagen. SC: Ich würde sagen, dass sich letztlich alles, auch die Musik, eigentlich nur um Hedonismus drehte. Sich abschiessen, auf dem Feld rumtanzen und so... Hätte man auf einer inhaltlichen Ebene Ernst gemacht, dann wäre vielleicht etwas draus geworden, aber niemand hat das je wirklich versucht. Das war alles nur Hedonismus, letztlich. CF: Nun, die Soundsystem-Kultur und die Rave-Idee haben für eine Zeit Eingang gefunden in das Direct Action Movement—die ganzen Ideen rund um Reclaim the Streets, Ende der Neunzigerjahre zum Beispiel. Ich fand das eine Zeit lang recht interessant, aber natürlich wurde auch das unmöglich. Einfach weil man einen Weg gefunden hat, das ganze polizeilich zu verhindern und dafür zu sorgen, dass es nie das Ausmass vom Juni 1989 erreicht. Und als dann Reclaim the Streets hier auch aufgenommen wurde, war das wieder etwas völlig anderes. Die hatten dann einfach Soundsystems mit Techno-Musik an einer legalen Demonstration. Das war dann eigentlich auch nichts anderes als eine komplette Travestie.

SC: Es gab ja dann schon auch einige militantere Strömungen. Ich nehme an sowas wie Underground Resistance. Diese Leute hatten zumindest eine radikale Aura. Aber das wurde dann auch nie spezifischer, oder? CF: Für eine Weile gab es schon noch einmal einen DIY-Gedanken; jede kleine Crew hat ihr eigenes Label gemacht und Platten getauscht... SC: Da wurde auch kein Marketing gemacht oder so. Die hatten weder Covers noch Labels. Als Produkt war das alles sehr temporär angelegt.

CF: Und unfertig; darauf ausgelegt, weiter manipuliert zu werden. SC: Aber heutzutage haben wir die komplette Fetischisierung von Produkten. Die Leute wollen ihre Boxsets haben; ihre siebgedruckten, limitierten Editionen...

CF: Und möglichst mit Download-Code, damit sie es auf ihren Handys hören und die Platte ungeöffnet ins Regal stellen können. SC: Das ist doch interessant—das Versprechen der digitalen Revolution war doch, dass sie einen Anonymisierungsprozess anstossen sollte. Ich meine, eigentlich hat doch jeder jetzt die Möglichkeit, Dinge zu machen; Das sollte alles ja eigentlich recht günstig, einfach und gemeinschaftlich sein—und das ist es ja eigentlich auch. Aber vielmehr scheint das Gegenteil eingetreten zu sein: Es hat die Leute dazu gebracht, noch mehr auf das Produkt und dessen Sammelbarkeit zu fokussieren, auf seine Einzigartigkeit.

CF: Warum meinst du, ist das der Fall? SC: Ich glaube, der Effekt ist doch ziemlich gut dokumentiert: Das Internet ist eine Homogenisierungsmaschine. Es sorgt dafür, dass Leute mit ähnlichen Meinungen aufeinandertreffen. Es sorgt also dafür, dass die Meinungen, Geschmäcker und politischen Haltungen der Leute eher verengt als dass es sie erweitern würde. Der gleiche Effekt wirkt auch auf die Musik, auch da wird der Geschmack der Leute eingedämpft. Wir hatten noch erwartet, dass so etwas wie Musik um einiges interessanter werden würde, weil die Produktion und Distribution, der Zugang zum Markt vereinfacht werden. Aber wiederum: Das Gegenteil ist eingetreten, es scheint, als sei die Musik banaler und homogener geworden als je zuvor. Und das ist dann doch ein ganz guter Lackmustest für das, was auch in der Politik geschieht. Wir sind alle im Arsch... Ich dachte, wir würden eigentlich noch ein Happy End finden für das und nicht alle runterziehen... Also, was ist die Lösung? Nigel?

even more completely part of the spectacle, so to speak.
SC Did you say spectacle [laughs]?
CF Yes [laughs]. There's always this development of things becoming a routine or a business or being taken over and that's not completely avoidable. It would be ridiculous if I were to claim that Praxis hasn't been touched by the culture industry at all, you know. You can't completely escape capitalism while there is capitalism. Even making records is obviously based upon, you know, the extraction of fossil fuels and as a raw material it's...
SC ...just more plastic that gets dumped in the sea! I mean would you say that if you do a party night in a squatted warehouse that it's like a contemporary autonomous-zone thing? Is that what you were thinking?
CF Yes, broadly speaking. But of course even a free party has a kind of economy behind it. You have to deal with equipment, logistics, transport, commodities. I know very well that it's impossible to completely escape the whatever-you-want-to-call-it culture industry, the spectacle, capitalism...but one aspect that is important to me is to try to at least formulate a critique within and against it.
SC I think the thing that disappointed me about the early rave scene is that it never took advantage of the spirit and moved on to something else. It just became commercial and bigger. These big squatted massive raves were actually quite new and quite revolutionary at the time. But it didn't move forward at all, which is a shame, because it had a lot of potential. Those mass gatherings were really scaring the government at the time!
CF Yeah, that is true to some degree. But on the other hand, I think it became impossible in Britain to do things on that scale, and then people were driven out of the country and started doing Teknivals in France and so on. And there, again, the same kind of process kicked in—the government woke up to it a couple of years later and then clamped down on it.
SC I would say that probably the musical content and the focus was just hedonism: get wasted, dance around in the field and stuff. If there had been some serious content behind it, it might have moved in a different way, but no one ever really tried to do that. It was always about hedonism, really.
CF Well, you had the soundsystem culture and the rave idea influencing the Direct Action movement for a while—like the idea of reclaiming the streets—from the mid 1990s to about 2000. I thought that was really interesting for a period, as well, but of course it also became impossible. I mean purely because they figured out how to police these kinds of events and prevent them from reaching the scale of June 1989 or something. And then when Reclaim the Streets was picked up here, for example, it was completely different. They just had some soundsystems with techno music at a completely legal demonstration. So, it was some other travesty of the idea.
SC But there were undercurrents of more militant stuff. What they call Underground Resistance, for example. Those kinds of people had the aura of something radical going on. It was never directly specified, was it?
CF I think for a while there was a DIY spirit again with putting out the records as well, like every little crew made its little label and was swapping records back and forth...
SC They even didn't do a lot of marketing. In fact, most of them didn't have covers or labels. As a product it was very temporary.
CF Or somehow unfinished, just a tool for further manipulation.
SC But what we're seeing nowadays is a complete fetishization of products. People actually want to have these boxsets of limited editions with screen prints...
CF And then the download codes, so they can just listen to the files on the mobile phone and keep the record untouched in the shelf...

NA: Ich denke, der Punkt besteht darin, einige Fragen über all das zu stellen und sich Momente des Durchbruchs und Momente der Erleuchtung anzuschauen, die man durch Musik finden kann, oder durch verrückte Zeiten und Ereignisse. Ich weiss nicht, ob es eine Antwort gibt. Aber man muss die richtigen Fragen stellen, nicht?

CF: Trotz den Problemen, Widersprüchen und Paradoxa, die wir in Bezug auf neue Technologien besprochen haben: Es handelt sich dabei um Entwicklungen der Produktionskräfte. Und alles in allem könnte das eine völlig neue Gesellschaft immer noch möglich machen...

SC: Eine Theorie besagt, dass die Linke wieder erfolgreicher werden könnte, wenn sie den Modernismus neu erfindet. Weil eigentlich hat der Neoliberalismus diesen völlig übernommen. Wenn du heute von Modernismus sprichst, dann geht's doch eigentlich nur noch darum, dass alle entlassen werden, dass man alles kosteneffizient gestaltet—das ist, was einem als Erstes in den Sinn kommt. Also müssen wir einen Modernismus erfinden, der etwas komplett anderes aussagt. Wenn es eine Lösung gibt, dann geht es darum, solche kulturellen Kernideen wieder in Anspruch zu nehmen. Ich glaube, Musik ist dafür durchaus ein geeignetes Vehikel.

SC That's kind of interesting, because the promise of the digital revolution was that it should boost an anonymization process. I mean, anyone should be able to do stuff now. It should be fairly communal, cheap, and easy—and it actually is! But it seems to have had the opposite effect of what you'd expect: it has made people focus much more on the product and its collectability, the uniqueness of it.

CF Why do you think that is the case?

SC I think there's a very well-documented effect: the internet tends to homogenize. It makes people of similar opinions come together. So it actually narrows peoples tastes, opinions, and politics more than expanding them. There's the same effect with music. We expected that something like music would become a lot more interesting because of the ease of production, the ease of distribution, the access to market, and so on—that the internet would allow more interesting music to flourish. But again, the opposite has happened—it seems that music has become much more banal and homogenous than ever. And that's a quite good litmus test for how things work in politics and so on. We're all screwed. But we should find a happy end to all of this, though, not bring everybody down [laughs]. So what's the solution? Nigel?

NA I think the point is to ask a few questions about all of this and to look at these moments of breakthrough and moments of enlightenment you can get from music, from odd times and odd events, through exploring the way the world is. I don't know if there's an answer to all of this. It's a deep philosophical question I don't have an answer to. But you need to ask the questions, really, don't you?

CF Despite the problems, contradictions, and paradoxes we've noticed about new technologies, these are the emerging developments of the productive forces. Overall they still could make a completely different society possible...

SC One theory to make the left successful again is that it needs to reinvent the idea of modernism. The neoliberal agenda has basically captured modernism. And when you say "modernism" nowadays it's always about firing everyone, making it cost-effective—that's what immediately jumps into your mind. So we need to reinvent a modernism for the left that means something completely different. Maybe if there's a sort of solution it is actually looking at recapturing those core cultural ideas. I think music is a well-placed vehicle for doing that.

Contribution — Jay Glass Dubs

JAY GLASS DUBS

HE NEEDED A NEW IDENTITY, A MASK TO WEAR IN HIS VIGILANT BATTLES, AND ONE DRUNKEN NIGHT, HE FOUND THE NAME AND THE CAUSE, IN THE GUISE OF:

AN EXERCISE OF STYLE FOCUSING ON A COUNTER-FACTUAL HISTORICAL APPROACH OF DUB MUSIC, STRIPPED DOWN TO ITS BASIC DRUM/BASS/VOX/EFFECTS FORM.

ATHENS, 21ST CENTURY

DIMITRIS PAPADATOS, A 30 SOMETHING MUSICIAN & RECORD STORE CLERK, WAS FEELING THAT THINGS HAVE TO CHANGE, AND THEY HAVE TO CHANGE NOW.

THE MISTS OF THE RECENT PAST WERE BLURRING HIS SIGHT. IT WAS TIME THAT HE CONFRONTED ALL THE USURPERS OF THE THINGS HE HELD DEAR. HIS BELOVED CHALICE, 'DUB MUSIC' HAS BECOME A LIFELESS IMAGE OF WHAT IT WAS IN THE HANDS OF CULTURAL APPROPRIATORS.

WHAT HAD STARTED AS AN ACCIDENTAL MIRACLE IN THE STUDIOS OF GENIUSES LIKE RUDDY REDWOOD HAS BEEN VIOLENTLY DRAGGED OUT OF ESSENCE BY TECHNO PRODUCERS WHOSE FOUR-ON-THE-FLOOR IGNORANCE HAD TURNED THE GENRE INTO A LAZY PROCESS, ARBITARILY USING 'DUB' TO CONCEAL THEIR LACK OF TALENT IN COMPOSITION AND THEIR POOR IMAGINATION ...

THE MISTS OF THE RECENT PAST WERE STARTING TO WEAR OFF, HOPE WAS IN HAND, BUT THERE WAS A LONG WAY AHEAD FOR HIM TO ROAM. HE HAD TO CHANGE FIRST, IF HE WANTED TO CHANGE THE WORLD ...

IT WAS HIM AGAINST THEM AND HE KNEW THAT HE HAD NO OTHER OPTION BUT TO CREATE A FAIR AMOUNT OF 3/4 **BANGERS!**

BUT ALAS, THE MISTS OF THE RECENT PAST HAD OVERTAKEN THE ATTENTION OF ALL HIS POSSIBLE AUDIENCE ...

IT WAS NOW CLEAR THAT HE HAD TO FIND LABELS THAT SHARED HIS VISION, PEOPLE WHO WERE WILLING TO PENETRATE THE MISTS WITH HIM, CREATE A TEAM OF MASTERMINDS OR JOIN ONE, TO SAVE EARTH FROM 4/4 IN 120 BPM.

AND FINALLY THE TRUTH REVEALED ITSELF TO HIM, AMIDST A GAMEPLAY BETWEEN GODS, AN IMAGE OF HIMSELF AS A CHILD APPEARED, AND A VOICE SPOKE TO HIM, HOLLERING ...

BE BRAVE JAY! BE BOLD!

BE BRAVE, I AND SEND OUT ...

UNSOLICITED DEMOS!!

SO HIS ROAMING BEGUN, THROUGH UNIVERSES UNKNOWN, AND DIMENSIONS UNFORSEEN, FROM THE EDGE OF JUPITER TO THE FAR SEAS OF VENUS, HE SEEKED AND HE SEEKED, FOR YEARS ON END

HE PASSED THROUGH TIDES OF TIME, AND FOUGHT WARS THAT WERE NOT HIS, WITH FORCES UNSUNG BY THE HEATHEN YARDS, AGAINST EVILS STRONGER THAN ANY HUMAN HAS EVER OPPOSED.

"SIGN JAY AND BE *DOOMED"

MEANWHILE, AN OLD COMRADE OF JAY, *GIZMO THE BLUE* WAS BUSY WORKING HIS WAY TO THE TOP OF THE MUSIC BUSINESS FOOD CHAIN. AN AMBIGUOUS PERSONALITY, MASTER OF THE *ANCIENT MONARCHY* ARTS AND CREATOR OF *HEROIC LULLABIES* ...

GIZMO WAS SPENDING HIS DAYS IN THE UNITED KINGDOMS BATTLING AGAINST LACK OF SENSE OF HUMOUR, BAD COFFEE, LACK OF CIGGIES, MAJOR LABEL LACKIES AND HIS OWN MISANTHROPIC VIEWS, THE LATTER BEING A GRAVE RESULT OF YEARS OF REPEATEDLY LISTENING TO *JJ CALE*.

* TRANSLATED FROM NORTHERN GREEK

GIZMO KNEW WHAT JAY WAS ABOUT TO DO AND HE WANTED TO ASSIST. HIMSELF AS WELL WAS FAITHFUL TO THE 3/4'S RETURN, AND WAS WILLING TO FIGHT AND IF NEEDED GIVE HIS LIFE TO THE CAUSE.

BUT HE HAD TO BE SURE. SURE THAT JAY WAS NOT A FAULTY BANDWAGON, THAT HIS AIM WAS TRUE AND NOBLE AND THAT HE COULD TRUST HIM WITH A VERY SPECIFIC AND IMPORTANT MISSION.

ON ANOTHER DIMENSION, A HERO FROM THE SOUTH, ANSWERING TO THE NAME OF *NOT WAVING* WAS BATTLEING HIS WAY THROUGH THE 4/4 TYRANTS IN FESTIVALS AND CLUB VENUES, SLOWLY INFILTRATING THE VIRTUES OF THE 3/4 BEAT, DEAF TO THE CRIES OF THE EVIL DOERS AND THE TECHNO SUPRESORS WHO USHERED HIM TO FOLLOW THEM IN THEIR FOUL WAYS.

HE KNEW THAT SOMEWHERE, SOMEHOW, A VOICE COMMON TO HIS WAS WAITING FOR HIS CALL TO ASSEMBLE AND FIGHT THE GOOD FIGHT ALONGSIDE HIM. HE WOULD HAVE TO FIND JAY AND OFFER HIM A 2LP RELEASE ON HIS LABEL OF *ECSTATIC* MUSIC ...

WILL OUR HEROES' STRUGGLE FOR MORE INTERESTING CLUBNIGHTS AND FESTIVAL LINE-UPS FLOURISH ? OR WILL THEIR PLANS BE OPPOSED BY THE EVIL FORCES THAT HARVESTED THE MISTS OF RECENT PAST AND KEPT 3/4 CHAINED FOR AGES ON END ?

TO BE CONTINUED

SOME KIND SOULS REPLIED TO THE DEMOS, RESULTING TO THREE FERRIC OFFERINGS OF THE JAY GLASS DUBS SOUND, BUT STILL, THE WEARY MUSICIAN HAD NOT FOUND WHAT HE WAS LOOKING FOR . UNTIL ONE DAY ...

HIS ATTEMPTS DRAGGED THE ATTENTION OF *BOKEH EDWARDS*, A POWERFUL MAGE WHO RESIDED IN THE FEROCIOUS NORTHERN UNITED KINGDOMS

HE APPROACHED JAY WITH A TEMPTING OFFER: "MAY THEE CREATE A MIXTAPE", HE UTTERED "INNA SLOWED DOWN DANCEHALL STYLEE"

EDWARDS WAS HIMSELF A MASTER OF THE *3/4 BANGERS* HE HAD COLLECTED AND EXCAVATED PROOFS THAT THIS FORM OF TRIPLE METER COULD BE ABSOLUTELY *DANCEABLE !!* HE HAD SEEN IT HAPPENING IN FRONT OF HIS *BARE EYES* ! CROWDS REACHING ECSTATIC LEVELS AFTER TWO OR THREE 87 BPM *MIXMAN* STEPPERS. HE KNEW THE TRUTH AND HE WAS GOING TO HELP JAY IN HIS AGON, HE WOULD BE A MENTOR AND A SUPPORTER, A FRIEND AND AN ALLY, A BROTHER IN ARMS FOR ALL THE SEEKERS OF THE TRUTH.

"AND MAY THE STYLEE BE NAMED : *GLACIAL DANCEHALL !*"

HE ORDERED

carhartt
WORK IN PROGRESS
Photo by Viktor Vauthier. © Carhartt Inc. U.S.A. ® carhartt and carhartt logo are registered trademarks of Carhartt Inc., Dearborn, MI 48121, U.S.A.
carhartt-wip.com